THE DANGEROUS HARBOUR

Revealing the Unknown Ships and Wrecks of the Halifax Explosion

BOB CHAULK

NIMBUS PUBLISHING
NIMBUS.CA

T0243654

Copyright © 2023, Bob Chaulk

All rights reserved. No part of this book may be reproduced, stored in a retrieval system or transmitted in any form or by any means without the prior written permission from the publisher, or, in the case of photocopying or other reprographic copying, permission from Access Copyright, 1 Yonge Street, Suite 1900, Toronto, Ontario M5E 1E5.

Nimbus Publishing Limited
3660 Strawberry Hill Street, Halifax, NS, B3K 5A9
(902) 455-4286 nimbus.ca

Printed and bound in Canada

NB1673

Editor: Paula Sarson
Editor for the press: Angela Mombourquette
Design: Jenn Embree

Nimbus Publishing is based in Kjipuktuk, Mi'kma'ki, the traditional territory of the Mi'kmaq People.

Cover, top: Norwegian steamship *Imo* beached on the Dartmouth shore after the explosion (NS Archives); below: an underwater image of what is likely the anchor from the *St. Bernard*, a lumber schooner that was obliterated during the 1917 explosion. (Sean McMullen)
Back cover: The author on one of his 1,200 dives in Halifax Harbour. (Sean McMullen)

Library and Archives Canada Cataloguing in Publication

Title: The dangerous harbour : revealing the unknown ships and wrecks of the Halifax Explosion / Bob Chaulk.
Names: Chaulk, Bob, author.
Identifiers: Canadiana (print) 2023043844X | Canadiana (ebook) 20230438466 | ISBN 9781774712405 (softcover) | ISBN 9781774712429 (EPUB)
Subjects: LCSH: Halifax Explosion, Halifax, N.S., 1917. | LCSH: Shipwrecks—Nova Scotia—Halifax.
Classification: LCC FC2346.4 .C43 2023 | DDC 971.6/22503—dc23

Canada NOVA SCOTIA Canada Council for the Arts Conseil des arts du Canada

Nimbus Publishing acknowledges the financial support for its publishing activities from the Government of Canada, the Canada Council for the Arts, and from the Province of Nova Scotia. We are pleased to work in partnership with the Province of Nova Scotia to develop and promote our creative industries for the benefit of all Nova Scotians.

We returned to our ship at 11 P.M. sick at heart with the appalling misery with which the city abounded, the glare from the fires lighting the harbour up like day.... Looking out on the flaming city from our ship I cannot help but marvel that we escaped sharing the fate of thousands of souls in this terrible catastrophe.

—Diary of Frank Baker, HMCS *Acadia*

TABLE OF CONTENTS

INTRODUCTION

The biggest avoidable disaster in Canadian history was caused by two ships. The second such disaster was caused by two ships. The third was caused by a single ship.[1] Ships have played a huge part, good and bad, in the story of Canada and the history of civilization in general.

Although this is a book about the Halifax Explosion, it is equally a book about ships and boats, and the men whose livelihoods were wrapped up with them—sailors, pilots, stevedores, shipwrights. When the Explosion occurred, of the approximately two thousand people who lost their lives that day, about 10 percent were sailors and men associated with ships. On that same day, there were around two hundred vessels in Halifax Harbour, from warships to fishing schooners. Remarkably few were destroyed. Ships are built to take a beating.

Ships have figured prominently in human history. Even with the passing of biremes, cogs, xebecs, galleasses, caravels, and a host of other types, ships have always been, and still are, the most sophisticated things built by civilizations, the biggest things that move, the first things to be propelled without the aid of animals or the wind, the first things to have engines. They changed the world, not always in good ways, making travel to faraway places possible and enabling the Europeans to become lords of the planet. Because of ships, German was spoken in Labrador, French was spoken on islands in the South Pacific, Spanish was spoken in the Andes, Portuguese was spoken in China, and English is spoken pretty much everywhere. Civilizations and languages have disappeared because Europeans showed up in ships and changed everything.

The influence of these craft has been so significant that the word *ship* pertains not only to the vessel, but to the moving of goods in general, regardless of the means. We ship by rail, we ship by road, we ship by air, and, of course, we ship by sea. And those who have sailed on ships throughout the centuries have coined hundreds of phrases we use every day. The English language has many colourful expressions, most of which come from four sources: the Bible ("read the writing on the wall"); Shakespeare ("vanish into thin air"); sports ("step up to the plate"); and sailors ("you scratch my back, and I'll scratch yours"). Whole books have been written about the subject of nautical expressions such as: shape up, by and large, over a barrel, out of the blue, at loggerheads, learn the ropes, hard up, the coast is clear.

And the English language was once filled with many words that have since disappeared. When I went rowing as a child, I climbed down the longers of the wharf and into my grandfather's rodney. Using the piggin, I bailed water from the dillroom, and then sat on the thwart (which was pronounced "tawt"). I gave each tholepin a whack to tighten it in the gunwale (pronounced "gunnel"), took each oar and popped the withes over the tholepins, untied the painter, and pushed the boat off. The chains on a sailing ship were rigid pieces of iron attaching the strakes to the deadeyes, which were used to tighten the shrouds. No wonder a newbie had to learn the ropes when they had names like vangs, sheets, halyards, and clewlines. A ship's knees did not flex, and neither the trestle trees nor the cross trees grow in a forest.

Only a ship had the space to carry the number of people who died in the worst sinking ever in terms of lives lost, the MV *Wilhelm Gustloff*. Formerly a German cruise ship, on January 30, 1945, it was evacuating German civilians from East Prussia. Soviet submarine S-13 sank it in the Baltic Sea with a loss of some 9,400 people. And only a ship could carry the amount of volatile material it took to make the Halifax Explosion. When things go wrong for big ships, the resulting disaster can be enormous. Things went dreadfully wrong for two ships on the morning of December 6, 1917. The catastrophe that ensued was colossal and agonizing.

A NOTE ABOUT TONNAGE FOR SHIPS

The size of a ship is usually expressed in tons, but understanding the size of a ship based on tonnage can be tricky.

In the beginning, a ton did not refer to weight, and therefore, a ship's tonnage did not refer to the weight of the ship. It was, instead, a means of calculating tax on cargo. It began in antiquity as a way to express how much cargo a ship could carry, based on tuns of wine, a "tun" being a wooden container like a large barrel, holding 252 imperial gallons or 964 litres. A 10-ton ship could carry 10 tuns of wine. But wine was not the only cargo carried, so it was decided that 100 cubic feet of cargo space would equal a ton of capacity. Regardless of shape or size, a ship that had 1,000 cubic feet of cargo space was a 10-ton ship. The space available strictly for cargo is the net register tonnage, or NRT. But ships have other space besides cargo space. So, the total space within a merchant ship—living quarters, engine room, fuel compartments, *and* cargo space—is called the gross register tonnage, or GRT.

Another method of expressing cargo capacity is called deadweight tonnage. This measures the number of tons of cargo the ship can carry to push the hull down into the water to the Plimsoll marks, an official indicator painted on the side of a freight ship showing the legal safe level to which the ship can be loaded.

To complicate matters further, naval vessels use a different system. They don't carry cargo, so they're measured in displacement tonnage, referring to the number of tons of water the ship displaces while afloat. HMS *Changuinola* was a freighter that was acquired by the Royal Navy (RN) and converted to a warship. It was 5,978 gross tons, 3,508 net tons, and 6,011 displacement tons.

To compare the sizes of two ships based on tonnage, you need to use the same classification system for both. This book uses GRT, unless otherwise indicated. In this book, ships are also noted by length where that information is available. It's difficult to picture a 4,000-ton ship. It's easier to picture a 350-foot ship.

A NOTE ABOUT MEASUREMENT SYSTEMS

Even though Canada uses the metric system, Canadians have not embraced it fully. While we are content to express the weather in degrees Celsius, we often buy fish by the pound, and we drive long distances in kilometres while measuring short distances in inches. This book reflects those inconsistencies. Ships' lengths are expressed in feet as they were in 1917. Water depths are given in feet because that is how a Canadian scuba diver's depth gauge reports them.

CHAPTER 1

KJIPUKTUK, THE GREAT HARBOUR

Halifax Harbour is called a harbour, but it's really a system of waterways, distinct and apart from one another. From the open sea, you enter and travel through the outer harbour, which is a 14-kilometre trip to the beginning of the inner harbour, where the channel narrows slightly between McNabs Island and the peninsula. Pass through and you think you've arrived, but you've barely started. Or, you can take a left for the Northwest Arm, where you can meander another 5 kilometres through the City of Halifax, or turn right to Eastern Passage and travel another 5 or 6 kilometres. Continue straight and you enter the inner harbour. It's another 6 kilometres to its end, but you're still not at the end of the waterway. Three more kilometres take you through The Narrows to a wide salt lake called the Bedford Basin, and then another 7 kilometres gets you to the Sackville River, where the harbour ends, 30 kilometres.

Because this is a book about ships, from here I dispense with kilometres and express distance in nautical miles, a mariner's measurement at sea (and a pilot's measurement in the air). A nautical mile is 1,852 metres or 6,080 feet, as opposed to the more common 5,280 feet in a land mile. On a terrestrial circle like the equator, the Earth is divided into 360 degrees. Each degree is subdivided into 60 minutes. A minute is the distance of a nautical mile. Ships' and airplanes' speeds are expressed in knots, one nautical mile per hour.

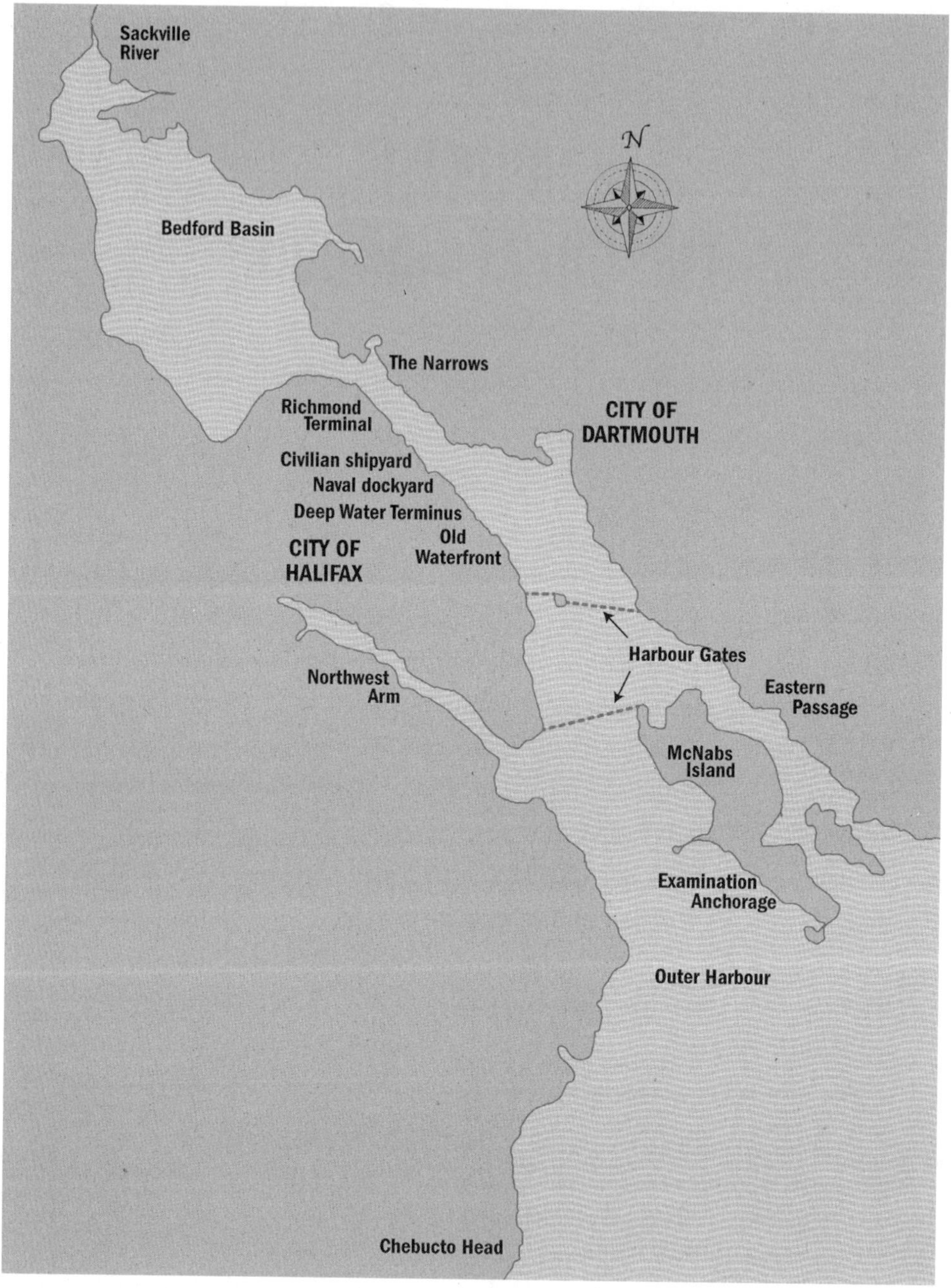

The waterways and waterfronts that comprise Halifax Harbour.

THE WATERWAY NAMED HALIFAX HARBOUR

During the First World War, goods and people moved between Europe and Canada through the ports of Montréal, Québec, Saint John, Halifax, and Sydney. The role of Halifax expanded throughout the war, dramatically so with the arrival of large convoys as a defence against German U-boats in the summer of 1917. Two-thirds of the 425,000 Canadian soldiers that went overseas during the war departed from Halifax.[2]

The harbour, which the Mi'kmaq named Kjipuktuk, is deep, spacious, and uncomplicated on the inside. The outside is speckled with shallow water and reefs, making it easy to defend—perfect for a naval base. The high number of shipwrecks around the outside speaks of the challenges of weather, geography, and enemy action over the years. The harbour is ice-free and can hold a huge number of ships safely away from the threat of enemies and storms. Of the large North American harbours, it's the one closest to Europe, which is why it has always been important during wartime. During the two world wars, it was marked by five lighthouses and a lightship. In its long history, the Sambro Light, purported to be the oldest operating lighthouse in the western hemisphere, has been equipped with foghorns and even cannon to counter the dense fog that can plague the entrance.

Halifax Harbour can be described more accurately as a system of waterways. That is why the people of Halifax, and especially those who work on the harbour, have names for the different parts: the outer harbour, inner harbour, The Narrows, Bedford Basin, Northwest Arm, and Eastern Passage, not to mention the many named coves situated off the harbour: Admiral, Back, Birch, Dartmouth, Deadmans, Dingle, Eisner, Fairview, Fergusons, Finlay, Herring, Ives, Long, McNabs, Melville, Norris, Purcells, Roach, Sleepy, Tufts, Timmonds, Wreck, and Wrights. There are thirteen islands within the harbour, six of which have been populated at different times.

ENTERING THE HARBOUR

A Halifax-bound ship goes first into the outer harbour, the roomiest area of all. A straight line of 7 miles from Chebucto Head to Hartlen Point marks the entrance. In this area a ship without a local pilot stands a better-than-even chance of running aground, for this is where virtually all the shallow water in the harbour is situated. There is plenty of water if you know the way, but the rocks and shoals will get you if you don't. Once a vessel gets to the inner harbour and beyond, there are vast expanses of deep water to hold hundreds of ships.

During wartime, gun batteries lined both sides of the channel coming in. From the Chebucto Head Light at the beginning of the harbour to the first submarine net that stretched across the channel during the First World War is a distance of 8 miles. The first, or inner, net was deployed in June 1915 from Halifax to Georges Island and from Georges Island to the Dartmouth shore near Fort Clarence. With its huge guns, Georges had always been the final stronghold for protecting the harbour against intruders. The arsenal also included a minefield stretching toward Dartmouth that was intended to snag any enemy ships that managed to travel that far.

Beginning in the 1870s, the Submarine Mining Establishment manufactured mines on Georges Island. The guncotton tanks are still there. That system was discontinued in 1906 for fear of blowing up local shipping. With the onset of the First World War, the defence was placed in the same area, except this time it was a steel net with a system of anchors at the bottom and floats at the top.

In May 1917, a second net went into place to strengthen the defences when convoys started in earnest. The nets kept submarines out, but surface vessels were an even greater threat.[3] With dozens of friendly ships entering the harbour some days, a reliable security system was required to check all ships coming in. The Examination Service handled that job, led by the chief examining officer, Acting Commander Frederick Wyatt. From offices aboard His Majesty's Canadian Ship (HMCS) *Niobe*, the service was responsible for controlling traffic entering and leaving the port. An arriving ship was met by a boat at the Examination Anchorage outside the nets off Fort McNab on McNabs Island. Only after a ship's cargo and paperwork had been verified was the vessel allowed into the port. Wyatt himself was an experienced navigator and pilot who had been a captain in the merchant marine. He had once been employed with the United Fruit Company and had been a member of the Royal Naval Reserve. When the war started, he became an officer of the Royal Canadian Navy (RCN) and was made chief examining officer in September 1915.[4]

The law of the sea has always been and continues to be that sailing vessels, being slower and difficult to manoeuvre, have the right-of-way over powered vessels. That did not apply when going through the gates of the nets. Instead, steamships had the right-of-way for the safety of the sailing ships, which were at the mercy of the winds and often required a lot of space in which to operate. In 1917, many schooners sailed in and out through the nets daily, which were open during daylight hours. Larger vessels were restricted to specific times at the beginning and end of the day.

THE INNER HARBOUR

The outer submarine net ran from Reids Rock, in an area that has since been infilled near Point Pleasant, to Ives Point, the innermost part of McNabs Island. The net was just inside the beginning of the inner harbour. From there, it is 3.75 miles to the Macdonald Bridge, where the width of the harbour shrinks dramatically into The Narrows, a 2-mile distance that leads to the Bedford Basin, the vast inland sea that was key to the harbour's ability to accommodate significant numbers of ships for convoy.

Below the Macdonald Bridge's location today was Jetty 4, which included the main coaling wharf for the navy. HMCS *Niobe* was permanently moored north of it and contained offices of many navy organizations, including the Examination Service staff. From there they could see ships entering the harbour and proceeding to and from anchorage. Jetty 4 was where ships recovering bodies from the *Titanic* in the spring of 1912 unloaded the corpses recovered after the sinking. Some were sent to relatives, but 150 were interred in three Halifax cemeteries.

A ship destined for a convoy sailed through the outer and inner gates into the basin and anchored with other vessels awaiting departure for Europe. En route it passed downtown Halifax on the left and Dartmouth on the right, the Halifax waterfront, the Deep Water Terminus, the dockyard, the shipyard, the sugar refinery, and the Canadian Government Railways Richmond Terminal. All these landmarks are key to understanding the events of the Halifax Explosion and its aftermath.

Once a ship had gone through The Narrows and was in the Bedford Basin, it was protected from hostile forces, whether natural or human-made. Even though there are other harbours that might compete with Halifax size-wise, few can offer the security a ship has while anchored in the basin. In December 1917, with two nets stretched across the entrance to the inner harbour, if a submarine were to slip through, it would have had its work cut out trying to cover the 6 miles to The Narrows entrance without being detected and then manoeuvre through the 2-mile squeeze to enter the basin.

Military ships usually went to the dockyard, situated today as it was then about halfway between the harbour entrance at Chebucto Head and the Sackville River, which marks the end of the harbour. There the naval craft tied up at the wharves. Today, the principal ones are referred to as jetties. By comparison, a similar structure used for commercial ships is usually called a pier. With just four jetties spread along the 875 yards of shoreline the dockyard occupied, cruisers and others of their size had to anchor offshore nearby in an area mariners call "the stream." Landlubbers might call that area "out in the middle." There are prescribed areas identified by buoys to mark where ships travel in the harbour. You can think of it like a road; in fact, some called it the "roadstead."

The convoy ships were merchant vessels mostly—cargo carriers, oil tankers, and passenger liners—carrying essential goods to Europe. These arrived singly and in company with others and steamed past the naval area to the innermost anchorage in the Bedford Basin.

THE NARROWS

On the way to the basin, ships would have passed numerous commercial establishments, including the shipyard, which was the main repair facility, and the sugar refinery, which had its own dock. North of that were some smaller wharves. The first belonged to the Lorne Amateur Aquatic Club on the site where the Royal Halifax Yacht Club got started in the summer of 1837.[5] The Royal Halifax Yacht Club went on to become the Royal Nova Scotia Yacht Squadron, which relocated in 1890, near where the submarine net came ashore during the First World War. Today, the squadron has its base in the Northwest Arm, having purchased property formerly occupied by the Atlantic Sugar Company. The Lorne Amateur Aquatic Club took its name from a boat owned in 1884 by the four founding members. Doubtless, they were influenced by the name of the Governor General of the day, the Marquess of Lorne, who was married to Queen Victoria's daughter Princess Louise.

Next to the Lorne Club was the wharf for the North Ferry, a private service provided by Charles Duggan, not associated with the main ferries run by the Dartmouth Ferry Commission between downtown Dartmouth and Halifax. The North Ferry, which carried passengers but no automobiles, shut down with the opening of the Angus L. Macdonald Bridge in 1955. It operated across The Narrows from Grove Street in Dartmouth to a small wharf and steep wooden stairs that led to Barrington Street. Next to that was St. Joseph's Boat Club.

What was still often called the Intercolonial Railway Terminal was the final commercial organization on the Halifax side of The Narrows. The terminal consisted of railway yards, warehouses, and docks for commercial ship loading and unloading. These were piers 6, 7, 8, and 9. From there, the shore steepened and opened abruptly into the Bedford Basin. Even though many still called it the Intercolonial Railway or ICR, the proper name at that time was Canadian Government Railways. Many of Canada's railways had begun to incur financial difficulties, and the federal government was obliged to take them over to continue the provision of an essential service.

Canadian National Railways dishes from different periods throughout the twentieth century, all recovered from the ocean. (AUTHOR'S COLLECTION)

A year later would see the amalgamation of these money-losing railways into one of the great organizations of Canadian history, Canadian National Railways. It would lead the way in the formation of several significant Canadian institutions, including Canadian National Telecommunications, Canadian National Express, Canadian National Hotels, Canadian National Steamships, the CN Tower, Canadian Broadcasting Corporation, and even Air Canada.

Most other vessels did not pass the dockyard. The passenger liners and freighters from Europe and the United States went to the Deep Water Terminus, the second set of docks and railyards in the harbour, between downtown and the dockyard. Smaller vessels carrying passengers and goods to and from other ports in Canada and Newfoundland were berthed south of the Deep Water Terminus docks at the wharves of the commercial shipping agencies like Pickford & Black, I. H. Mathers, and T. A. S. deWolf. They were at the old waterfront off downtown, along with other marine operators such as towing companies like G. S. Campbell and stevedoring companies like Furness Withy.

The old Halifax waterfront had been the centre of trade for a century and a half, until steamships outgrew the docks. That led to the building of the Deep Water Terminus in the 1870s, then referred to simply as Deepwater, located north of the site of the Halifax Casino today, but it, too, had become inadequate. By 1912, the federal government was funding an extensive system of docks, sheds, and railway yards near the entrance to the harbour. A century later, the Ocean Terminals, as the development is called, continues to grow as Halifax competes with American ports to the south for an increasing share of the North American shipping trade.

THE NORTHWEST ARM

The Northwest Arm is an unusual body of water in that it is 3 miles long and narrow enough in places to yell across and be heard. It is also deep enough for the largest recreational craft and even for a small ship. It is popular for recreation, and in summer is full of people on paddleboards and in racing sculls, canoes, and small sailboats. Because of where it is situated, it cuts Halifax in two and greatly complicates the movement of traffic.

The minesweepers patrolling the harbour entrance during wartime operated from the Northwest Arm.

EASTERN PASSAGE

Eastern Passage is another long and narrow body of water that separates the harbour's biggest island from the mainland. Huge car-carrying ships travel into Eastern Passage to unload hundreds of thousands of vehicles annually. Because of the shallow water in the outer harbour outside of McNabs Island, the ships are obliged to enter the inner harbour, do a 180-degree turn around the island, and head back out toward the horizon. Then they turn around, dock at Eastern Passage, and start unloading.

HALIFAX WATERFRONT IN 1917 AND TODAY, NORTH TO SOUTH

NAME OR OWNER	BUSINESS THEN	AT THE LOCATION TODAY
CGR Pier 9	Commercial shipping	Richmond Terminals
CGR Pier 7 & 8	Commercial shipping	Richmond Terminals
CGR Pier 6	Commercial shipping	Richmond Terminals
St. Joseph's Boat Club	Amateur competitive rowing	Irving Shipyard
North Ferry	Pedestrian ferry to Dartmouth	Irving Shipyard
Lorne Amateur Aquatic Club	Amateur competitive rowing	Irving Shipyard
Acadia Sugar Refinery	Manufacturing	Irving Shipyard
Shipyard Wharves	Docking for repairs and for tugs	Irving Shipyard
Halifax Graving Dock	Ship repair	Irving Shipyard Graving Dock
Magazine Wharf	Canadian Militia	Dockyard
Hospital Wharf	HMC Dockyard	Dockyard
Wharf 4	HMC Dockyard Coaling Wharf	Dockyard
Wharf 3	HMC Dockyard	Dockyard

Wharf 2	HMC Dockyard Anchor Wharf	Dockyard
Wharf 1	HMC Dockyard	Dockyard
CGR Deep Water Terminus Pier 5	Commercial shipping	Dockyard
CGR Deep Water Terminus Pier 4	Commercial shipping	Dockyard
CGR Deep Water Terminus Pier 3	Commercial shipping	Dockyard
CGR Deep Water Terminus Old Pier 2	Commercial shipping	Dockyard
CGR Deep Water Terminus Pier 2	Commercial shipping	Dockyard
Black & Flinn	Produce wholesalers	Dockyard
William Roche	Coal dealer	Dockyard
Mackay-Bennett	Telegraph cable Ship base	Casino
DeWolf's north	Shipping line agent	Casino
DeWolf's south	Shipping line agent	Casino
Liverpool	N/A	Casino
S. M. Brookfield	Construction	Casino
H. R. Silver	Commission merchants	Casino
Cronan's north	Dry goods	Casino
Cronan's south	Dry goods	Casino
Commercial	General wharfage	Purdy's Tower 1
Furness Withy & Co.	Shipping line agent	Purdy's Wharf
A. O'Connor Co.	Dry goods merchant	Hotel
William McFatridge	Diving and marine salvage	Hotel
Ordnance	Imperial use	Hotel
Central	General wharfage	Hotel
Pickford & Black	Shipping line	Historic Properties

Cook	Construction	Historic Properties
Imperial Oil	Oil wholesalers	Law courts
Dwyer's	N/A	Law courts
John Tobin & Co.	Wholesale grocers	Harbour ferry
Stayner	N/A	Harbour ferry
Dartmouth Ferry	Dartmouth steam ferry	George Street
Market	Public use	George Street
Western Union Cable Co.	Telegraph cable ships	Cable Wharf
City	Public use	Queen's Marque
King's Wharf	Imperial use	Queen's Marque
Engineers	N/A	Queen's Marque
W. & C. H. Mitchell	West India merchants	Queen's Marque
N. and M. Smith north	Fish wholesalers	Maritime Museum
N. and M. Smith south	Fish wholesalers	Maritime Museum
Plant Steamship Line	Shipping & passenger service	Naval memorial
Farquhar	Marine salvage and construction	Naval memorial
Bentley	Wood products	Parking lot
Levi Hart	N/A	Parking lot
F. W. Bissett	Fish and fish oils	Parking lot
G. S. Campbell	Ships agent & tugboat service	Foot of Salter Street
Joseph Wood & Co.	Ship agents and brokers	Boardwalk over water
Phelan	N/A	Boardwalk over water
Robin, Jones & Whitman	Fish exporters	Boardwalk over water
George E. Boak & Son	Coal merchant	Boardwalk over water
Hugh D. McKenzie	Coal merchant	Bishop's Landing

A. N. Whitman	Fish exporters	Bishop's Landing
John McInnis & Son	Lumber merchants	Bishop's Landing
Boutilier	Fish dealer	Bishop's Landing
North Atlantic Fisheries	Fish dealers	Bishop's Landing
Hart's north	Commission merchants	Cunard Building
Hart's south	Commission merchants	Cunard Building
Dominion	N/A	NS Power HQ
Dominion Coal Co.	Coal shipping terminal	NS Power HQ
Halifax Electric Tram Co.	Transportation	Pier 20

Sources: McAlpine's Halifax City Directory 1917*, harbour charts, and photographs.*

Many dock owners rented space to other companies at their docks or in buildings nearby. Having space on the waterfront was essential for many businesses; however, space was at a premium in the days before trucking became common. Trains went to relatively few locations, and there were no airlines. That meant there was a bustling maritime trade along the Nova Scotia coast and to other provinces, Europe, Newfoundland (not yet part of Canada), and the US, all centred on the Halifax waterfront.

View south at the waterfront from the grain elevator at Pier 2, with Georges and McNabs Islands upper right, c. 1900. The white yacht at lower left may be Waterus, *which became HMCS* Hochelaga. (TOM LYNSKEY)

View north from the grain elevator, c. 1900, with the sugar refinery jutting above the horizon left of centre. The explosion occurred just past the sugar refinery. The large buildings centre right belong to the Naval Dockyard, with the Mast House prominent. (NS ARCHIVES)

CHAPTER 2

CANADA'S NAVAL WOES

When Britannia ruled the waves, it had the four corners of the North Atlantic covered. In addition to the island of Great Britain with its many naval bases, it had imperial fortresses to the south at Gibraltar, southwest at Bermuda, and northwest at Halifax. Prior to the First World War, it had handed the assets of the Naval Dockyard to the Canadian government with the proviso that they would be maintained in case the RN needed to return. In the meantime, Canada was left to figure out how to handle the defence of its coastline and ports.

A NEW WARSHIP ARRIVES

In the pre-dawn of a cold December morning, the lookouts aboard HMS *Changuinola* were studying the beam from a lighthouse off their port bow. By 5:00 A.M. the pattern of flashes and eclipses told them it was the Sambro Light, bearing north northwest. The ship had just crossed the Atlantic Ocean from the United Kingdom and was in the approaches to Halifax Harbour. It was December 5, 1917, the third year of the First World War.

The day before *Changuinola* arrived, the armed merchant cruiser HMS *Victorian* of the Allan Line had led the steamships *Pak Ling*, carrying a general cargo; the *Northumberland*, with a load of frozen mutton and lamb; and the Canadian Pacific Ocean Services passenger liner *Metagama* out of the harbour toward the British Isles. The tanker *Orangeleaf* joined the convoy the next day.[6]

The *Northumberland* had come all the way from New Zealand, bound for Great Britain, via the Panama Canal and up to Halifax to avoid crossing the Atlantic Ocean alone, where it might encounter a German submarine. Such was the effort required to keep the European Allies fighting the war, calling for many ships, brave sailors, complex planning, and a, deep secluded harbour in which to gather convoy ships. That harbour was Halifax.

At 6:38, *Changuinola* slowed and crewmen retrieved the paravanes, which reduced the danger of running into a mine. Within an hour, it passed the Chebucto Head Light, with HMCS *Baleine* and *Patrol Vessel*-VII in sight.[7] The two minesweepers were just beginning their daily sweep of the channels leading into the harbour. They travelled about 500 yards apart with a single wire strung between them to snag any mines that got set overnight.[8]

Changuinola was entering the outer harbour, gliding between the Lichfield and Neverfail Shoals, with more than 6 miles to go before reaching the inner harbour. Off the starboard bow, several ships were anchored, awaiting the dawn so they could be permitted entrance into the harbour. The searchlights and guns on McNabs Island came into view on the vessel's right, at Fort McNab, Fort Hugonin, and Ives Point, and on the left at Sandwich Battery, Connaught Battery, and Point Pleasant, testifying to what an ordeal it would have been for an enemy ship attempting to fight its way in. None had ever bothered to try.

Capt. Howard Wilcox was in command of *Changuinola.* Appointed on August 7, 1917, he took over from Henry Brocklebank, who had spent the previous three years with the ship as part of the 10th Cruiser Squadron blockade that kept neutral ships from trading with Germany while monitoring movements of German Navy ships. Brocklebank's job had been to patrol the area between Greenland and the British Isles, stopping ships and confirming who they were, what they were carrying, and where they were bound.

The 411-foot-long *Changuinola* was 51 feet wide and displaced 6,011 tons. Like HMS *Victorian,* it was an armed merchant cruiser, built as a cargo carrier but modified to do some of the work of a warship. Launched on July 30, 1912, from the Swan Hunter & Wigham Richardson shipyard at Newcastle for the Hamburg America Line, it was a banana boat for the United Fruit Company when the RN requisitioned it in December 1914. The decks

Changuinola *in dazzle pattern, designed to mislead submarine captains into taking up an incorrect firing position when planning their attack. Most British naval and merchant ships received dazzle patterns in 1917 and 1918.* (© IMPERIAL WAR MUSEUM [SP 2036])

were reinforced, guns mounted, and the ship was reconfigured for fighting rather than freighting. Wilcox commanded a complement of 27 officers with 190 in the crew. *Changuinola* had departed from Glasgow for Halifax on November 21, beginning a new role as a convoy escort ship.[9]

Under the guidance of a Halifax pilot, Captain Wilcox conned the ship past the Examination Anchorage, where the merchant ships awaited their turn to enter the harbour. As a British warship, *Changuinola* was not required to submit to examination. With the coming of dawn, the Examination vessel was flying the Canadian Blue Ensign and the special pilot flag with a red-and-white horizontal stripe surrounded by a blue border, indicating the harbour was open to traffic. *Changuinola* continued alongside McNabs Island off to the right and slowed to pass through the gate of the outer submarine net that stretched across the entrance to the inner harbour between McNabs Island and the breakwater at Point Pleasant. As *Changuinola* passed through, Assistant Examining Officer Roland Iceton, aboard HMCS *Niobe*, received a telephone call from the gate ship confirming that *Changuinola* had passed through.

Large fishing schooner. Note the sizes of the men in the stern relative to the heights of the masts. (NAVAL MUSEUM OF HALIFAX)

With his ship safely steaming into the inner harbour, Wilcox noted a sprawling construction site next to Point Pleasant on the left. Barges and cranes were moving vast amounts of stone into place in the water as Cook Construction Company and Wheaton Brothers worked on building the Ocean Terminals docks. Work had begun before the war started and would continue for another decade before the whole project was completed. Within minutes, *Changuinola* went through the inner submarine net, which triggered another call to Iceton. On the ship's left, a forest of masts appeared from three dozen fishing and freighting schooners tied up on the Halifax waterfront.

Changuinola continued north through the inner harbour, with downtown Halifax and the waterfront on its left and Dartmouth on its right, past the Deep Water Terminus, and up to the area where the naval infrastructure resided—the dockyard, jetties, graving dock, ship repair facilities, and railway yards of a nation busy coping with a new kind of war at sea, for which the country was ill-prepared. London had warned Ottawa to expect a significant increase in submarine activity and seemed to expect Canada's woefully inadequate navy to deal with it. The matter was so urgent that Ottawa had just sent a delegation to London to find out what they needed to do to prepare.

By 9:00 A.M. on December 5, *Changuinola* was anchoring off the Royal Canadian Naval Dockyard, southeast of HMCS *Niobe*. The only real Canadian warship stationed at Halifax, moored just north of Jetty 4 at the south entrance to The Narrows, HMCS *Niobe* was no longer capable of going to sea. By then, Roland Iceton could see the ship and made a note of its location, anchored in the stream south of HMS *Highflyer*, a light cruiser, waiting to escort a convoy of merchant ships to Europe. *Changuinola* was also expected to be leaving with a convoy in a week's time.

Changuinola's crew immediately prepared to take on water and fuel. Before long, fresh water was being pumped aboard from a lighter owned by the Halifax Water Boat Company attached to the ship's port side (at ten cents per 1,000 gallons[10]). Twenty-year-old Gerald Doody, a popular hockey player and respected young businessman, was the managing director of the Halifax Water Boat Company. He had just twenty-four hours to live.[11] Coal was also coming aboard from a barge on the starboard side. The water lighter left near 6:00 P.M., but the coaling went on until 11:30 that night.

This was the age of steam. Coal was king, and Nova Scotia was flush with it. Barques, brigs, and terns had been all but replaced by ships with engines refined over the past century, driving huge coal-powered vessels at unprecedented speeds, while consuming astounding amounts of coal. The ships in Halifax were mostly working vessels, although the glamorous passenger liners with names like *Mauretania* and *Olympic* appeared in the harbour from time to time. They were not, however, carrying the rich and famous to Europe. They were carrying soldiers by the thousands.

MASTERY OF THE ATLANTIC

The war at sea had taken a new turn, and the Allied war machine was adjusting. *Changuinola*'s change from blockade enforcer to convoy escort was a piece of the transformation. The new reality was signalled when the SS *Stephano*, a passenger liner owned by the New York, Newfoundland and Halifax Steamship Company, was sunk off Nantucket, one of five that went down that day. It was not the sinkings that were unusual. What got everybody's attention was that the vessel targeting the five ships was a U-boat—in North American waters! It was a shock. Up to then, German submarines had operated only in Europe. Now it was clear: they were able to operate anywhere on the Atlantic. With two-thirds of the food consumed in the British Isles imported, the British merchant marine had a lot of ships that needed protection. Forty-three percent of the world's merchant vessels—9,200—were of British registry, compared to just 4 percent of American registry.[12] Most of them were operating on the North Atlantic, and they were all at risk.

The British were concerned, but they were also severely annoyed at the enemy's brazen conduct. The 240-foot U-53's captain had had the gall to pay a courtesy visit to Newport, Rhode Island, in the neutral United States. While it was ashore, Americans were even treated to a tour of the sub. When it departed, the US Navy (USN) decided to shadow it and witnessed a bizarre scene on October 8, 1916, as U-53 sank the *Stephano*, travelling from Halifax to New York, off Nantucket. Officers, crew and 146 passengers, most of whom were American citizens, were allowed to leave the ship and were picked up by the American warships on the scene. The Germans then boarded and looted the British-registered ship, before sinking it without interference from the Americans.[13]

In 1884, Bowring Brothers of St. John's started the New York, Newfoundland and Halifax Steamship Company, with the SS *Miranda* and SS *Portia*. Under the name of Red Cross Line, they provided a St. John's–Halifax–New York passenger service, which eventually included the *Stephano.* The ship was a moneymaker that took well-heeled New Englanders north in the summer and fall. In late winter the vessel's innards were gutted, the china and silverware were taken ashore, and the hardwood floors were covered with planking. Then it was loaded with sealers and sent "to the ice," that violent, bloody, deadly, immensely profitable business that destroyed a lot of seals and sealers.

At the time of the *Stephano*'s sinking, an air of desperation was growing around the tables of German war strategists. Not that the Allied generals were outfoxing them—they had no Wellington or Montgomery—but the Germans likewise had no Frederick the Great or Erwin Rommel. They shared the common unenlightened strategy of throwing trainloads of young men into the fray; however, the Germans were running low on young men to sacrifice. The Allies could always bring additional shiploads of soldiers from New Zealand or South Africa or Canada or Algeria. They had a boundless supply that needed to be cut off, along with the war *matériel* and food. The Germans' answer was the submarine, which had been accomplishing their objective in European waters. Now, U-boats were heading to North America, and Canada was scrambling to prepare.

CANADA'S UNDECLARED WAR

Everything that Canada did during the war was at the bidding of the British. Nobody in Canada decided that their country would go to war with Germany or Austria or the Ottoman Empire. It was a given that when the government of the United Kingdom declared war on Germany, Canada was also at war. It was part of the authority that European nations exercised over much of the Earth, collectively built up over the centuries as they acquired empires. It gave the British the right to take men in India, put them into uniforms, and send them to attack German colonies in Africa. Germany then responded by taking Africans from their colonies to fight the Indian soldiers. Although there was no animosity toward one another—and little understanding of why all this was happening—these men were then obliged to kill or be killed. Such were the strange times and ways of the First World War. Black men in Africa

Red Cross Line dishes recovered from the site of G. S. Campbell's Wharf in Halifax Harbour. The spoons are engraved with the names of SS Stephano *and SS* Florizel. (AUTHOR'S COLLECTION)

had been put into French uniforms, trained, and then taken to Europe to kill white Germans.

With these baffling goings-on, it's not much of a stretch to expect the descendants of British settlers in Australia and New Zealand to return to Europe, after more than a century away, and travel tens of thousands of miles to take up arms against Turkish soldiers they had never heard of until they faced them at Gallipoli. No matter. The enemy of the Mother Country was the enemy of her dominions.

As a dominion, Canada's role was to supply what the British needed and do what the British wanted. Right now, Ottawa needed to know what was required of the country's tiny, ill-equipped navy. The Germans knew that time was not on their side, and they saw the solution not in the trenches but rather on the Atlantic. At the beginning of 1917, they announced unrestricted submarine warfare starting on February 1. They advertised that the ships of any nation, neutral or otherwise, including American, carrying cargo to the United Kingdom or France would be sunk.

The strategy was a wild success. Over a four-month period, the Germans averaged 189 ships sunk per month. In April 1917, the Allies lost 395 ships in the worst month of the war.[14] All told, Germany put 365 U-boats to sea against the Allies in the First World War, of which 178 were sunk.[15] The RCN did not participate in any of the sinkings. It had nowhere near the firepower for such undertakings.

As of November 20, 1917, the Liverpool Shipowners Association reported that 231 ships—from Liverpool alone—had been lost to the war, with a total tonnage of 1,465,046, while new vessels added to the fleet numbered 131. The replacement cost of those vessels was estimated to be £103,500,000, which would be more than £2.6 billion today.[16]

The British knew they could not sustain such losses. They responded by sailing ships across the Atlantic in groups, instead of alone and vulnerable to attack, with a protective escort of naval ships like *Changuinola*. The first convoys consisted of two or three troopships with an escort, usually an armed merchant cruiser that also carried freight. For example, the AMC *Orama* loaded cargo, and then on August 1, 1917, it departed from Halifax in convoy with the AMC *Carmania*, troop carriers *Adriatic* and *Orduña*, and SS *Bermudian* of Canada Steamship Lines.[17]

The most impressive convoy was convened at the beginning of the war, when the 1st Canadian Troop Convoy, carrying 30,000 young Canadians, assembled at Gaspé Bay, leaving there on October 3, 1914, in thirty-one ships. Off Cape Race, the sister ship of the *Stephano*, the SS *Florizel*, joined them, carrying a contingent of 500 Newfoundlanders, the group known to this day as "The First 500." There would be many more.

The cargo convoys started during the summer of 1917. RN Rear Admiral Bertram Chambers, port convoy officer for Canada, wrote later that convoys first went from Sydney, NS, on July 10.[18] The last Sydney convoy that year departed on November 6, after which the movement of east coast convoys transferred to Halifax's ice-free harbour.[19]

The first convoy from Halifax under Admiral Chambers's command left on November 21, just fifteen days before the Halifax Explosion.[20] One after another, from Canadian and American ports, ships found their way to Halifax, where they were taken into the Bedford Basin to anchor until departure day. By the summer of 1917, 89 percent of the cargo space in ships leaving Canadian ports was used for government service in support of the war, with most heading for British ports.[21]

STRIVING FOR NAVAL PROFICIENCY

Life was complicated for the fledgling RCN and its Halifax base. It was ten years since the British government had shut down the dockyard, opened in 1759 and the reason Halifax had been founded. In the fall of 1917, Halifax was trying to morph from a port controlled by the British to one controlled by Canadians. It was not going well. With a century and a half of RN presence, Canadian governments had been happy to leave the defence of Canada to the British. But, by January 1, 1907, the British had gone home, and the dockyard lay empty. The next three years would be the only period in its history that Halifax was without a naval presence. Building a navy for Canada would be painfully slow.

The Admiralty, the bureaucracy that ran Britain's RN took the approach that Canada's naval needs would best be served through financial contributions to build ships for its navy. As the cost of maintaining the vast and complex RN increased, the British pressured the colonies to share the cost, but with the danger of an invasion from the United States declining, Canadian governments, like Wilfrid Laurier's, managed to keep skirting the issue. However, the British made it clear that with German naval expansion, they intended to withdraw the battle fleets from overseas to home waters. And they did.

It would take more than three years to even start building a navy.

The problem was twofold: Canadian politics and the evolving nature of naval warfare. French Canadians didn't want a navy that would give Canada the mobility to get entangled in British wars elsewhere, while English Canadians were scornful of anything that wasn't up to the standards of the RN. They were in denial. Truth be told, Canada was not a maritime nation. With the vast majority of the population living hundreds, if not thousands, of miles from the ocean, Canadians gave it little thought. Short shrift for a naval presence was manifested when the Second World War became inevitable. As the federal government prepared the budget, it allocated $29.8 million for the air force, $21 million for the army, and just $8.8 million for the navy.

Navies were alarmingly expensive. The decades-long switch from sail to steam had provoked a host of new vessel configurations and weaponry. Submarines, torpedo boats, destroyers, all-big-gun battleships, steam turbines, and internal combustion engines radically complicated the equipping of a navy. Battleships became so costly that nations would soon be afraid to send them to sea because to lose one would be catastrophic.

Wilfrid Laurier's government took small steps in the direction of a Canadian navy. If there was to be one, there had to be a commander. On May 15, 1908, Guelph, ON, native Capt. Charles Kingsmill, who had commanded multiple RN warships, came home to Canada. He was transferred from the RN to Canada's marine service with the intention that he would command the soon-to-exist Canadian navy. To prepare, he was promoted to rear admiral. That was the easy part. Then he encountered the foot-dragging and infighting among the various interest groups. He didn't have a navy, but he had an impressive rank and title that came with a jaunty uniform. He soldiered on.[22] Finally, on January 12, 1910, Prime Minister Laurier introduced the Naval Service Act of Canada.[23] The bill passed in May, not because of widespread concurrence but because the government's majority carried it in Parliament.

To stay ahead of the opposition, the government rushed to get everything in place before the next election, expected in the fall of 1912. Kingsmill found a couple of cruisers in England, one for each coast in Canada, so officer training could start. HMCS *Niobe* arrived at Halifax on October 21, while HMCS *Rainbow* travelled the 15,000 miles around Cape Horn en route to Esquimalt, British Columbia, and arrived on November 7.[24] Some RN officers transferred to Canada to fill the key posts. Ten new warships were planned, and Canadian Vickers Limited was incorporated in June 1911 with the hope of building them in Montréal. Things were going swimmingly.

Then, the bottom fell out. The inevitable election came on September 21, 1911, a year earlier than anticipated. It produced a Conservative win under Halifax native Robert Borden, and major changes followed. The optimistic enterprise to build a navy that had started under Laurier was suddenly at a standstill. On November 5, 1912, the Borden government introduced the Naval Aid Bill, which proposed a $35 million contribution to the construction of three battleships for the RN. The debate lasted all winter, but the bill passed on May 15, 1913, just a year before the First World War. Then, the bill went to the Liberal-dominated Senate and got defeated. Utterly taken aback, the government had no Plan B.

By then, the First World War was ramping up. Canada would not be able to provide any naval response. Other dominions such as Australia, with a battle cruiser, four light cruisers, three destroyers, and two submarines, and New Zealand, with a battle cruiser and three light cruisers, had Canada entirely outclassed.[25] Men had enlisted in Halifax, but with just one ship—*Niobe*—that spent more time in dry dock than at sea, there wasn't much to do, so they soon drifted away. Between 1911 and 1912, what there was of a navy recorded 112 enlistments and 149 desertions.[26] The RCN started the First World War with fewer than 400 officers and men.[27] They were unable to crew even the two aging warships the government had procured for them.

At the beginning of the war, Canadian government attempts to confer with the British in finding a naval role for Canada were met with the disdainful response to forget about the navy and concentrate on the army. With the war underway, Borden suggested in November 1914 that the new Canadian Vickers plant at Montréal could be used to construct destroyers or submarines for the defence of Halifax. His proposal received a similarly dismissive response: Halifax did not need any further protection.

The war would not wait. Canadian sailors went into the RN instead. Officer training had gone forward when fourteen midshipmen entered the Canadian naval college in January 1911, but by 1917 all of these had become officers in the RN. Soon, the Canadian government, which supposedly had its own navy, was recruiting men for the RN instead. As of March 31, 1917, 1,331 had entered the Royal Naval Canadian Volunteer Reserve and 1,188 were serving on RN ships. And other RN services were also scooping up Canadian sailors to man British war assets.[28]

The low point came with the discovery that the British government had quietly contracted with Vickers, in Montréal, to build ten submarines for the RN, beginning in January 1915. Nobody bothered to advise the Canadian government.

When, all of a sudden, German submarines appeared in the western Atlantic, the Admiralty was in a flap and started demanding Canada increase its patrols. For the officers who had been repeatedly denied Admiralty support for increasing the Canadian navy's scanty anti-submarine forces, these new directives from London had a hollow ring. The Canadian government flatly rejected the notion that the sad state of the dominion's anti-submarine force was in any way Ottawa's fault.[29] The government also conveniently forgot that it had scuttled Laurier's work following the passing of the Naval Service Act.

It took a lot of to-ing and fro-ing to get the relationship off the rocks, but by February 1917, plans were in place to rapidly and dramatically expand the RCN's fleet. Plans were fine, but with limited time available to build ships and a scarcity of guns to equip them, the RCN would not get what it had been hoping for throughout the war. And so, with pressure mounting to do something, but with no ships and no clear directives, Admiral Kingsmill sent a delegation to England to consult with the RN as to how the British saw the U-boat threat, what they expected from the Canadian navy, and what equipment they were willing to provide.

For the month of December 1917 and into January 1918, Capt. Edward H. Martin, who was responsible for the naval defence of Halifax and its immediate approaches, was away. Fifty-eight years old, he had retired from the RN in 1909 after more than thirty-six years of service and joined the RCN upon its formation. Martin left fifty-four-year-old Capt. Frederick Pasco, also a retired RN captain, in charge of the dockyard, making Pasco the senior RCN officer in Halifax. Second in command was another ex-RN man, Walter Hose, the captain of patrols, in charge of the mishmash of Canadian naval vessels that guarded the entrance to Halifax and patrolled Canada's east coast. In 1921, Hose succeeded Kingsmill as director of the Naval Service.

These men had nothing to do with the convoys. Those were handled by the RN, under Rear Admiral Chambers. Another key person in the harbour was also an RN alumnus, forty-year-old Acting Commander Frederick Evan Wyatt, the chief examining officer who controlled all movements of ships into and out of the port. The other individuals who were key to running the harbour were Harbourmaster Francis Rudolf, responsible for the non-naval vessels that used Halifax, and the Halifax pilots, who moved ships in and out of the harbour.

CANADA'S SHIPS OF WAR

Until the fall of 1917, all the ships of the RCN were either hand-me-downs from the RN, vessels scrounged from other government departments such as Marine and Fisheries, or a variety of other craft that were purchased and converted for patrolling the seacoast.

The only real warship was HMCS *Niobe*, which arrived after its best-before date and whose wartime service was, therefore, brief. With nowhere near the number of personnel required to put the ship to sea when it arrived, it was stationed at Halifax and manned by 16 RN officers and 194 RN ratings. These were supplemented by 28 RCN and Royal Naval Canadian Volunteer Reserve officers, and 360 ratings. That still wasn't enough until the government of Newfoundland—which was still thirty-five years away from becoming a Canadian province—agreed to assign one officer and 106 ratings from the Newfoundland Division of the Royal Naval Reserve. That gave a ship's company of 705. It was more than four years since the founding of the RCN and Canadians comprised just over half the crew of Canada's first sizable warship.

Canada's first real warship, HMCS Niobe, *in the Halifax dry dock, after running aground July 30, 1911. It was out of action for more than a year.* (NS ARCHIVES)

From October 1914 to July 1915, *Niobe* sailed with British cruisers patrolling the American coast, including off New York Harbor, where thirty-eight German ships had become trapped when the declaration of war came.[30] But ten months at sea spelled the end of the worn-out cruiser. By September

1915, its deteriorating condition meant that *Niobe* had to be removed from operations to become a depot ship at Halifax. Guns were removed, engines partially dismantled, and roofing erected over the quarterdeck and battery to provide space for offices. The gable roofing made it appear the way we imagine Noah's ark looked. It was a sad sight. There, *Niobe* remained for the rest of the war, anchored just north of Jetty 4. It became head office for the RCN in Halifax, where some 1,200 naval, transport, intelligence, and communications staff were housed. It was held in place 20–30 feet from shore with a total of five anchors buried in the shoreline and the bottom around the ship. People came and went along a short wooden jetty, called the hospital wharf, which ran out from shore to the gangway.

HMCS *Niobe* was the first and last significant Canadian warship to sail from Halifax during the First World War. The RCN had its hands full keeping the key port of Halifax running as the headwinds increased. Author Janet Maybee has written: "The dangers and challenges multiplied with the onset of the First World War and the huge increase in shipping as convoys gathered in Bedford Basin to transport troops and supplies to Europe. There were no more pilots added to the roster, no additional pilot boats, and a high degree of confusion about who was in charge of the harbour: the convoy commander? The captain superintendent? The pre-war harbourmaster? The British navy? The very modest and barely hatched Canadian navy? The chief examining officer?"[31]

The RCN was left with a mishmash of smaller craft, including converted yachts and small passenger liners, fishery patrol vessels, hydrographic survey ships, trawlers, drifters, tugs, and motor launches. These vessels performed the work of coastal patrol, minesweeping, guarding ports and facilities, and acting as gate vessels and tenders. The fastest was HMCS *Grilse*, a converted yacht whose 6,000 hp turbine engines gave it a respectable top speed of 32 knots, making it one of the few RCN ships capable of catching a U-boat on the surface. *Tuna*, a torpedo boat, was another.[32]

There were even a couple of submarines, CC1 and CC2, built at Seattle for the Chilean government. The deal fell through, and British Columbia premier Sir Richard McBride decided to purchase them for the navy. In 1914,

Niobe *permanently moored at the Hospital Wharf, north of Jetty 4.* (NAVAL MUSEUM OF HALIFAX)

they were commissioned into the RCN. In 1917, they were ordered to Europe, leaving for Halifax with their support ship *Shearwater* on June 21, 1917. They were the first Canadian warships to transit the Panama Canal. Unfit for a transatlantic crossing, they remained in Halifax, taking up dock space, and were sold for scrap in 1920.

Other than *Niobe*, the armament on RCN ships was limited. They carried 6- and 12-pounder guns, depending on the size of the vessel. The QF

12-pounder 12 cwt gun was a 76 mm (3-inch) calibre naval gun introduced in 1894. The barrel was 3 inches in diameter measured on the inside. Twelve-pounder referred to the projectile weight and 12 cwt or twelve hundredweight (112 pounds) referred to the weight of the barrel and breech—12 cwt × 112 pounds, which equates to 1,344 pounds. QF meant quick firing; they could fire up to fifteen rounds per minute. The other common gun used on Canadian naval vessels was the QF 6-pounder 8 cwt, a 57 mm (2.24-inch) gun introduced in 1885 and meant for use against torpedo boats and submarines, when they came along. Compare that with the obsolete *Niobe*, which was equipped with sixteen 6-inch guns, twelve 12-pounders, and five 3-pounders.[33] When the RN's Grand Fleet squared off with the Imperial German Navy's High Seas Fleet at the only noteworthy sea battle of the First World War, Jutland, the biggest guns had a diameter of 15 inches.

As an indicator of just how limited Canada's fleet was in 1919, of the ships that had been gathered together, only two had been assigned international distinguishing signal letters, compared to Australia, which had seventeen such vessels, consisting of cruisers, destroyers, and a tanker. Canada had no destroyers and the only cruiser on the east coast was *Niobe*, which had not been to sea in more than two years and would soon be condemned. The other was *Rainbow*, far removed on Canada's west coast at Esquimalt.

CHAPTER 3

THE STRESSED HARBOUR

When *Changuinola* entered the harbour the day before the Halifax Explosion, ships and boats were anchored or tied up everywhere. The First World War was in its fourth year, and nowhere in Canada were its effects felt more than at Halifax, the mainland North American naval port closest to Europe and a world-class harbour. Ships were in constant movement, arriving and departing with goods that had to get to Europe to support the war. December 5, 1917, would see the arrival of the merchant steamships *Calonne*, *Corfe Castle*, *Saint Bede*, *Polyphemus*, *Olaf Kyrre*, *Noruega*, *Mississippi*, *Eolo*, and *Mont Blanc*. The steady stream of merchant ships carried foodstuffs, weapons, ammunition, machinery, clothing, and every item imaginable for the war in Europe. Some carried fuel. Some carried passengers.

New soldiers were heading across the Atlantic Ocean, while the wounded and those maimed in body and spirit were returning to begin new and very different lives from the ones they had left. The famous liner RMS *Olympic*, sister ship of the ill-fated *Titanic* and the busiest of the twenty-five ships that carried Canadian soldiers to Europe, was a regular in Halifax.[34] Just a week previous to December 6, the Cunard Steamship Company liner *Saxonia* had arrived with returning soldiers who disembarked at the immigration centre in Deepwater Pier 2. The ship was under the command of Arthur Rostron. As captain of RMS *Carpathia* in 1912, Rostron had raced his ship through the night to save some 705 *Titanic* survivors. The week before Rostron's arrival in the *Saxonia*, his old ship the *Carpathia* had arrived at Halifax from New York and departed again for England on November 26, 1917. The following July 17, 1918, three torpedoes brought an end to the famous vessel, off the coast of Ireland.[35]

SS *IMO*

Far in the harbour, about to take on coal, was a ship that looked something like a downsized *Titanic*. The ship was smaller and older but the lines were the same. It was the *Imo*, built in the same shipyard as the *Titanic* for the same owners, White Star Line.

The *Imo* began its life as the SS *Runic*. It was constructed in Belfast by Harland & Wolff, the builders of the *Titanic*. Even though the *Titanic* was a much larger vessel, compared end to end, the similarities are evident as Harland & Wolff stuck to their proven hull designs originated by Edward Harland in the Oceanic class of ships of the 1870s. Launched in 1889, the *Runic* carried a dozen or so passengers but most aboard on any given voyage were of the four-legged variety—cattle. The West India & Pacific Steamship Company purchased the ship in 1895 and renamed it *Tampican*. In 1912, it again changed owners when a Norwegian firm, Southern Pacific Whaling Company bought it and renamed it *Imo*.

The SS *Imo* arrived in Halifax from Rotterdam on December 3, with a stop at Haugesund, Norway, to pick up crew members. It was carrying only ballast. As a neutral ship, it was headed to New York for a cargo of food, but the British required non-aligned ships to undergo an inspection to ensure they were truly neutral. The examination of such ships was eventually moved to New York, but in December 1917 it took place in Halifax, having begun there in February 1917.

The *Imo*'s captain, Haakon From, decided to take on additional fuel while awaiting the inspection. On December 4, he ordered the ship's agents, Pickford & Black, to obtain 50 tons. Vast amounts of coal were being consumed from Halifax dealers, and the usual supplier, Dominion Coal, was unable to deliver. The *Cruizer* had not yet arrived from Louisbourg with the regular shipment, and their available stock was allocated to *Changuinola*. That caused a delay for George Smith of Pickford & Black. He went to their alternative supplier, William Roche, with an understanding that it would be loaded in time for the *Imo* to sail the next day, December 5.

Captain From was under pressure to keep his visit to Halifax as short as possible. Like many Norwegian sailors, the captain was a whaler, and a driver.

At forty-seven, he had spent more than a quarter of a century at sea, twelve years as captain. He had been to the Antarctic at least twice. He didn't like delays.

The *Imo* was under charter to the Commission for Relief in Belgium and had a huge sign on its side containing the words "Belgian Relief" inscribed in red. After invading Belgium at the beginning of the war, the German occupiers began requisitioning their food to help feed the German army. Because the tiny country grew less than a quarter of the food its citizens consumed, Belgium suffered a food shortage, and there was a risk of mass starvation.

Bringing in food from elsewhere was complicated by the fact that the British had imposed an economic blockade on Germany and its occupied countries, and they knew that the Germans would requisition any food that went in. A group of concerned people, primarily in the US, formed the Commission for Relief in Belgium (CRB) usually referred to simply as Belgian Relief. Under the leadership of its chairman, future US president Herbert Hoover, they declared that any food imported by the CRB remained the property of the American ambassador to Belgium and he could do whatever he wanted with it. With resentment from both sides of the war, Belgian Relief constantly navigated a tightrope and its ships were sometimes the targets of German U-boats. In April 1917, with the US on the verge of entering the war on the side of the Allies, the German government agreed to guarantee Belgian Relief vessels safe passage.

The job of keeping a whole country, albeit a small one, from starving was a significant undertaking. Belgian Relief ships, such as SS *Ganelon*, SS *Petra*, SS *Maumee*, and SS *Princess Clementine*, were in and out of Halifax Harbour regularly. On August 8, 1917, for example, there were four separate Belgian Relief vessels entering or leaving the harbour.[36] RN ships like *Changuinola* routinely stopped and inspected the relief ships in the mid-Atlantic to make sure they were following the rules. In fact, while serving with the 10th Cruiser Squadron, sailors from *Changuinola* had boarded the *Imo* on a previous trip at sea when it was carrying a cargo of wheat from Philadelphia to Rotterdam.[37]

The *Imo*'s Norwegian owners had originally used it as a whaling supply ship but it was now chartered to the CRB to transport relief supplies. On his ninth trip to Belgium, Captain From planned to proceed to New York, pick up his load, and be on his way. Once the inspection at Halifax was completed, the *Imo* could leave essentially when the captain wished without needing additional clearance from the RN, which concentrated on the movements of ships travelling in convoys.[38]

On the morning of December 5, while *Changuinola* was coaling, George Smith picked up Captain From in the Pickford & Black launch and took him to *Niobe* to get his route instructions and orders to proceed to New York.

Captain From expected the coal to be aboard his ship when he returned. The *Imo*'s inspection had been completed, and the Naval Control Office had notified customs that the ship had been cleared to sail when ready. At 1:30 P.M. harbour pilot William Hayes received a call at his home from Edward Beazley at the Halifax Pilotage Commission office on Bedford Row. Hayes would be taking the *Imo* to sea that afternoon and was instructed to be at the Pickford & Black Wharf at 2:00 P.M. to be taken to the ship. When his assignment was completed, one of the two pilot schooners owned by the commission would pick him up from the *Imo* outside the harbour. From there he might pilot an incoming ship into the harbour or be returned to Halifax.

At the same time, customs officer Arthur Lovett departed King's Wharf in downtown Halifax and went to the guard ship HMCS *Acadia*, at anchor in the Bedford Basin, to advise the officers that the paperwork was in order. With that done, Lovett headed to the *Imo* to deliver the ship's papers to the *Imo*'s captain. Around 2:30 the Pickford & Black boat was in the basin with Captain From and pilot Hayes aboard.

"Although it has not yet been definitely decided to drop Halifax as a port of call and search for all vessels bound for British and European neutrals, it is understood that as soon as an understanding is reached with the British authorities this will be done. An immense saving in coal, time, and tonnage will be accomplished, for the detour to Halifax and the delay there commonly consumed anywhere from five days to two weeks. It has been a source of great annoyance to shipping men."
—*Acadian Recorder*, January 16, 1918 (from New York, January 10)

On arriving at the *Imo*, they discovered that the barge with the 50 tons of coal they had been waiting for was just pulling alongside. By the time the coal was transferred, the nets guarding the harbour entrance would be closed for the night, and they would not be able to leave. Pilot Hayes had no option but to go back downtown in the Pickford & Black boat and return at first light.[39]

Another delay! Time was getting on and Captain From's patience was wearing thin.

In the meantime, a new ship appeared at the harbour entrance.

SS *MONT BLANC*

The French ship *Mont Blanc* had arrived after five days' steam from New York. As midnight approached on December 1, 1917, the *Mont Blanc* had slipped out of New York and begun its solitary passage to Halifax. The ultimate destination was Bordeaux. The holds and deck were crammed with a noxious cargo of flammables and explosives: TNT, picric acid, and guncotton, which looks like cotton but is a lethal and volatile compound employed in solid rocket propellants and other explosives. That was topped by a deck covered with 494 drums of a flammable substance called benzol.

Although the 3,279 GRT *Mont Blanc* was a French freighter, it had been built in England by Sir Raylton Dixon & Company at their Middlesbrough yard for Société générale de transports maritimes à vapeur, Marseilles, and launched in 1899. E. Anquetil of Rouen acquired it in 1906. It was then briefly owned by Gaston Petit, also of Rouen, and its last owner, as of 1915, was la Compagnie générale transatlantique, or CGT, of St. Nazaire. What Cunard and the White Star Line were to the British, CGT—often simply called the French Line—was to the French. While Cunard had famous ships like the *Lusitania* and *Queen Mary*, and White Star had the *Olympic* and *Titanic*, CGT had SS *Normandie* and SS *France*, to name just two of the fast and elegant vessels the line put to sea. In the first decade of the twentieth century, CGT began to accumulate what became a significant fleet of cargo ships, of which *Mont Blanc* was one. After a series of mergers, the company today is called CMA CGM, one of the world's premier container shipping companies. Their massive vessels call at Halifax regularly.

Mont Blanc's trip to Halifax was challenging for thirty-eight-year-old Capt. Aimé Le Médec and his officers and crew. Travelling in a ship well worn by eighteen years of hard labour was bad enough, but when they discovered the nature of the cargo that went aboard they were horrified. Then they were told they would not be sailing with a convoy from New York because their old clunker, with a top speed of 7.5 knots, would be unable to keep up with a fast convoy out of New York. They would have to go to Halifax, where both fast and slow convoys originated.

The German strategy in the war was to starve the British and French by cutting their lines of supply, ultimately leading to their defeat. The historical way to implement such a strategy was with a naval blockade to keep ships from entering or leaving port. This was not an option against a nation with so many ports and the world's most powerful navy, which the United Kingdom possessed. In fact, the Germans themselves were being blockaded by the RN. The Germans used submarines instead, their first extensive use in a war. Slow-moving freighters were easy prey, and many were sunk. The Germans would perfect the strategy in the Second World War, about which Winston Churchill once wrote that "the only thing that ever really frightened me during the war was the U-boat peril."[40]

The RN dabbled with small convoys of three or four troopships with an AMC escort, but losses of commercial freighters were so high by mid-1917 that the navy was forced to get serious. Convoys of freighters from Sydney began in July, switching to Halifax with the coming of winter.

Most of those ships had to find their way to Halifax, which became increasingly difficult in 1917. That meant the officers and crew of the *Mont Blanc* and their volatile cargo were on their own to slink their way along the coast between New York and Halifax, their only protection one gun forward and another aft. To handle those guns, they had a couple of artillery soldiers supplied, presumably, by the French Army.

Before entering the harbour, foreign merchant ships were required to

Royal Mail Ship (RMS) Virginian *stopping outside Halifax Harbour to pick up a pilot.* (AUTHOR'S COLLECTION)

engage the services of a Halifax pilot and have the approval of the examining officer. On the afternoon of December 5, 1917, Halifax pilot Francis Mackey took a ship from the Bedford Basin out through the harbour to the open sea, where he was picked up by the pilot boat, which cruised in an area called the pilot station, out from Chebucto Head. That vessel then took him to another ship nearby that had just arrived from New York and needed a pilot. Mackey climbed aboard the *Mont Blanc* and was taken to the bridge, where he met Capt. Aimé Le Médec. It was the captain's first trip on the *Mont Blanc* and his first visit to Halifax. Before guiding the ship into the harbour, Mackey directed it toward the Examination Anchorage, where they anchored below the guns of Fort McNab.

Just after 4:30, Lieutenant Terrence Freeman boarded the *Mont Blanc*. An hour later, after scrutinizing everything he needed to see and satisfying himself that the *Mont Blanc* did not pose a risk to the harbour—at least from a military perspective—he signalled the *Mont Blanc*'s arrival to the chief examining officer, Commander Wyatt on board HMCS *Niobe*, along with details of its cargo. One of Wyatt's assistants, Mate Roland Iceton, took the information as Wyatt had gone for the day.

That consumed the last hour of daylight. The nets were closed and would reopen at sun-up the next day. The ship was slated to enter the harbour first thing the next morning.

Going home was out of the question, so Mackey was obliged to spend the night aboard the *Mont Blanc*. He was philosophical; it was part of the job.

HMCS *ACADIA*

At 7:23 A.M. on December 6, the sun rose over the ocean outside Halifax. Crew members of *Changuinola* were already at work preparing their ship to load cargo. At 7:30, pilot William Hayes once again arrived in the Pickford & Black boat at *Acadia*, which lay anchored in the basin at the entrance to The Narrows, on the Dartmouth, or eastern, side. He reported to Lieutenant-Commander Jones of the Royal Navy Volunteer Reserve that he would be taking the *Imo* to sea. The boat then took him to the *Imo*, where he again greeted the captain and instructed him to raise the flag that would display the ship's international signal letters, NYXG, the indication to *Acadia* that they were ready to depart.

For HMCS *Acadia*, serving as the guard ship was a temporary assignment. *Acadia* was a hydrographic survey ship that had been repurposed as a patrol vessel, but after hard service at that, the vessel was in need of an overhaul. While waiting in the lineup for a space at the shipyard, on December 4 *Acadia* had been anchored and put to work as a guard ship and base for staff of the RN assigned to control the movement of neutral and Allied ships working for Belgian Relief. *Acadia* was replacing *Gulnare*, which was also awaiting repairs and was anchored across The Narrows entrance on the southwestern side of the basin. Personnel had already moved from *Gulnare* to *Acadia*, but telephone communications had not yet been set up between the headquarters ship *Niobe* and *Acadia*, so to communicate with *Niobe* a message had to be

HMCS Acadia *not far from where it was anchored on the morning of December 6, 1917.* (AUTHOR'S COLLECTION)

sent by semaphore from *Acadia* to *Gulnare*, and from there it was telephoned to *Niobe*.[41]

Despite its displacement of a modest 1,067 tons, *Acadia* was still one of the newer and more substantial ships in use by the Canadian navy in the First World War. Launched in 1913 from the yards of Swan Hunter & Wigham Richardson, Newcastle, it went into the RCN at the beginning of 1917 as HMCS *Acadia*, where it served until the end of the First World War. It returned to survey work, but in October 1939, it was back with the RCN for the duration of the Second World War. After that, it returned again to survey work until retiring from service on November 28, 1969.

Today, it lies tied on the Halifax waterfront as part of the collection of the Maritime Museum of the Atlantic. It's an interesting little ship, displaying the characteristics of iron and steel ships from the age of steam, with its riveted hull, triple-expansion steam engine, massive coal bunkers, oversized smokestack, majestic ventilators, straight bow, radio masts, external helm, fantail stern, and taffrail. It is the only ship afloat that served with the RCN for both world wars. It is also the only ship afloat to have survived the Halifax Explosion.

IMO DEPARTS

On December 6, 1917, there were nearly fifty ships resting at anchor in the Bedford Basin, many expecting to depart in convoy either the next day or on December 10. On the morning of December 6, one of the first pieces of business aboard *Acadia* was to raise two flags—one displaying the *Imo*'s international identification letters NYXG and a second with TXC, meaning "Proceed when ready."

A modern-day ship's captain would be uncomfortable with the way events were unfolding. Pilot Hayes and Captain From were about to take a long and somewhat awkward ship through a narrow waterway. Today—assuming there was no war to necessitate secrecy—they would already have been listening to marine radio and heard that the *Clara* was partway through The Narrows as pilot Edward Renner made regular radio checks to advise Halifax Traffic Control of their progress. They would have heard the *Mont Blanc* enter the harbour and state its intention to Halifax Traffic, and they would have heard the *Stella Maris* advise that it would be transiting The Narrows. Pilot Hayes would have advised Halifax Traffic of their own intentions to take the *Imo* to sea—along with a host of other information, including departure time and intended route—and Hayes would have known that any vessel, large or small, in the harbour that had a radio would have heard him provide all that information. Halifax Traffic would then have provided details about what was moving in the harbour, what ships were anchored along the *Imo*'s route, any ships about to enter the harbour, and much more. Everybody aboard ships would have known everything.

Instead, the four captains and pilots of the *Mont Blanc*, *Imo*, *Clara*, and *Stella Maris* respectively knew nothing except their own plans. As well, the sun was in Hayes's and From's eyes, there was glare off the water, there was patchy haze in the air, and ships were anchored all over the place. The captains would have to figure out for themselves which of those were anchored and which were moving. It was not a matter of looking up The Narrows and seeing the solitary *Mont Blanc* coming their way. Rather, they would see the *Clara* up close, followed by the *Stella Maris* along with Burns and Kelleher's workboat, CD-73, the North Ferry, and in the distance the *Mont Blanc*, *Changuinola*, *Highflyer*, and a batch of smaller navy craft at anchor. When they first saw the ship, they probably had no idea that the *Mont Blanc* was moving.

The *Imo* got underway at 8:10 A.M. with Johan Johansen at the helm in the presence of the captain and pilot on the bridge. As the anchor wound its way up and hung below the bow, the ship started toward The Narrows entrance. Second Officer Peter B'Jonnas was on deck, directing the recovery and stowing of the anchor, which did not go neatly into the hawsehole at the ship's bow as with most ships of the day, but had to be taken onto the deck in the style of older ships.

The exit from the Bedford Basin lay to the southeast. Pilot Hayes gave the order for a long sweeping turn to port as they weaved their way from their anchorage north of Birch Cove on the west side of the basin around the anchored ships, followed by another turn to starboard that would take them into The Narrows. As the *Imo* moved along, its four tall masts were visible above the Richmond piers in The Narrows, and Francis Mackey, aboard the *Mont Blanc*, made a mental note that a ship was about to enter the other end of The Narrows. That was the first he knew of the *Imo*'s presence.

Pilot Mackey had spent the night aboard the *Mont Blanc* outside the submarine net, which opened at daylight to let the waiting vessels into the crowded harbour. His ship was second in line. Mackey watched as an American ship, SS *Clara*, piloted by his colleague Edward Renner, went through the open gate. In the engine room, Chief Engineer Antoine Le Gat glanced at the clock that read 7:50 as the order came from the bridge for half speed. Under the experienced eye of Francis Mackey, who had received his master pilot certification in 1899,[42] they began to wind their way to the anchorage in the basin. The *Mont Blanc*'s route would take it through the second submarine net past *Changuinola* and other ships lying at anchor and through The Narrows into the Bedford Basin. Then the crew could anchor and finally relax, if that were possible while sharing their home with a very prickly cargo.

Capt. William Sitland was out early, as usual, leaving his house at 6:00 A.M. He boarded Hendry's tug *Lily* on the Halifax waterfront. The engineer was already shovelling coal into the furnace to get up a head of steam that would give life to the tug's engine. With daylight, Sitland headed the *Lily* south to see if he could engage one of the ships leaving the Examination Anchorage. He went up to the *Mont Blanc*, just approaching the gates, but pilot Mackey signalled that he was going to anchor in the basin and would not be needing a tug.

Meanwhile, the coal barge returned to *Changuinola*, followed at 8:15 by the coaling crew. By 8:30, more coal was coming aboard. At many ports, coal was loaded by workers carrying 50-pound baskets up a long ramp from the coal barge and into the ship's side. Substantial vessels like *Changuinola* had the service of a coal elevator, a long corkscrew that was inserted into the coal aboard the barge and rotated by an engine. As the corkscrew turned, a steady supply of coal wormed its way up to a conveyor belt running across to the ship, where it tumbled into the bunkers—an early example of mechanization cutting out labour jobs.

The daily harbour routine had begun, with ships getting fuel and supplies, workboats taking repair crews to jobs, ferries crossing the harbour, minesweepers and patrol ships putting to sea. Besides the ships, there was a constant flow of people associated with shipping, both naval and commercial. Some, such as those working on tugs and duty boats, worked strictly in the harbour, helping ships to dock, pulling them away from the docks, transporting people and messages, and towing all manner of floating conveyance with food, fuel, fresh water, and workmen to anchored ships.

People were arriving for work at the dockyard and neighbouring establishments like the shipyard, Hillis's foundry, the brewery, the railway yards, and docks while their children were off to school and homemakers were beginning their daily routines. A parade of young women clocked in at the Dominion Textile plant up the hill from where the two ships would soon confront one another. Life for everybody was about to change.

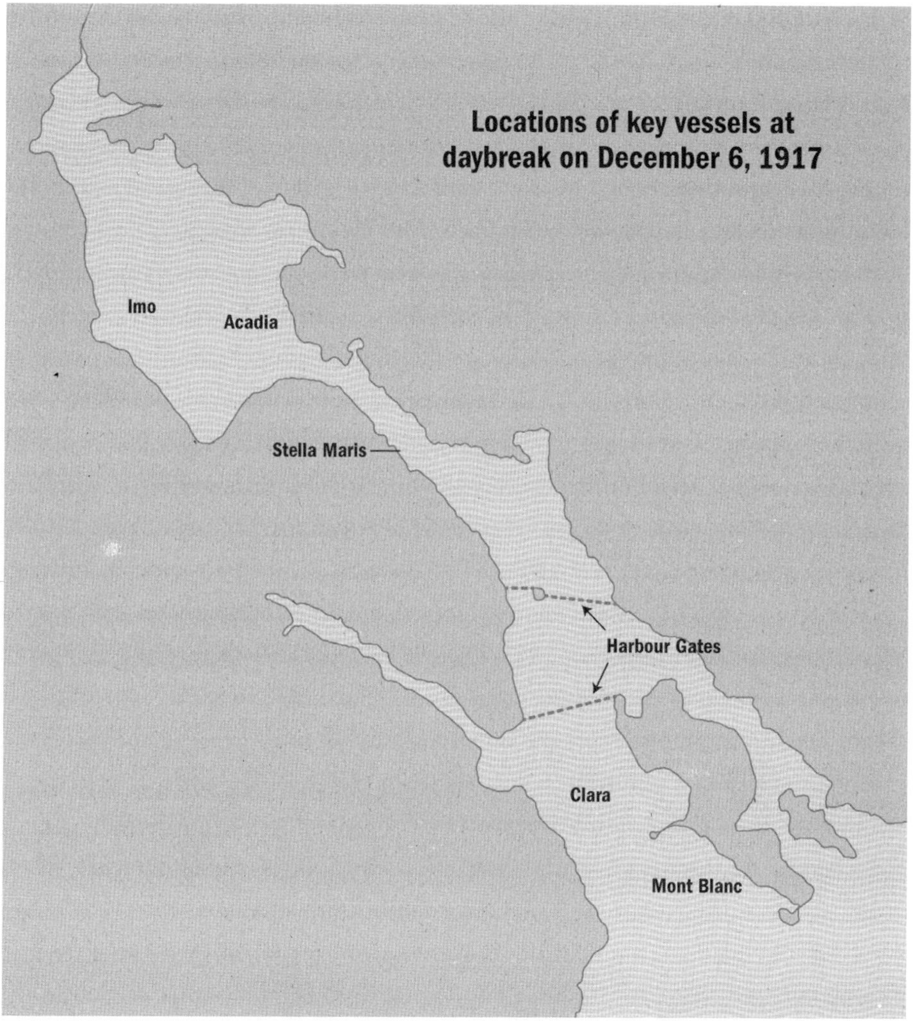

This map shows where the key vessels were in Halifax Harbour at daybreak on the morning of the explosion.

SS *STELLA MARIS*

One of the most powerful tugs in Halifax Harbour in December 1917 was the *Stella Maris,* meaning star of the sea, commanded by forty-five-year-old Horatio Brannen, a native of Woods Harbour on the South Shore of Nova Scotia, and owned by the Stella Maris Steamship Company, Halifax. Like many other captains in the harbour, Brannen had to contend with the challenges of finding good crewmen. Being from a fishing community and an ample family, he had always relied on brothers, cousins, sons, and nephews. The previous evening, while *Changuinola* was taking on coal and water, and pilot Hayes was heading home after his abortive attempt to take the *Imo* to sea, Brannen's brother-in-law Walter Nickerson, a seasoned salvage diver and sailor from Clarks Harbour, arrived to join the crew of the *Stella Maris.*

He had worked with Brannen in the past, when Brannen commanded a salvage vessel engaged in the recovery of lost ships and their cargoes. It was a dangerous, chancy, inconsistent living suited to a particular type of individual—one who didn't mind the risks and liked the rewards. Brannen was captain of the salvage vessel SS *Deliverance* when he, along with a batch of relatives, joined the war effort in the early part of 1915. He was known for having gotten HMCS *Niobe* off the rocks after it ran aground near Cape Sable Island in 1911.[43] In June 1917, in the middle of the outer harbour, he was in charge of HMCS *Deliverance,* which had been repurposed as a minesweeper, when it was cut down by the Norwegian ship SS *Regin* in thick fog and sent to the bottom near Herring Cove. Everybody was rescued. Recreational divers found the wreck in the late twentieth century and recovered some historic dive gear.

A valuable man like Horatio Brannen wasn't out of work for long. He took over command of the *Stella Maris* from his younger brother Arthur on June 15, 1917. The vessel had been built in 1882 at the Samuda Dockyard in London, England, and was one of the last vessels built at the yard, located near where Isambard Kingdom Brunel built the revolutionary *Great Eastern.* The *Stella Maris* was 124.5 feet long with a beam of 23.6 feet and had a wooden hull on an iron frame. Built as a gunboat for the RN, HMS *Starling* was eventually converted into a tugboat.

December 6, 1917, began for the *Stella Maris* with a routine trip to the basin. In tow were two scows—commonly called barges today—each containing a load of ashes from the dry dock. Burning coal was how heat was produced in those days—to warm a building, fire a forge, or fuel a boiler for a steam engine that drove machinery. The by-product was a lot of ashes that had to be disposed of. The tug was taking the scows to the middle of the basin to dump them. A crew of thirteen men from the shipyard was aboard to shovel the ash overboard. The *Stella Maris* had its own crew of eleven, making a total of twenty-four aboard.

Captain Brannen's second son Walter was at the helm with his father next to him on the bridge, conning the vessel. Twenty-one-year-old Walter was the first mate of the *Stella Maris.* To ease the process of getting the scows out from behind the dry dock and around several ships rafted together at the dry dock wharves, the scows had been pulled tightly up to the stern of the tug. They had to wait for the SS *Clara* to go by on its way to the basin, travelling closer to the Halifax side than expected. With the *Clara* past, Walter eased his vessel out from shore at about the halfway point of the 2-mile-long Narrows. It was a tricky manoeuvre because he had to avoid three ships that were docked in tandem at the shipyard pier to his left.

On the inside was the coal carrier *J.A. McKee.* Tied alongside its outer side was the *Middleham Castle,* and tied to the *Middleham Castle* was the armed tug *Musquash.* All three were waiting for repairs at the shipyard. Chief Steward Joseph Babineau watched from the *Musquash* as Walter successfully got around their stern with the two scows in tow and made a left turn to head north toward the basin. Deckhands began to let the tow lines pay out. The 125-foot-long tug had a similar-length line stretching to the first scow, which measured 30 feet. Then, a 30-foot-long line went from the first to the second scow, which measured 20 feet more—325 feet in total.

With everything in line, Captain Brannen called for increased speed and the tug steamed at about 4 knots past the ships and the sugar refinery, which had the tug *Ragus* and the SS *Picton* tied to its wharf. The *Picton,* a sizable ship like the *Middleham Castle,* was tied in front of it. Another tug, the *Douglas H. Thomas*, was also tied at the shipyard, as were the shipyard tugs *Wasp B* and

Sambro. As the *Stella Maris* passed the *Picton*, Captain Brannen saw, through the haze, the starboard side of the *Imo* coming on a right turn into the channel. When it straightened up, a blast came from its whistle. Wondering if the blast was meant for the *Stella Maris*, Brannen looked back and saw the *Mont Blanc*, about a third of a mile away and obscured by the sun's glare on the water. He decided the blast was meant for that ship.

CHAPTER 4

"LOOKS LIKE SOME TROUBLE COMING THERE"

Concerned about the speed of the *Imo*, Brannen ordered Walter to pull the *Stella Maris* over toward the Halifax side to give it more space. Tied to the north side of Pier 6 was the three-masted schooner *St. Bernard*. The tug passed it, then passed the *Curaca* at Pier 8 and the *Calonne* at Pier 9. This collection of piers, along with sheds and railway tracks, constituted the Richmond Depot of the Canadian Government Railways. By the time the *Stella Maris* got to the *Curaca*, the *Imo* was 150 to 200 yards across The Narrows from them. Suddenly, it let out three blasts and the water boiled off its stern as the propeller spun in reverse.[44]

HANDLING A SHIP

Automobile drivers instinctively know the time and distance required to slow or stop their vehicle, or to back it up. A ship is not that agile. They are ponderous and they pack a lot of momentum, floating on a fickle surface at the mercy of external forces like wind, tide, and waves that change from hour to hour and day to day. Ships need a lot of room to turn and they have no brakes, so the officer of the watch has to carefully plan every move. They have to get it right because everything happens in slow but unchangeable motion. Learning to do it properly takes years.

Handling a steamship in 1917 was a slow, methodical, instinctual process

HMCS Acadia *Engine Room Telegraph.* (AUTHOR'S COLLECTION)

that worked well on the open sea but could be stressful in the confines of a harbour, where space on the surface was minimal, other vessels were present, and communication between ships was extremely limited. There was no putting a ship in gear and stepping on the gas. It was a team effort. An officer ordered others to take action and then evaluated the results, with a careful eye to ensuring that his ship went where he intended it to go, at the intended speed. He was on the bridge, but his directives were executed far away in the engine room. He communicated using a mechanical device called the engine room telegraph.

It provided a basic menu of options like which direction to go in—forward or reverse—and at what speed to run the engine. On the *Mont Blanc*, the options were Stop, Stand By, Slow, Half Speed, and Full Speed for forward and reverse.[45] Somebody in the engine room read the selection and made it happen. There was no speedometer. If the officer wanted to know how fast the ship was going or how much water was below, he had to send somebody to measure it and wait until that person returned with the information. Knowing how much water was below was often a guesstimate.

It was when manoeuvring that the most risk occurred. All the ship had was the basic rudder that pushed the stern left or right to change direction. While moving slowly, which was a must in a crowded harbour like Halifax, steering was least efficient and could be sluggish. In tight spots, a ship would require a tug to move it around. One trick often used to get additional steerage without needing too much space was to throw the ship in reverse—no small feat, considering there was no reverse gear. The whole engine and drive train had to be put into reverse. That caused the prop to go counter-clockwise, shoving the stern to the left, which made the bow pivot to the right, a bit like a lever going sideways. The phenomenon is called transverse thrust. That's what the *Imo*'s commander was up to when he startled those aboard the *Stella Maris* by sounding three blasts to indicate the ship was in reverse, causing the prop to create turmoil in the water.

The weather was decent that December morning: clear with little wind. The lack of wind caused some haze as coal furnaces in houses and other buildings came to life and engines in factories and ships started chugging. There was a lot of traffic on the water and not everybody—like the pilot of the *Clara*—was following the rules of the road.

Two motorized vessels meeting in tight quarters like The Narrows normally pass the same way two automobiles pass on a road (in North America). A vessel going toward the Bedford Basin—coming in the harbour—was expected to stay on the Dartmouth side (to the east), and a vessel leaving the basin was to stay on the western, or Halifax, side. The closest land for each one should have been on their right according to the direction they were travelling. Because the *Imo* was coming from the west side of the basin—the Halifax side—it took a right turn to enter The Narrows. The American ship SS *Clara* had just come up through The Narrows on the Halifax side.[46] That meant the two ships were positioned opposite to what the rules specified.

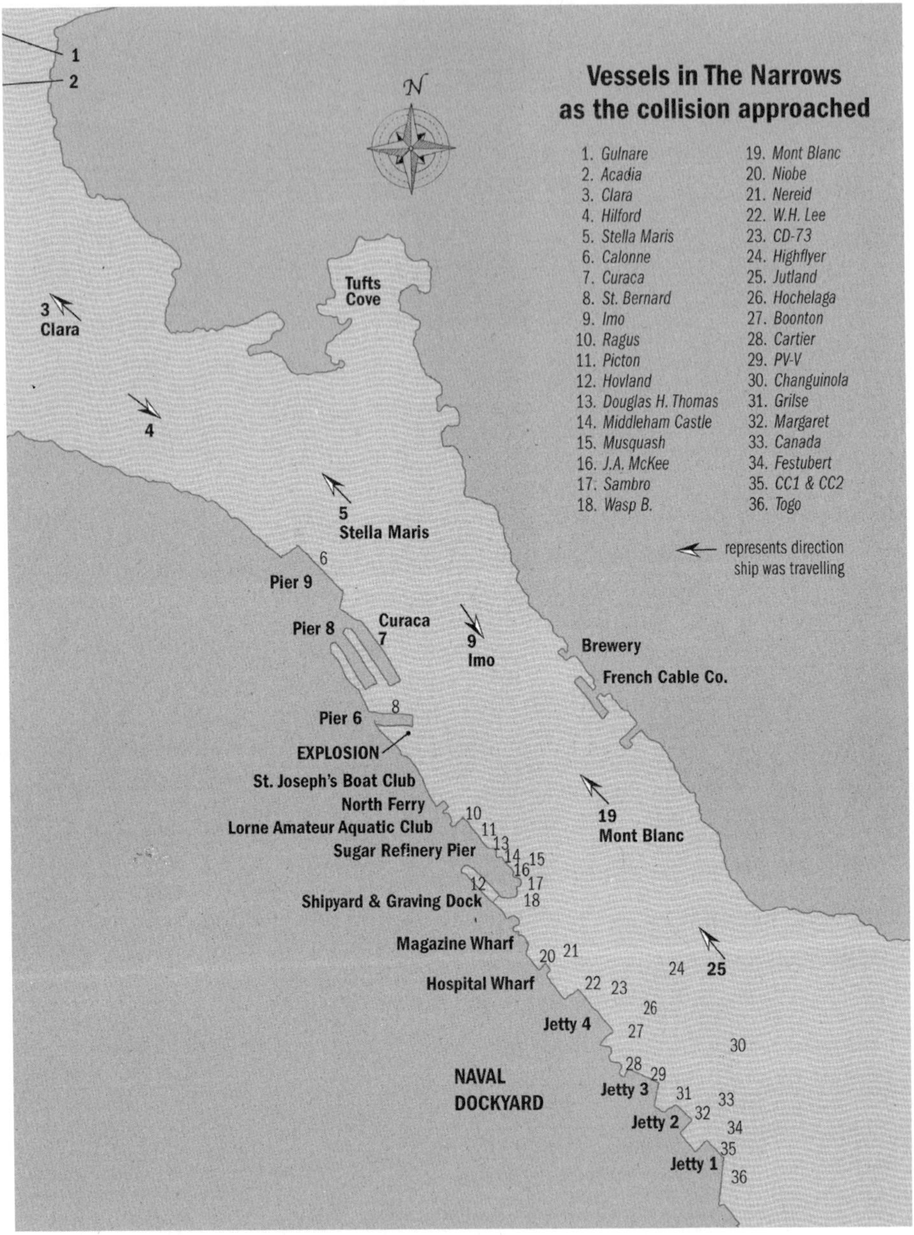

Ship locations are approximations, based on testimonies, official reports, newspaper stories, photographs, and other sources from the period following the disaster.

THE STANDOFF

The *Imo*, a long and narrow ship like most of the liners built by Harland & Wolff at that time, had a wide turn radius so it was an especially tight turn to get in position to pass port-to-port. The pilots, Renner and Hayes, signalled one another and agreed to pass starboard-to-starboard. Using his megaphone, Renner hailed across and told Hayes that another ship was coming, evidencing that Renner knew Hayes was probably unable to clearly see the *Mont Blanc*. The *Clara*'s presence kept the *Imo* tending toward the Dartmouth side to the east. Soon afterwards, the question of getting the *Imo* to the Halifax side was further confounded when it encountered the *Stella Maris*, which was near mid-channel going to the Bedford Basin.

The *Imo*'s captain decided to slow the ship to avoid going closer to the Dartmouth shore. To do that the engine had to be put into reverse. With transverse thrust, this enabled the ship to be steered more sharply to the right to get the bow heading away from the Dartmouth shore and keep the ship on course. The manoeuvre was not to avoid the *Mont Blanc*, which, at that point, was still more than half a mile away.[47]

With the *Clara* and the *Stella Maris* out of the way, the *Mont Blanc* came into view as the next obstacle for the *Imo* to get by.[48] Pilot Mackey, in the *Mont Blanc*, had already seen the *Imo* while it was entering The Narrows. We have no way of knowing when those on the *Imo* saw the *Mont Blanc*. Along with the haze, the sun had come up at 7:40 A.M. and was also obscuring the view for those on the *Imo*. Third Officer Peter B'Jonnas would testify that visibility was only about a quarter of a mile.[49]

THE COLLISION

Clifford Jenkins, signalman aboard HMS *Highflyer*, provided a succinct description of the collision.

> The French ship *Mont Blanc* passed the *High Flyer* [*sic*] at about 8:50. She was going up to Bedford Basin. Just after we had got her name and she passed I saw the Belgian Relief ship just coming through the entrance of Bedford Basin.
>
> The two ships it could be seen were not able to pass one another if they kept on their courses so the *Mont Blanc* turned about 4 points to starboard to clear the *Imo* but the *Imo* did not seem to alter course at all. To try and clear herself again or stop herself from going ashore, the *Mont Blanc* turned to port, thus laying herself across the harbour and heading for the Halifax side. The *Imo* then altered course to starboard and was heading straight for the *Mont Blanc*. She sounded three short blasts on her whistle for going astern but was too late to stop herself.[50]

To communicate to one another, the captains of the *Mont Blanc* and *Imo* only had their steam whistles: one blast, two blasts, three blasts. Not only were they constrained in what they could communicate but there were other vessels in the vicinity whose captains might be wondering, *Was that blast meant for me?* as Captain Brannen, aboard the *Stella Maris*, had asked himself. And the railway tracks that ran alongside The Narrows had trains often blowing whistles.

The ships' horns, being very loud, attracted many witnesses to testify after the fact. However, which ship blew how many blasts and when was a subject of much contention. When the dance between the two ships began to unfold, a lot of people were watching with a growing sense that a collision was imminent.

Early on, each of the two captains was aware of the other vessel, but the view from the *Imo* had to have been obscured somewhat, as noted earlier. The view from the *Mont Blanc* was that, from the beginning, the *Imo* appeared to

Starboard means right, toward Dartmouth, and _port_ means left, toward Halifax when going north, toward the Bedford Basin. Rule of thumb: _left_ and _port_ both have four letters.

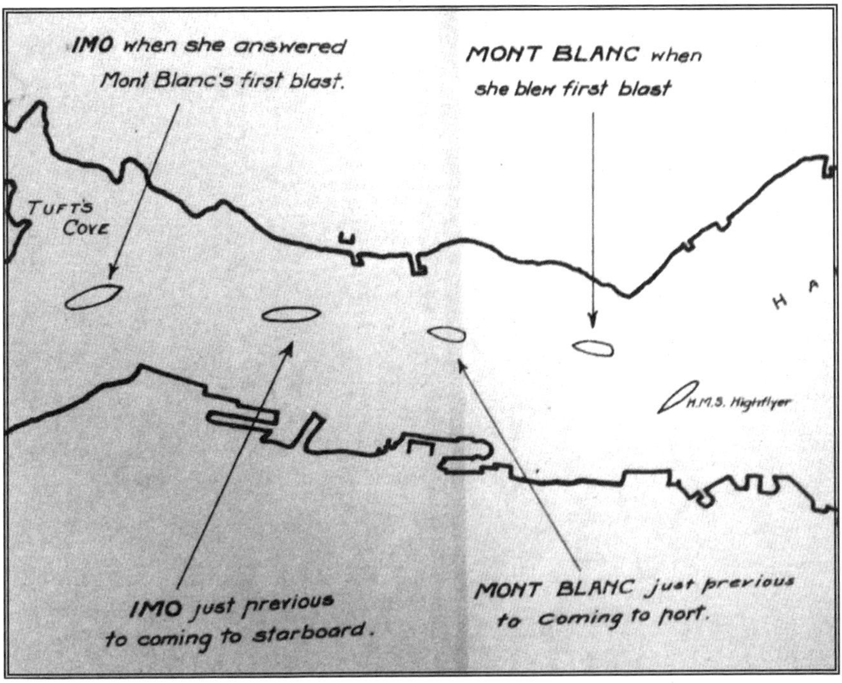

This sketch, from the inquiry report, describes the final minutes before the collision. (MARITIME MUSEUM OF THE ATLANTIC)

be on a course that would intersect with that of the *Mont Blanc*. The *Imo* had already exchanged horn blasts with the *Clara*. The *Mont Blanc* captain took action that he thought would get the two ships off the collision course. He stayed on the right and indicated his intention with horn blasts. The *Imo* did not respond as expected but continued on its course. As the vessels closed in, both ships took evasive actions, but the *Mont Blanc*'s captain was convinced that a collision was inevitable unless he ran his ship ashore or turned to the left. He gave up on the idea of a port-to-port passing and, while there was still time, decided to go in front of the approaching *Imo* and do a starboard-to-starboard pass. He went for it, only to see the *Imo* take a right turn into their path. The two ships collided.

It appears that the *Imo* was trying to stop and/or go to the right to avoid the collision. Unfortunately, it did not look like that to those on the bridge of the *Mont Blanc*. The *Mont Blanc*'s captain decided to make the counterintuitive swerve to the left because he couldn't figure out what the *Imo*'s captain was up to.

Many explanations have been put forth to try to make sense of what happened next. I offer these considerations:

- There was not one but two experienced and competent pilots. It is unlikely that either was acting irrationally, as was implied after the fact.
- Hayes and From had been distracted by the *Clara* and *Stella Maris*, as well as the poor visibility caused by smoke and glare on the water. When they looked out the harbour, they would have seen several large ships at anchor in addition to the *Mont Blanc*.
- This was the first trip for Le Médec in the *Mont Blanc*, so he was barely familiar with his ship. He was under considerable stress because of the cargo his ship was carrying. Could Le Médec have overreacted and Mackey went along?
- There was a language issue aboard the *Mont Blanc*, which was manageable under normal circumstances. But in the certain excitement of the last moments, there was probably a communications breakdown between pilot and captain.

Watching events unfold, not from the sidelines like most others, but directly in line with the route the two ships were on, was Herbert Whitehead. To the south of the two ships, his vessel, CD-73, was approaching *Niobe* to pick up provisions for the fleet of drifters in the Northwest Arm and Dartmouth Cove when he heard the exchange of whistle blasts. The helmsman pointed up The Narrows and commented, "Looks like some trouble coming there."

Whitehead would later testify: "After the helmsman pointed out there was going to be some trouble, as he said, I watched them: both ships." He noted that they were 600–700 yards apart, and added, "They seemed to me at that time to be almost headed on to each other."[51]

The *Mont Blanc* had sent a single short blast, meaning, "I am going to starboard," toward Dartmouth. The *Imo*'s answering whistle was two short blasts,

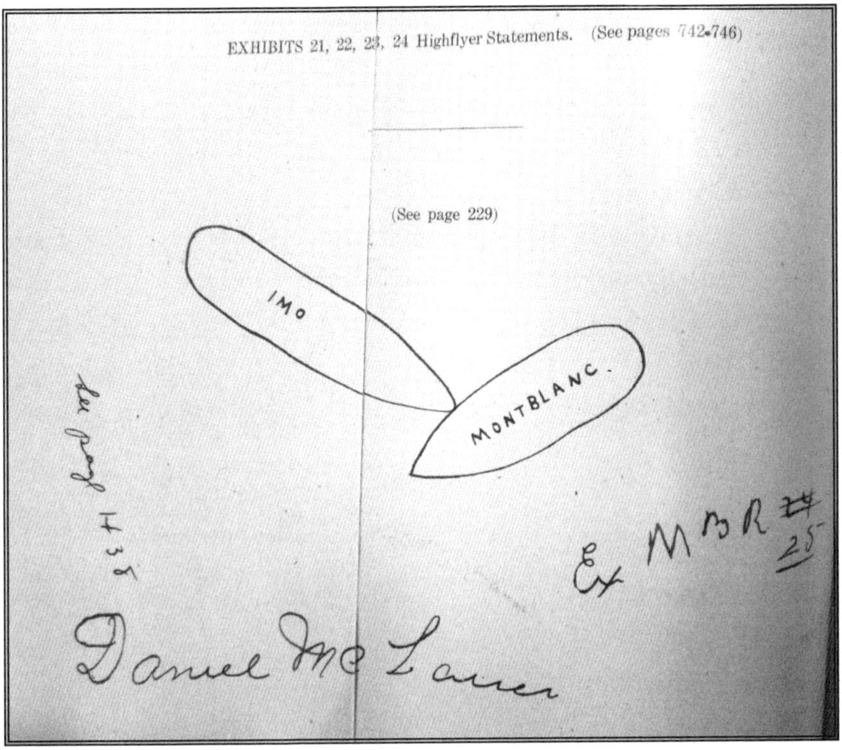

Sketch from the inquiry report illustrates where the Imo *struck the* Mont Blanc. *Note the signature from Daniel McLaine, captain of the tug* Douglas H. Thomas, *who testified at the inquiry, presumably attesting to its accuracy.* (MARITIME MUSEUM OF THE ATLANTIC)

meaning, "I am going to port." For the *Imo,* that was also toward Dartmouth. Both ships were trying to slow down. Yet, nobody watching believed they could avoid a collision.

That was how Francis Mackey and Captain Le Médec felt aboard the *Mont Blanc.* Drastic measures were called for. Le Médec took the only option he felt they had: to go left and pass the *Imo* starboard-to-starboard. Just then, the *Imo* let out three blasts, meaning, "I am putting my engine full astern." Transverse thrust kicked in and the *Imo* started turning to starboard as it slowed. This sounds like the logical decision for Captain From to make, to slow the ship and get to starboard as quickly as possible. Obviously, he was not expecting the *Mont Blanc*'s turn to port.

The inevitable occurred as the bow of the *Imo* sliced into the starboard bow of the *Mont Blanc*. It opened a gash that extended from the surface of the water to the deck. Witnesses such as George Abott aboard a dockyard dispatch boat testified that they could look in through the gash and see steel drums stacked inside the hold.[52]

The superintendent of the shipyard, Launcet Spence, after thoroughly examining the *Imo*'s bow a few days later, estimated it could have penetrated the other ship by as much as 12 feet, making a gash 17 feet wide at the deck.[53] That is greater than the estimates made by others appearing at the inquiry, but so many witnesses testified that there was disagreement over just about everything.

It is interesting to note that of the fifty or so commercial steamships in the harbour at the time of the explosion, the *Imo* had the highest length to beam ratio, which is an indicator of the length relative to the width of the ship. The *Imo*'s ratio was 9.6 to 1—it was 9.6 times as long as it was wide—while the average was a shade below 7.5 to 1. The *Imo*'s builder, Harland & Wolff, was known to build ships that were longer and narrower than the norm. That means the *Imo* had a sharper bow, which would have made it more destructive to the *Mont Blanc*. It was also 100 feet longer and had a GRT of 5,256 compared with the *Mont Blanc*'s 3,279. Of all the freighters that could have come out of the basin that day, the *Imo* was the worst one to face off with.

IGNITION

Aboard *Niobe*, the administrative centre for the RCN in Halifax, the ship's first lieutenant Allan Baddeley was just sitting down to breakfast, when a signalman approached to say, "Two steamers in collision, sir, about half a mile upharbour." He provided all the details he had.

Baddeley replied, "Tell the Officer of the Day to call away the steam pinnace, and ask Mr. Mattison to speak to me." Five minutes later the 40-foot steam-driven launch cast off with six men aboard, under command of Acting

Niobe*'s pinnace is the launch with two smokestacks. The others are whalers, like the one that arrived at the burning* Mont Blanc *from* Highflyer. (NAVAL MUSEUM OF HALIFAX)

Boatswain Albert Mattison, whom the First Lieutenant had referred to as "my excellent Mate of the Upper Deck." They headed toward the two ships. Baddeley returned to his breakfast.

Minutes later, the signalman was back. He reported the crew of the French ship were taking to the boats, some even jumping into the water in their haste to get off the ship. Baddeley gulped down his coffee and headed to the upper deck to see for himself.

Fire had started immediately in the picric acid, close to the water level. With a grinding and tearing, the *Imo* backed away from the *Mont Blanc,* which started to slowly drift toward the Halifax side of The Narrows. Then, the fire ignited the benzol. Captain Le Médec knew there was nothing the crew could do, so he gave the order to abandon ship. As they lowered the boats, the RCN duty boat CD-73 drew near. Capt. Herbert Whitehead yelled through his megaphone to the *Mont Blanc* crew members to come aboard and he would take them into the basin, out of harm's way. Nobody seemed to understand. Instead, they boarded the boats and started rowing for the North Ferry Wharf on the Dartmouth shore—strange behaviour to those watching from shore, but the *Mont Blanc*'s crew knew it was futile to try to fight the fire so they were trying to get as far away as possible.

> **"I had one of the stokers who was a French Canadian on the lookout at the bow and he speaks French and he said he never heard any warning given in French and I never heard any in English."**
> —Herbert Whitehead, captain of CD-73[54]

Seeing the drums of benzol burning on the deck made Whitehead nervous, and when three small explosions occurred, he concluded that the ship was loaded with oil. He decided that with everybody having abandoned ship, he should get away to protect his crew and boat. He headed back toward *Niobe*, where Baddeley was watching a column of black smoke, for he could not see any ships because his view was blocked by the dockyard buildings.

It was obvious that a tug was needed to tow the burning ship away from the land so it could burn out, but the first lieutenant knew tugs were not his concern. He already had 1,200 personnel aboard *Niob*e to worry about.

> Whose concern they were I did not clearly know; so many diverse and interlocked authorities ruled Halifax since the German submarine campaign had brought the convoy system into being. There was, with an office somewhere along the waterfront in the heart of the town, an Admiral exercising the functions of Port Convoy Officer for Canadian ports. Somewhere ashore was a Convoy Admiral, waiting to escort the next convoy to England. In supervision of ships' entry and departure through the gate in the harbour's net defences was the Chief Examining Officer. At times, though not at the moment, the Commander-in-Chief of the North America and West Indies

> Squadron flew his flag in port in [HMS] *Leviathan*; and in his absence one or another of the cruisers and armed merchantmen in harbour would be Senior Officer Afloat. The dockyard and its resources were in the charge of the Captain Superintendent. Somebody, I concluded, would send the urgently needed tug.[55]

Another boat, the *Jutland*, owned by metalworking firm Burns & Kelleher, was also going by at the time of the collision, heading to the basin to work on several ships at anchor. Like CD-73, it stopped while those aboard watched the goings-on and considered that an explosion might be in the works. Seeing there was nothing they could do, they too continued to the basin.

A brief article in the *Acadian Recorder* of December 10, 1917, makes an interesting observation about this encounter:

> An employee of a brass foundry was going into the Narrows on a motor boat to work on a steamer just as the Belgian Relief steamer came down. He went in the cabin, when the boy shouted to him to come on deck, as he thought the steamers were going to collide. When they did, it struck him that one might be a munition ship, so they put on all speed and were a half mile away when the explosion occurred. He says the Belgian steamer acted as though there was something wrong with the machinery or steering gear.

As with a great deal in the intervening testimony, accounts differ as to whether the engineers had shut down the *Mont Blanc*'s engine. If they did, inertia would still have kept the ship moving. With nobody at the helm, it began to slowly drift, or move under its own reduced power, across The Narrows toward the Halifax shore and a number of valuable targets that a burning ship could severely damage or destroy. The line of ships stretching from the sugar refinery north to Pier 9 included the tugs *Ragus*, *Douglas H. Thomas*, *Musquash*, *Wasp B*, and *Sambro* with *Hilford* heading toward the scene from the basin. The freighters *Middleham Castle*, *J. A. McKee*, *Picton*, *Curaca*, and *Calonne* along with the tern schooner *St. Bernard* were also tied up. The North Ferry was in the vicinity and there were probably others. Eventually, the burning ship neared Pier 6, where the *St. Bernard*, a wooden schooner built at Parrsboro, NS, was tied to a wooden pier with a load of lumber—lots of combustible material, more than enough to set the city ablaze. Hundreds stood on the docks and streets nearby watching the fire. Nobody was thinking about an explosion.

Estimates of the time between the collision (with the start of the fire) and the explosion vary, but most centre on seventeen to eighteen minutes. During that time, the lookout aboard HMS *Highflyer* signalled *Niobe* that a ship was on fire. They phoned the acting captain superintendent of the dockyard, Capt. Frederick Pasco, who was just five days into the job. He gave orders to send the firefighting tugs *W. H. Lee* and *Gopher* to the scene, but the fire was already beyond fighting. Lieutenant Baddeley's words say it all: "Where at first there had been a lazily rolling column of turgid blackness glinting in the morning sunshine, was now a leaping of flame, an uprushing of red in the heart of black in an increasing vehemence of viciousness…an uprising which was developing into a rapid series of belchings, of which the ear as well as the eye was not aware."[56]

Aboard the *Stella Maris*, Captain Brannen was close enough not only to see but also hear the collision. His second mate, William Nickerson, reported, "We saw white smoke—we thought it was steam—and a black gust of smoke came, and about that time we saw the flames, just after the black smoke."[57]

Brannen gave orders to anchor the scows near the Dartmouth shore and to ready the tugs' hoses to fight the fire. They turned and headed downstream at full speed. On the scene, Captain Brannen manoeuvred the *Stella Maris* as close as was practical, to within about 50 yards of the burning ship.

As he was considering his next step, a substantial rowboat arrived. Called a whaler, it had come from *Highflyer* and carried the executive officer, Lt.-Cmdr. Thomas Triggs, and a crew of five: Leading Seaman Claude Rushen, Able Seaman James Dowling, Able Seaman Samuel David Prewer, Able Seaman Joseph Murphy, and Able Seaman William Becker, along with Lieut. James Ruffles. Triggs went aboard the *Stella Maris* and conferred with Brannen. It was apparent to both of them that hosing water on the fire was pointless, so they decided that the tug should try to tow the burning ship to the basin. The *Stella*

Maris then towed the whaler to the *Imo* so Triggs could assess the situation there and report back to Captain Garnett aboard *Highflyer*. Brannen returned to the *Mont Blanc*. He decided to ease the *Stella Maris* under the stern of the *Mont Blanc*, attach a towing hawser, and pull it from the pier.

Lt.-Cmdr. James Murray, who was responsible for liaising between the Port Convoy Office and the merchant ships arriving in Halifax to join a convoy, was in the Bedford Basin aboard the *Hilford*, visiting some of those ships. He had just left the Union-Castle Line steamer *Corfe Castle* when he saw the smoke. He told the captain to speed up so he could investigate. They raced past Pier 9 where Murray's office was located and arrived just as the *Mont Blanc* crew were abandoning ship. Pilot Mackey saw him and yelled to him about the burning cargo. Murray had Capt. Arthur Hickey spin the *Hilford* around and head back to Pier 9 so he could sound the alarm of the explosion that he was sure was imminent. He leapt off the *Hilford* onto the *Calonne*, which was tied at Pier 9 and rushed to his office, while the crew tied the *Hilford* to the outside of the steamship.

Just then, the steam pinnace arrived from HMCS *Niobe*, with Acting Boatswain Albert Mattison and a crew of six men: Ernest Baird, Charles McMillan, Freeman Nickerson, Albert Saunders, George Veal, and George Yates. They were ordered aboard the *Mont Blanc* to secure a hawser in the hope that the *Stella Maris* could tow the burning ship away from the pier.[58] There are accounts of at least two being seen on the *Mont Blanc*'s deck, but we don't know if any others succeeded in boarding.

Captain Brannen sent the first mate to bring a 10-inch hawser. Boatswain William Spenser Nickerson was in the hold retrieving the line while the first mate Walter Brannen was on the ladder assisting as the *Mont Blanc*, just 150 yards away, continued to move shoreward. It stopped as it nosed into the beach and grounded just south of Pier 6.

Able Seaman Edward McCrossan of the *Curaca*, which was tied at Pier 8 close by, reported: "The tide seemed to drift her in and it was several minutes before she slid in alongside the pier and stopped."[59]

People stopped; heads turned, necks craned, and oars creaked as two boats pulled desperately for the Dartmouth shore.

CHAPTER 5

THE HARBOUR'S WORST DAY

Nothing attracts a crowd like an intensifying fire. This one, long past being controlled, was like a snorting, avaricious dragon, devouring the *Mont Blanc*, snaffling its way from stempost to gudgeon as it wolfed down the succulent cargo, farting and belching as it went. Men at work, children heading for school, toddlers propped on chairs near a window; nobody within viewing distance could take their eyes off the demon and its vile machinations. Like a magnet it drew their gaze; from across The Narrows, from the brow of the hill, from the roof of the sugar refinery bystanders gawked in rapt fascination. Burst after burst of flame lunged through a cloud of smoke as drums of benzol boiled, burst, and exploded in a cacophony of vivid colour grasping for heaven itself.

Edward McCrossan later testified to the inquiry: "All the crew of our ship were standing at the stern watching the fire. I counted at least seven explosions and after each one something would shoot away up in the air and burst."[60]

DISCHARGE

Finally, the inevitable came, as what is believed to have been the worst non-nuclear man-made explosion in history erupted, releasing enormous energy that expanded gases at 1,500 metres per second. A sharp change of pressure at the outer edge of the blast wave drove air, water, and debris, taking out ships, infrastructure, docks, buildings, people, animals, and anything else in its path. The mass got pushed outward and upward across a 5-mile range.

View north from Jetty 4, with HMS Ariadne *taking on coal ca.1898. The explosion occurred beyond and to the right of the sugar refinery, the tall building belching smoke, and would have gone up through the top of the smoke. HMCS* Niobe *was docked, facing north, in the space between Jetty 4 and the sugar refinery.* (NS ARCHIVES)

The ensuing violence took many forms, ravaging the unfortunate people of Halifax and Dartmouth and shocking them with multitudinous ways to die or be maimed. First, the blast went outwards in all directions, uprooting people and structures. That removed all the air, which was immediately replaced at hurricane speed by returning air. The result was a series of brief typhoons. There are many accounts of people being picked up and flung by these twisters. Among those at work at Pier 8 was Fred J. Collings, a metalworker from the firm of Collings and Sons. The blast hurled him 70 feet and knocked him unconscious, but he awoke. He commented that there were close to a hundred men working in the area, and he was one of the very few to survive.[61]

Then, the water got pushed into what the people of the day called a tidal wave; today, we call it a tsunami. That sent water up the hills of Richmond and across The Narrows, spilling over the Dartmouth side, snatching people and dragging them into the icy water. Finally, the immense amount of material that the blast sent upward had to come down again, so there was a torrent of red-hot metal returning to Earth. I have seen some of it on the bottom of the harbour near the blast site. Pieces of the *Mont Blanc* rained down, coated with vaporized fuel and chemicals, and spread a dark, oily film everywhere.

"When I recovered consciousness, I was stretched out on the fidley all covered with something that smelled like benzene. It took me five days to get my face clean."
—Alfred Kayford, SS *Calonne* [62]

THE *MONT BLANC*'S FINAL INDIGNITY

Much of the ship fell from the sky, landing over a huge area that took in the cities of Halifax and Dartmouth and beyond. What went up sped down at a terrific rate. *Niobe*'s first lieutenant had the presence of mind to yell, "To the conning tower!" and he and his companions rushed from the bridge to the conning tower of the old cruiser, finding refuge behind the 12-inch steel walls designed to withstand an artillery barrage. "Into the cramped dimness crowded the Chief Yeoman of Signals and another signalman, the Captain of Patrols, myself and messenger. Within a few seconds, before any of us found anything to say, came the crash of debris and wreckage all around outside."[63]

Captain Garnett of *Highflyer* reported, "I was standing under the Shelter Deck and After Bridge with the Marine Officer close to me, and my Coxswain just behind me, and later my Coxswain brought to me a jagged piece of double riveted strap plating which he informed me had come through the deck and fallen between us."[64]

The situation was similar for Percy Hardy, the engineer aboard Minesweeper 13. Along with the cook and steward, he got buried in the cabin when coal stored on the dock tumbled down on them. Hardy recalled, "I collected myself together and got up the ladder pushing coal and doors away like a mad man. Then, when I reached the deck, chunks of steel all sizes from a cent to a suitcase came flying all around. I have the piece that nearly got me."[65] With his own boat damaged and immobile, he boarded CD-9 as it headed up The Narrows to assist the injured.

Getting hit by even a small piece of this debris—say, bullet size—would have been lethal because of the speed at which it would have been falling. The piece of the *Mont Blanc*'s anchor shaft that landed less than a mile from where my house is situated today drilled 6 feet into the ground. Bits and pieces of debris were picked up over the years and became souvenirs in Halifax homes, pushed into sight above the ground by the heaving frosts of more than a hundred winters.

THE WAVE

The blast roiled the water near the explosion site but not to the extent claimed by some early reports or speculated by others. To this day, people say that the bottom of the harbour was made visible (to whom?); others think that a crater was formed in the bottom, and some went so far as to say the harbour was deepened in the area. As a person who has dived in The Narrows many times, I often get asked if I have seen any results of the Explosion. The answer is yes (more on that later), but no craters. Because the *Mont Blanc* was ashore, the explosion drove the water onto the Halifax shore and some 60 feet up the hill from the waterfront, according to first-hand accounts. Based on more recent modelling, the maximum wave height is estimated to have been 14 metres which then fell rapidly to 4 metres by the time it had travelled for two minutes, reaching the entrance to the basin and where the Macdonald Bridge crosses the harbour today. It would have taken eight minutes to reach Bedford and fallen to 2 metres in height.[66]

There are remarkable stories of survival through the ravages of the tsunami. One is perhaps more about the ravages of the explosion and the relatively good fortune some experienced amid the disaster as recounted by Joan and Lewis Payzant in their history of the Halifax-Dartmouth ferry service. This incident was about the operator of a boat associated with the North Ferry.

> George Holmes of Tufts Cove was operating his ferry boat on that day. The last thing he remembered was heading for the burning *Mont Blanc* to pick up passengers or crew from the ship. It was not until Christmas Day, three weeks later, that he regained consciousness, finding himself onboard the U.S. Hospital ship *Old Colony*, and with not the slightest recollection about how he came to be there. He had been gathered up with other casualties and placed in a morgue, where an acquaintance, looking for her husband's body, was startled by a groan! Recognizing Holmes, she immediately advised the hospital staff who quickly arranged for transfer and hospital care. He ended up spending months in hospitals.[67]

The Payzants tell of another incident about the North Ferry and what sounds more like the work of the tsunami than the way it is related by Helen Duggan: "Charles Duggan and *Gray Starling* [were] blown clear out of the harbour, and the boat, with Charlie still in it, still alive but unconscious, ended up in a north Dartmouth field. It was some hours before Charlie Duggan regained consciousness and lived to tell of his experiences as a harbour ferryman."[68]

Other accounts of the tsunami along the Dartmouth shore indicate there was a run-up as far as Windmill Road. Indeed, the locations where some vessels landed were initially assumed to have been a result of the blast when they were actually caused by the tsunami.

Philip Mitchell was on the Dartmouth shore nearby, watching the commotion with the two ships. When the explosion came, he found a piece of board and held it over his head to protect himself from falling debris. When the tsunami struck, he wrapped his arms around a power pole and held on. The water swept over his head, and as it receded, he noticed a boxcar from a train nearby was dripping salt water, indicating it had been immersed. He held on as a second wave flooded up to his armpits. Afterwards, he made his way home to find it damaged and proceeded to assist in extinguishing a fire next door.[69]

Perhaps the most amazing story of the tsunami happened to men involved in my favourite pastime—except for them diving was their job. Just astern of *Niobe*, a naval diving party under the supervision of John T. Gammon, master-at-arms, was engaged working with two divers and a support crew constructing the concrete foundation for a crane bed. Those were the days before scuba, when divers breathed through an air hose from the surface. The air was pushed down into the diver's helmet from a hand-operated pump. One diver was already under the water and a second was descending the ladder to the bottom. Each diver had two men pumping air and a third keeping his connecting lines clear, a total of six men.

Then came the explosion. In Gammon's words:

> I was blown on my stomach, and on regaining my feet I saw the buildings collapsing and shrapnel falling. To my horror the house in which the pump was secured was demolished, the men all blown away from the vicinity by concussion, and the pump was stopped. I first thought we were being bombarded by a German submarine which had crept through the gates and was shelling the Dockyard. My next thoughts were the divers. I sprang to the ladder where they would have to ascend and noticed that the water had receded eight or ten feet. I saw no men in sight, but noticed that the diving pump was intact. At that moment a man [Able Seaman Walter Critch] picked himself up about twenty yards away. I shouted to him to man the pump. He did so single-handed, holding the roof of the building with one hand and turning the handle of the pump with the other.
>
> On getting close to the bottom of the ladder, I got the diver, took his glass off and pushed him up the ladder. I grasped the air pipe and

Horatio Brannen's first command of a salvage vessel, SS Coastguard, *with a diver down. Atop the aft house, two men turn the pump supplying air through the hose that runs down to the deck. The man there keeps it steady and uses it to signal to the diver below.* (MARITIME MUSEUM OF THE ATLANTIC MP181.1)

> breast rope of No. 2 diver and pulled him back to the ladder, but unfortunately the air pipe got entangled and with one hand I had to haul down the slack from above and pull the other. I thank God I was able to get him to the ladder and took his glass off and assisted him up the ladder, and he fell exhausted. This took several seconds and I was expecting any moment for the water to return and drown us both.

The divers had managed to survive the interval before Critch started the pump because there would have been residual air in their suits and helmets that kept them alive. Removing each diver's glass refers to unscrewing the circular glass faceplate, which would have provided a flow of fresh air from outside.[70]

With that done, Gammon steeled himself for a more personal life-and-death ordeal: the long hike to his house on Union Street, where a brief couple of hours before, he had left his wife and four children. When he finally got home, the situation was bad. There was no sign of life—just a demolished house. It was no better at the school, where his two oldest would have been.

What could he do but return to work? After spending the worst twenty-four hours of his life, the next morning he heard some good news. His seven-year-old daughter was alive. Later that day, his five-year-old turned up. Feeling encouraged, he decided to run an ad in the newspaper. It generated some hopeful news: it looked like his baby daughter was alive, but when he arrived at the hospital, he discovered she was not.

The next day, he found his wife in a hospital bed, just out of surgery and barely alive, but alive nonetheless. That was to be the extent of his new, diminished family. Even though he continued to run ads, he never heard anything about his two youngest children.

He later learned that he had been made a Member of the Order of the British Empire. Walter Critch received the Meritorious Service Medal.

In one respect, William Sitland in the tug *Lily* was fortunate. After being turned down for a tow from Pilot Mackey of the *Mont Blanc*, he found another vessel in need of a tug and was in the process of docking it at Woodside, at the entrance to Eastern Passage. He felt the shock of the explosion but did not know how serious the situation was until he saw through his binoculars that the Richmond area was a mass of flames. That's where his house was, and his family. He rushed back to the wharf. Everybody was gone. He headed north but soon was overcome by the thick smoke; he was unable to reach his home until close to 4:00 P.M. All that remained was the foundation of his house. He later found that his wife was in hospital but five of his six children, ages ten, six, five, three, and just eight months were gone, along with a relative who had been visiting.

THE ADMIRAL'S TOUR

RN Rear Admiral Bertram Chambers was just getting up from the breakfast table when the whole house shook violently as an ear-splitting roar descended. No windows broke because they were far enough away, in the area of Citadel Hill, and they faced away from the blast, but his wife was convinced a bomb had fallen in the front yard. Throwing on his coat, he set out on foot, walking through broken glass from the houses on the street. Trees were bent and twisted and telegraph poles were down. He hailed a passing commercial vehicle and reached the Port Convoy Office in the Metropole Building on Hollis Street, where he learned about the explosion.

Wanting to get a first-hand view of the situation, Chambers, along with his deputy, Capt. James Turnbull, and the admiral of the next scheduled convoy, Vice-Admiral Evelyn Le Marchant, boarded the tug *Maggie M*. The vessel, under charter to the Port Convoy Office, was the property of Capt. James Gordon, then in his seventies, who was at the helm when they stepped aboard. They headed to *Changuinola*, the nearest RN ship. Captain Wilcox had already raised signal flags calling for the landing of all available medical and relief parties. In the confusion of the first moments following the explosion, nobody was aware of what had happened. Given that one of the most important Allied ports had just been blown up, Chambers ordered Wilcox to also signal that all ships were to get up steam immediately and prepare to cast off should the need arise. They then loaded *Changuinola*'s relief party and took them ashore so they could face the disheartening job that awaited.

Looking up The Narrows all the way to Pier 9, a distance approaching 3 miles, Chambers could see nothing but wreckage afloat and devastation ashore. At the dockyard, they landed Admiral Le Marchant to see what assistance the RCN might need. He later reported that they had things under control, and any assistance the RN could render elsewhere would be critical.

With that done, Captain Gordon steered the *Maggie* to *Highflyer*, where Admiral Chambers reviewed the damage to that ship and conferred with Captain Garnett, who had already sent a party ashore. It was clear to Chambers that the RN had abundant resources to offer so he sent a detail from *Changuinola* north to the ships closest to the explosion site. He then asked Captain Gordon to push the *Maggie* through the floating debris so he and Turnbull could witness what he suspected would be the worst of it.

At the entrance to the Halifax side of The Narrows just north of Pier 4 sat *Niobe*, looking disrobed and shorn of everything movable. Under its bow was the militia's magazine, which was in the shadow of several fires. An officer and detail of men were hurriedly moving high explosive artillery shells down to the shoreline so they could be quickly dumped overboard should the fires consume the magazine.[71]

After pushing through debris all the way to Pier 9, Admiral Chambers was stunned to see the tug *Hilford* sitting high and dry on top of the pier. It had been tied outside the steamship *Calonne* and had somehow managed to vault over the *Calonne* and onto its side on the pier. Chambers's second assistant, Lieutenant-Commander Murray, had taken the *Hilford* to the area to survey the situation while the fire was raging. Given the state of things, there was no telling where he might be now. The *Maggie* pressed on into The Narrows so Chambers could check in with the guard ship *Acadia*, still at its anchorage just inside the basin. He was relieved to learn that the convoy ships anchored in the basin had escaped serious damage, as had *Acadia*, although it sustained a severe shaking up, despite being 1.5 miles away and shielded by a high landform.

One of the crew, RN sailor Frank Baker, wrote in his diary, "A shower of shrapnel passed over the forecastle, shattering the glass in the engine room and chart room to smithereens, which came crashing down into the alleyways... The fires all burst out on to the floor of the stokehold and it was a marvel that the stokers were not burned to death, but all of them escaped injury as did all the others of the ship's company."[72] A steamship like the *Acadia* was built with the expectation that it would be thrown about on the ocean, but having the furnaces belch burning coal practically onto the feet of the men shovelling it in takes being thrown about to a new level. The stokehold is very tight with only one way out—up! Even though the ships anchored in the basin escaped severe damage, there are many stories like this one.

The two starboard furnaces of HMCS Acadia. *Trimmers delivered the coal from the bunkers and dumped it on the floor. The stokers then shovelled it off the floor into the furnaces.* (AUTHOR'S COLLECTION)

Chambers directed Gordon to turn the *Maggie* around and retrace their route out of the harbour. As they passed the carcass of the 65-foot *Hilford*, they were hailed by survivors on the shore in bad need of help. While those aboard the *Maggie* aided the dazed and dying men caught up in the destruction of the dock, Chambers had the shock of discovering the body of Lieutenant-Commander Murray, pinned under a heavy beam. It was a sad moment for the admiral. Murray, who had once been the captain of the Canadian Pacific liner *Empress of Britain*, was well regarded, not only by Admiral Chambers but also by all who dealt with him. For a brief period, he also commanded the *Empress of Ireland*, a famous ship in Canadian history. He finished his command on April 24, 1914. On May 29, the *Empress of Ireland* collided with the coal carrier *Storstad* and sank in the St. Lawrence River with a loss of over a thousand lives.

Everybody living was gathered aboard the *Maggie*, which headed for *Highflyer* as more rescue boats were arriving. Among them was *W. H. Lee*, a naval motor vessel that supported the minesweepers moored in the Northwest Arm, keeping them supplied with stores and shuttling crews back and forth. The *Lee* had arrived from the Dockyard Coaling Wharf—Jetty 4—and set to work fighting the numerous fires.

Late that afternoon, Admiral Chambers sent out an advisory suspending all convoy activity at Halifax and requesting all centres not to send any convoy ships until further notice.

IT GETS WORSE

As darkness fell on December 5, HMCS *Lady Evelyn* had headed out to sea. The ship was one of eight patrol vessels covering the east coast. With the coming of winter, the convoys had begun operating from the ice-free port of Halifax. That called for more ships to keep the sea lanes clear around Halifax, so *Lady Evelyn* was part of the motley assemblage of vessels the navy managed to pull together.[73]

Launched as *Deerhound* in 1901 from the English yard of John Jones & Sons in Merseyside, near Liverpool, the ship carried passengers on the west coast of England, before the Canadian postmaster general's department acquired it in 1907. Given a new name, its job was to meet transatlantic mail steamers in the St. Lawrence River and take off the mail for transfer to trains, which would speed up the delivery. With the coming of war, the new Canadian navy was desperate for ships and *Lady Evelyn* became HMCS *Lady Evelyn*. After serving with the navy, it survived in commercial service on Canada's west coast until shortly before the Second World War.

Lady Evelyn was not considered a sufficiently robust vessel for offshore work during the challenging winter season, so it was limited to patrols closer to shore near the Halifax approaches. Little did they know that *Lady Evelyn* was in for a thorough shaking down over the next couple of days. By 10:00 P.M. on December 5, the vessel had steamed to the outer approaches to watch for ships and anything else that might be a threat. It was a quiet night and the

HMCS Lady Evelyn. (NATIONAL DEFENCE, PUBLIC DOMAIN VIA WIKIMEDIA COMMONS)

weather was good. It continued into the morning until just after 9:00 A.M., when the blast erupted.

It was wartime, there had been a terrible explosion, and the tiny *Lady Evelyn* was a warship, so for the captain the next step, while unfamiliar to him, was also obvious. He ordered action stations—and everybody waited. The anxious gun crews were not called upon that day to fire their modest weapons in anger, but for all aboard the situation in their home port appeared to be very bad indeed. They continued patrolling when an unscheduled ship appeared on the horizon. It must have been with trepidation that they challenged the newcomer. It was the USS *Tacoma* heading to Halifax to see if they could lend a hand.

The explosion was heard and seen many miles away from Halifax. When it occurred, the *Tacoma* was 52 miles out, returning to the US after its third trip escorting troopships and convoys to Europe. The officer of the watch felt a concussion so strong that the ship's company also cleared for action. The column of smoke and the volume of the blast caused the captain, Powers Symington, to change course and bear up for Halifax. When noon arrived, they encountered *Lady Evelyn* on its lonely vigil patrolling the outer approaches to the harbour and were guided in.

First-class dish from a Norddeutscher Lloyd ship, recovered from Halifax Harbour. (AUTHOR'S COLLECTION)

Half an hour later, another much larger American warship was coming in the harbour to take on coal. This was the USS *Von Steuben*, a converted German armed cruiser that had been interned in Philadelphia and was seized by the United States government when the US entered the war. It was the former *Kronprinz Wilhelm* of the Norddeutscher Lloyd Line, built at Stettin by AG Vulcan in 1901. GRT was 11,476 and the length was 637 feet. It was converted by the Germans to an armed merchant cruiser with displacement of 24,900 tons. In 1915, desperate for coal, it put in to Norfolk. Ship and crew were interned and could not leave because of a British blockade. When the US entered the war on April 6, 1917, they seized the ship and commissioned it as the USS *Von Steuben*. A fast four-stacker, the *Kronprinz Wilhelm* had been the holder of the coveted Blue Riband for the fastest crossing of the Atlantic Ocean, putting it in a league with such illustrious ships as *Deutschland*, *Lusitania*, *Queen Mary*, *Normandie*, and *United States*.

Now, with a ship's company of 975, making it the biggest ship in the harbour that day, the *Von Steuben* dropped anchor in the stream at 2:30 P.M., just after the *Tacoma*. Most of the piers had been destroyed or had derelicts leaning against them. An anonymous American soldier wrote, "By this time the naval men had lowered all their boats while anything that could float on water was pressed into service to take the wounded to places where succor could be given."[74]

The tug *Boonton* had towed the USS *Old Colony* to Jetty 4 where it had been tied up and was getting fitted out as a hospital ship. Using equipment borrowed from the US Coast Guard ship *Morrill*, from the destroyed RCN hospital ashore, and even from the Victoria General Hospital, they soon had two operating rooms and accommodation for some three hundred patients. Moving the wounded by water was the only practical way to get them shelter and medical attention.

Also in the area that day was a familiar ship with a new name. Built as SS *Senlaç* in 1904 at Saint John, NB, the *Acadien* was about 15 miles away when the explosion sent two bumps at the small wooden coastal steamer. The captain, W. M. A. Campbell, took a sextant reading to determine the height of the blast cloud. He estimated it to be about 12,000 feet high, with fire visible at the top and at points within the smoke along the column. It lasted about as long as a lightning flash but, of course, the smoke remained.

The *Acadien* was scheduled to arrive at Halifax by noon on the sixth. It had been carrying a load of salt from Halifax to Saint Pierre, but got diverted to North Sydney because of a leak. The freight was transferred to the SS *Pro Patria*, which took it to its destination, while divers went down to examine the *Acadien*'s hull. Repairs were made and the vessel was returning to its home port of Halifax.

In a previous life as the *Senlac*, it had provided freight and passenger service between Halifax and Lunenburg, Liverpool, Lockeport, Shelburne, Barrington, and Yarmouth.

The rest of the day for *Lady Evelyn* was quiet but come evening the wind began to breeze up and the barometer started to fall. By midnight, the wind was approaching gale force. By dawn, the little ship was taking a beating from high northeast gales blowing out of Halifax Harbour with heavy snow obscuring the way in. The crew spent the day and night in the shallow waters of the Examination Anchorage, where they managed to get the vessel anchored, running out a significant amount of chain to keep the anchors from dragging.

Meanwhile, an ocean liner inbound to Halifax was forced to anchor outside the harbour and spend a very stressful night. At 17,500 GRT and almost 600 feet long, *Calgarian* was the biggest and newest ship in the Allan Line fleet. Their ships' names all ended in *-ian*. As a regular visitor to Halifax, the captain knew that he could not take his ship in under the existing conditions. He anchored just 2 miles southeast of Portuguese Shoal. From there, he would have been obliged to navigate around the shoal to get into the harbour, which would have been impossible under the circumstances. To be on the safe side, he ordered that the depth be checked every fifteen minutes throughout the night in case the anchors might drag under the strain. Pity the poor seaman who had to lean out over the side of the heaving ship with the snow beating in his face to lower and retrieve the leadline from 84 feet of icy water four times per hour.[75]

By morning on December 8, with the storm over, the *Lady Evelyn*'s crew hove in the anchors and steamed into the channel. To the right, they observed the SS *Saranac* aground after dragging its anchors, and nearby the *Northern King* had dragged its anchors into another ship, SS *A. E. Ames*. Later, the *A. E. Ames*'s owners, Canada Steamship Lines, would bring an action in the Vice-Admiralty Court for salvage and damages for $200,000 against the *Northern King* and its owners.[76] It was not the only incident for the *A. E. Ames* in 1917. On June 29, it had had the misfortune of colliding with the *Keybell* in Lake Ontario, while sailing from Port Colborne to Montréal.

Shortly after *Lady Evelyn*'s arrival in the channel, a signal from the Examination boat told the officer of the watch that they were cleared to return to port, where the ship's company got their first sight of the shocking destruction, much of it lying silently beneath waist-deep snow, along with the bodies of the dead and perhaps a few casualties clinging to life. Men with families in Halifax could finally begin the harrowing task of tracking down their loved ones. Everybody else was to stay aboard. There was nowhere to go anyway.

Calgarian was anchored by 11:00 A.M. and had a crew ashore by 11:30. Two very busy weeks lay ahead.

Even though the newspaper's office building had been hammered and they had no windows, the *Morning Chronicle* had the story on the street in the middle of the blizzard the next day, Friday, December 7. The screaming black headlines that tried to cram in too much information were impressive, but on the left side of page 1, an understated request said it all. Under the heading "Missing" was the sub-heading, "Will anyone knowing of the whereabouts of the following kindly communicate with *The Morning Chronicle*." Streaming down to the bottom of the page was a long list of names—children, men, women, whole families.

CHAPTER 6

THE SCORCHING BREATH OF THE DRAGON

The horrendous blast unleashed the full force of bound-up energy aboard the *Mont Blanc*, and lashed against a small number of the many vessels and sailors on the harbour that day. They were the ones tied up at the shipyard, sugar refinery, and Piers 6, 8, and 9, along with the smaller craft that were attempting to deal with the fire.

MONT BLANC RAINS DOWN

Ironically, the tremendous concussion and the pieces of the ship that fell out of the sky missed all but one of those who had been aboard the *Mont Blanc*. It was as though the death ship, as it was immediately dubbed by the press, had finally set them free. The only fatality was one of the gunners, named Yves Gueguiner.

OH, FOR A HERO!

At times like these, a hero might step forward, telling everybody to leave the ship while he steers it to the basin to avoid having it blow up in a populated area. Nobody stepped forward. Nor did they row to Halifax where the people were so they could warn them; instead, they went to a mostly wooded and sparsely populated area of Dartmouth. Witness after witness testified that they did not hear any warnings about an impending explosion. On the contrary, from those who survived from the *Mont Blanc*—which was all but Gueguiner—there was much protesting about the loud and voluble warnings they sounded to all within earshot.[77]

None among the ship's company seemed able to speak English, and the closest the record comes to identifying a warning was the repeated word, "Explosion! Explosion!" yelled by arm-waving members as they pulled away. Whether they did or didn't—they probably did; why wouldn't they?—it is indeed ironic that there was so much death and suffering near and far while those aboard the source should escape so readily. Of course, the people of Halifax and those who governed them were not interested in irony; they were interested in who to blame.

Harbourmaster Francis Rudolph told the inquiry that Francis Mackey indicated to him that he and the captain had attempted to take the *Mont Blanc* into the basin, away from the city. He called for full speed on the engine room telegraph, but got no response. He concluded that everyone in the engine room had abandoned their posts and were headed for the boats, so he and Le Médec did the same.[78]

ST. BERNARD DISAPPEARS

The 90-foot tern schooner *St. Bernard* was probably the closest moored vessel to the exploding ship, tied up at Pier 6, where the *Mont Blanc* had drifted. It had arrived from Canso and tied up at Hendry's Wharf on December 3, before moving to Pier 6 on December 4 to load lumber. Hendry's had recently sold the schooner, but they were still the agents. It had been built and registered in Parrsboro in 1901.

Capt. Joseph Evans and two crew members scrambled to get the schooner away from the wharf, but their efforts were futile. All three perished.

STELLA MARIS ENDURES

The *Stella Maris* was pointing toward the burning *Mont Blanc*, which probably saved it from total destruction. It took a severe mauling and got thrown about by the ensuing tsunami. The superstructure and wheelhouse were blown away, and it ended up with a gaping hole described as 6 feet in diameter. It was aground where Pier 6 had been. Considering that the *Curaca*, many times the size of the *Stella Maris*, ended up across The Narrows at the entrance to Tufts Cove, it is interesting that the *Stella Maris* came to rest within a few feet of the explosion site, pushed there, no doubt, by the tsunami. It remained where it had landed until the following spring.

Pier 6 was gone, as was virtually every building within a 3-mile radius. Captain Brannen and eighteen other men were dead or dying but—here's another surprise—the first mate Walter Brannen and the second mate William Spenser Nickerson survived with only minor injuries. So did Walter Nickerson, chief engineer Alex Cameron, and water boy Roy Hudson. Cameron remembered the vessel going underwater just before he lost consciousness. When he came to, he was lying on the deck with his clothes and coveralls blown off, clad only in his underwear and boots. (There are numerous accounts of people having their clothes blown off, but they always seemed to prudently hang on to their underwear.)

"There are some things I remember that seem strange," Cameron recalled for the *Halifax Chronicle Herald* on December 6, 1973. "For instance, that morning I had been cleaning my rifle in my cabin. I left it there, and when it was found the stock had disappeared and the barrel was twisted out of shape by the force of the explosion, right down there in the cabin. Yet, fully exposed on deck, I came out of it living."[79] The ship was eventually salvaged, rebuilt, and returned to work, with Cameron once again in charge of the engine room.

What remains of the Stella Maris *sits forlornly on the bottom at the explosion site. The sunken* Curaca *is in the background.* (MARITIME MUSEUM OF THE ATLANTIC, MP 207.1.184/46)

Walter Brannen had been on the ladder to the hold and was blown back down by the explosion. Briefly knocked unconscious, he and second mate William Nickerson were taken off the wrecked ship by crew from the SS *Cruizer*, an ocean-going tug that had arrived from Louisbourg the previous day towing the coal barge *Laugen*. It was the second mishap for the *Cruizer* in a matter of months. On June 29, while travelling from Louisbourg to Halifax, it had collided with the ship *Eva*. Shortly after the Halifax Explosion, Walter Brannen became captain of the tugboat *Delbert D.*, used by the Admiralty in Halifax Harbour.

The first of the men to die when the *Mont Blanc* went up were the men whose sense of duty compelled them to go immediately to the burning ship. While the crew of the *Mont Blanc* were scrambling to get away and save their own lives, Captain Brannen and his crew of the *Stella Maris* were anchoring their scows and returning to try to extinguish the fire and then pull the vessel from the pier. To be fair, the men from the *Stella Maris* were not aware of the *Mont Blanc*'s cargo, while those aboard the *Mont Blanc* were.

The memory of Samuel Brookfield's feisty *Stella Maris* prevails in the annals of the Halifax Explosion not only because of the heroic efforts of those aboard but also because of the high price they paid. The tug suffered the highest losses of a locally owned vessel and most likely the greatest number of deaths of Canadian crewmen.

Five days after the explosion, Brookfield had not succeeded in recovering the bodies of his deceased employees from the wrecked *Stella Maris*. The day after the explosion, he had set out to drive to the site and retrieve them, but when he reached Young Street, he and his auto were commandeered to take an injured man to hospital. (Emergency regulations required automobile owners to make their vehicles available when called upon.[80]) That assignment turned out to be a challenge. After being turned away at two locations, Brookfield was finally able to get the man admitted to Camp Hill Hospital. By then, darkness had fallen. He tried the next day to resume his original mission but again was obstructed, and three days later was still working on it.[81] By December 7, Captain Brannen's headless body was at Snow's Funeral Home, where 150 *Titanic* victims had been embalmed a short five years earlier. Today the building is a popular seafood restaurant.

In 1905, after service as HMS *Starling*, the *Stella Maris* had been sold to Halifax interests. In 1916, with registration in St. John's, ownership was transferred to the Stella Maris Steamship Company. Because of the work tugs did, they were often in dangerous situations and their owners were sometimes sued. Many tugs have been sunk in Halifax Harbour and the lives of many crewmen lost over the past two centuries. To minimize risk of liability, owners often formed separate legal entities to own each tug.

In 1920, registration changed to Windsor, NS, under Farquhar & Co. Ltd., Halifax. With the *Stella Maris*'s registration still at Windsor, the owner changed to Halifax Trading and Sealing Co. Ltd. and remained there until the registration was closed in 1927. The tough little vessel, its bones brittle from age and a violent life, finally succumbed, as did many wooden ships of Eastern Canada, to the pressures of the hard spring ice. On a sealing voyage in March

1925, it foundered 80 miles north of my ancestral home of Fogo Island, NL. Capt. George Whitely and his ship's company of ninety were all saved. Most of those men would have been sealers, not crew.

The *Stella Maris* was not the only ship arriving at the *Mont Blanc* on December 6. The whaler from *Highflyer* arrived, as did *Niobe*'s pinnace. Men from both of these vessels received medals for bravery, but there was nothing for anybody from the *Stella Maris*, not even a pension for the widows of the men who died.

With the explosion imminent, Vincent Coleman, a dispatcher for Canadian Government Railways, staying at his post to the end, was sending a message to warn an arriving train not to proceed any closer. His justly deserved heroism is recognized with his name on a prominent building on Bayers Road in Halifax even though, according to Joseph Scanlon, Coleman's message did not have any effect on the incoming trains. Nevertheless, the message was picked up farther down the line and as a result, word got out and help was soon being organized.[82]

HIGHFLYER'S WHALER SINKS

During the explosion, *Highflyer*'s whaler was supposedly hurled into the air. Lieutenant-Commander Triggs was already dead from the blast, but some of the crew had a brief chance to fight for their lives. Unfortunately, the beating the whaler took was too much for them. William Becker was the only one who survived to tell their story.

The first time I heard a comment from another diver that he had seen a whaler on the bottom of The Narrows, I wondered how it might have gotten there. It had to have been from an accident of some sort that sank it quickly. Otherwise, help would have been available, considering that it was in a high-traffic area. I recall at least two divers over the years claiming to have seen it. I might have seen it because I have done a lot of harbour dives, and seeing small boats and other types of wreckage was a common occurrence.

A rowboat generally is a curiosity for a minute or two but it would not have crossed my mind that it could have been from the Halifax Explosion.

NIOBE'S STEAM PINNACE GOES TO THE BOTTOM

Everyone on *Niobe*'s pinnace was killed. It is likely that at least two men had just started to board the *Mont Blanc* to attach the hawser from the *Stella Maris*. There are reports of two men running toward the stern.

In describing the Halifax Explosion, the online *Canadian Encyclopedia* declares authoritatively, "At 9:05, *Mont-Blanc* exploded in the largest man-made, non-nuclear explosion in history. The force of the explosion blew *Niobe*'s pinnace and its crew to pieces." Given the circumstances, that is not an unreasonable assumption, but it is still an assumption because, as far as we know, nobody saw what happened.

There is a strange aspect to the disaster that many overlook. While people miles away from the epicentre died, there are documented cases of men quite close to the *Mont Blanc* who survived the explosion. With the obvious exception of the *Mont Blanc* itself, all the iron and steel ships in the destruction zone were repaired and put back into service, some sailing for decades thereafter. In fact, besides the *Mont Blanc*, Transport Canada reports only two vessels being completely destroyed: the wooden schooners *Lola R.* and *St. Bernard*. Five men from the *Stella Maris* survived, as did their vessel. On the bridge of the *Imo*, at point blank range, stood three men: the captain, pilot, and quartermaster. Two were killed and the quartermaster, standing alongside them, survived. Farther forward, Third Officer Bjarne Birkeland also survived. The whaler from HMS *Highflyer* was flung into the air and crashed into the water, but one of the men still managed to live on.

Besides the unlikely survival of these individuals, I believe *Niobe*'s pinnace lies on the bottom of The Narrows. All seven men aboard were lost, and it has always been assumed that the boat was destroyed. But there is a boat 90 feet below the surface, near the site where the explosion occurred, far enough away and deep enough to not get swept up in the dredging and rebuilding of the piers after the Explosion. For many decades, one and then two floating dry docks hovered close above the site, but they are gone now.

The wreckage turned up as the result of a survey of the bottom of Halifax Harbour that the Canadian Hydrographic Service conducted in the summer of 1992, using the CCGS *F. C. G. Smith*.[83] Some incorrectly identified the wreck as the tern schooner *St. Bernard*, which was the closest of all vessels to ground zero. It is not the *St. Bernard*.

On December 1, 2017, the Canadian Broadcasting Corporation posted on its website a story about the mystery boat and the efforts to identify it, noting that divers had checked it out not long after its discovery and were unable to identify it.[84] The article described the anomaly as the wreck of a schooner. I was a member of what the CBC grandly called the "Heritage Dive Team" and first saw the wreck on June 12, 2004. The dive was challenging, in the middle of the traffic lanes of The Narrows where a lot of ships go through, including the huge container carriers heading to the Fairview Cove Container Terminal and the bulk carriers coming from the National Gypsum terminal. The currents were strong, and it was dark in the shadow of the giant Panamax floating dry dock that had a ship cradled in the air while workers moved beneath it. At the time, I never stopped to realize that we were below the spot where the collision had occurred.

That darkness left a lasting impression on me. Non-divers think it's dark underwater. It is sometimes, but I have seen my shadow on the bottom at 70 feet in The Narrows with the sun shining above. On that June dive, however, the silt was dark and it absorbed the light. I was interested to learn later that in the debris falling after the *Mont Blanc* exploded, there was material described as black rain. According to Joseph Scanlon, "It consisted of a mixture of oil, iron filings and dirt and it poured from the sky, covering everything—including victims—in black. It pushed dirt into many of the open wounds, causing infection that would lead to death. A layer of black can still be found in the soil in Halifax's North End."[85]

Despite the poor light on that dive, as soon as I saw the wreck, I knew it wasn't a schooner. It was too small and it was sitting upright, indicating it had a flat bottom. A wrecked schooner lies on its side because its bottom is rounded, with the keel jutting down. There was no sign of any masts or rigging but that could have been concealed by the deep, dark silt that covered the area in dunes like the Sahara Desert. The waves of silt had most of this vessel buried, and there was a plastic tricycle plunked in the middle of it along with more plastic and other rubbish from our throwaway society.

After the dive, my buddy and I agreed that it was definitely not a schooner. Trying to convince myself that it was a sailing craft, I thought that perhaps it was a sailing yacht named the *Cygnet*. We were offshore from where the Royal Halifax Yacht Club, the forerunner of the Royal Nova Scotia Yacht Squadron, got started in 1837. The *Cygnet* had sunk while racing in the area on September 2, 1876. Three men had drowned, two of whom were never found.[86]

Still curious, we went back for a second dive to see if we could get a better look at the site. In the poor visibility, I got disoriented and had burned through half my air before I finally found the wreck—an all-too-common vagary of wreck diving—so I learned nothing new from that dive. We had not considered that the boat could have been associated with the Halifax Explosion mainly because, at the time, our level of knowledge about the event was limited to the basics. That was the last I saw of the wreck, but for years I wondered what it might be. It was certainly not a run-of-the-mill workboat or fishing schooner like the many in the harbour the day the *Mont Blanc* was destroyed.

Given the significant numbers of scuba divers that frequent the harbour, I assume others have visited the site since we were there. Years later, I saw a picture of *Niobe* with the pinnace alongside long before it sank. That settled the mystery for me.

But how could a perhaps 40-foot-long wooden boat in the firing line of such a destructive blast survive? Well, the *Stella Maris* was wooden, and close by, and it survived. The *Highflyer*'s whaler was wooden; it did not disintegrate even though it supposedly was sent through the air. HMCS *Niobe*'s pinnace is believed to have been against the side of the *Mont Blanc* unloading the brave men who were boarding the deserted ship to connect a towing line; the ship would have towered above. With the pinnace sitting so low, much of the force of the concussion would have been above it, and a piece of the disintegrating *Mont Blanc* could have literally shoved the little craft under the water and swamped it, after which the violence of the water would have twisted and turned it to the location where it was sitting when the side-scan sonar picked it up. It was lying more or less intact on the bottom, heavily decayed, or at least it was when I saw it in 2004. The worms may have finished it off by now.

For their heroism, Acting Boatswain Mattison and Stoker Petty Officer Ernest Edmund Baird were posthumously awarded the Albert Medal for gallantry in life-saving at sea. They were named and recognized in Parliament, along with the other five men: Leading Seaman Charles McMillan; Ordinary Seaman Freeman Burnley Nickerson; Able Seaman Albert Saunders; wireless telegraph operator George Veals; and Stoker George Roley Yates. It's fitting that Mattison and Baird were honoured in such a way, but how did their bravery differ from that shown by the others? Were they the two men seen running along the deck toward the stern of the burning *Mont Blanc*? How can we ever know?

PICTON AND THE TUGS

Docked at the sugar refinery wharf was the SS *Picton*, which was severely bashed about by the explosion. It sustained twenty-two deaths aboard, but did not sink. However, considering all the fires going on in the neighbourhood, the cargo of 1,500 tons of artillery shells was a problem.

On the way into Halifax, the *Picton* had struck bottom and sustained enough damage to its rudder and stern post to require repairs at the shipyard. The ship was fully loaded and ready to join a convoy but that had to be delayed and, instead of anchoring in the basin to await the convoy, the *Picton* had to await its turn to enter the graving dock. The shipyard wharves were already packed three abreast so it was tied next door at the sugar refinery, where there was space to unload some of the cargo of food, such as bags of flour and oats and canned goods, to lighten the ship. A gang of stevedores was seeing to that, when the disastrous collision occurred just offshore from where they were working.

Within minutes of the collision, the tug *F. W. Roebling* was racing to help extinguish the fire aboard the *Mont Blanc*. Instead, those aboard became casualties of the explosion. As they approached, the explosion threw the vessel's bow upward. The mast crashed back, destroying the pilot house and crushing Capt. Charles Mood. The cook was also severely injured, and the chief engineer, Henry Doane of Yarmouth County, was killed. Just the day before, on December 5, 1917, he had sent a postcard to his wife, Etta, asking what he might buy their son for Christmas.

Hendry's, the agents for the wooden schooner *St. Bernard*, also acted quickly, dispatching their tug *W. M. Weatherspoon* to put a line on the schooner and tow it away from the burning *Mont Blanc*. It lost the race and was soon picking up survivors. Captain Ormiston took five or six from the *Douglas H. Thomas* to Pickford & Black's Wharf and turned around to go back for more. Meanwhile, the tug *Gladiator* was on the way, and the *Merrimac* arrived from the Bedford Basin. The first thing the *Merrimac* encountered was the *Curaca*, barely afloat in the middle of The Narrows. They took off all the survivors they could find, just six men. With another twenty aboard from the *Calonne*, many of them badly injured, the tug headed downtown and dropped them at Campbell's Wharf before returning to help deal with the *Picton*.

The *Picton*'s cargo of artillery shells was not uncommon considering it was wartime. But a ship burning so close to that cargo was a major problem so the man in charge, Frank Carew, ordered the men out of the holds and had the hatch covers put back down. But worse was coming. Almost all eighty men at work disappeared in the explosion and were still missing five days later.[87] On the tenth, the *Acadian Recorder* published an ad listing the names of fifty-seven stevedores employed by Furness Withy and Co. who were missing, along with eight other employees, including Mr. Carew.

Furness Withy was a British shipbuilding and ship-owning firm with stevedoring facilities in Halifax. The company was also the Halifax agent for the *Picton*. When the explosion happened, the marine superintendent for the company, James Harrison, being aware of the cargo and having seen the proximity of the burning *Mont Blanc*, feared the explosion might have been aboard the *Picton*. Learning that was not the case, he knew there was still a chance his ship could blow up, given all the fires nearby. Unable to get to the ship through the chaos, he managed to hitch a ride aboard the *Weatherspoon*. It had just arrived at the Furness Withy Wharf with a load of injured survivors from the *Middleham Castle*, which was tied up at the dockyard wharf next door to the sugar refinery wharf, where the *Picton* was.

By then the *Merrimac* was returning from dropping off its twenty-six survivors at Campbell's Wharf. Capt. Angus Rudolph described the subsequent events this way:

> When we got back, the *Curaca* was ashore in The Narrows. We then went to help with the *Picton*. The *Weatherspoon* and the *Gladiator* both had hold of her. We cut a line that the *Picton* had to the shore, and then put Captain Harrison, of Furness Withy and Company, and two of the *Weatherspoon*'s men on board the *Picton*. They cut away the steel cables from the wreckage of the pier, and we hauled the steamer out into the stream, where she was anchored. On Saturday the *Weatherspoon*, the *Gladiator*, and the *Merrimac* took the *Picton* down to Eastern Passage, as she had explosives on board, and it was thought best to have her out of the way.[88]

After the move, the *Picton* continued to be troublesome. Besides the artillery shells, there were problems with the smoke-screening gear aboard, which had been trashed in the explosion. (Many words and expressions of the English language have nautical roots and "smokescreen" is one of them. During wartime, many ships had the ability to create a huge cloud of smoke in which they could hide from enemy warships. They carried a supply of chemical cartridges that could be ignited to produce a cloud of thick black smoke.) The cartridges on the *Picton* were now in disarray, some with their volatile contents spread around. Just walking on it could ignite them.

With all that unstable material lying aboard, the *Picton* couldn't stay where it was. It was too tempting a target, and before long there were some young locals aboard seeing what they might make off with. Smoke was soon belching from the marooned ship, and the citizens nearby were fleeing through the pouring rain, fearing another blast. As a result, the *Picton* was again towed out and anchored, where it continued to cause trouble, with the smoke cartridges still producing smoke. The ship had become notorious.

On December 10, 1917, the *Halifax Daily Echo* declared, "The naval authorities afterwards took charge of the vessel and towed her away. She was taken out to sea, her cocks drawn, and allowed to sink.... Now that the *Picton* has been disposed of there is absolutely no danger of another explosion from any vessel in port."

But, stop the presses! The *Picton* was still very much afloat and as irksome as ever. With reporting like that, it's no wonder the people of Halifax were jittery. The *Picton*'s adventures were far from over. The last incident took place on January 29. The wearisome ship had been towed to the new Ocean Terminals piers where the submarine net came ashore, near the entrance to the inner harbour. The ammunition was being unpacked and inspected to determine if it could be shipped to Europe. As one of the heavy boxes was dragged across a surface it caught fire. The phosphorus that had leaked from the damaged cartridges had mixed with cordite, causing a box to ignite. The small blaze was quickly put out, but December 6 was still fresh in the public's mind, causing schools and houses in the vicinity to empty. The panic eventually died down, and the ship was forgotten. It was later tied up at the Furness Withy Pier until it got into the shipyard for repairs on April 27.[89] It finally left Halifax on August 14, 1918, for Sydney and then on to England.

MUSQUASH DITCHES ITS AMMO

Rafted on the outside of two ships, the *Middleham Castle* and *J. A. McKee,* was the tug *Musquash*. Red-hot fragments of metal rained down and it was soon ablaze. Being a minesweeper, it had a gun aboard, which meant there was also ammunition, so there was some urgency to get matters in hand as the vessel was coming loose from its mooring to the *Middleham Castle* and in danger of drifting into the anchored *Picton* nearby.

Two British sailors, Thomas Davis and Robert Stones, volunteered to go aboard the *Musquash*. They secured a line and the *W. H. Lee* towed the minesweeper stern-first into the middle of The Narrows. Then the two sailors went forward, pulled the ammunition—by now badly scorched—away from the flames and threw it overboard. They broke down doors to enable *Lee*'s hoses to put out the fire. The sailors' actions subdued the fire and prevented further damage and loss of life, as the ammunition could have exploded at any time.[90]

This was just one of many fires the *W. H. Lee* had to deal with that day. The two sailors were awarded the Albert Medal for bravery.[91]

Five men were lost on the *Musquash*, including the sixteen-year-old steward Edward Pieroway. He was buried at Sandy Point in St. Georges Bay, on the west coast of Newfoundland. That once-prosperous community—James Farquhar's ship *Harlaw* had a regular service from Halifax—was gradually abandoned because of sea level rise. It is in an area of long sandy beaches and had been connected to the mainland, but once the connection eroded away, the community was threatened. Despite efforts to shore up the perimeter, the residents were soon on a low, flat, sandy island, left with no option but to move from the two-hundred-year-old community. The last residents moved away in the 1970s.

There is an identification challenge with the *Musquash* because there were two steam tugs so named in eastern Canada at that time. There was *Musquash*, vessel number 131307, built at Garton near Liverpool, England, in 1910, with a 100-foot-long steel hull, registered at Québec in 1914 and owned in Montréal. And there was *Musquash*, vessel number 133677, built at Portsmouth in 1894, with a 51-foot-long wooden hull, registered at Halifax in 1914 and owned in Chatham, NB.

I believe the one involved in the Explosion story is 131307, mainly because it had a sister tug named *Gopher*, vessel number 131308. They were built together to the same specs at the Garston Graving Dock & Shipbuilding

Company in 1910 for the same customer, the Mersey Towing Company in Liverpool. On June 3, 1914, they left Liverpool and arrived at Montréal on June 20 as the property of the Quebec Salvage and Wrecking Company, partly owned by Canadian Pacific Steamships. On December 6, 1917, there was at Halifax the same *Gopher* and a tug named *Musquash*. It seems very likely that this was the same *Musquash* that had been in company with *Gopher* in the past, especially when we consider that in 1920 the Quebec Salvage and Wrecking Company sold their *Musquash* to a Halifax firm named Atlantic Salvage Company.

During the night of August 4, 1921, this same *Musquash* was in heavy seas towing a barge, probably containing coal, from Louisbourg to Halifax, when the line parted and the barge went adrift. While attempting to reattach to the barge, the *Musquash* was holed by a derrick on the barge and rapidly took on water. The crew were forced to take to the lifeboat and the vessel sank near St. Esprit in Cape Breton, with no loss of life.[92]

DOUGLAS H. THOMAS, A DERELICT

The Dominion Coal Company of Glace Bay, owners of the *Douglas H. Thomas*, described their star tug as "a first-class ship in every respect, powerful, dependable and good looking." Named after a prominent Baltimore banker with ties to local shipping and built in 1892 at the Sparrows Point Yard of the Maryland Steel Company, the 116.5-foot tug was an ocean-going vessel that saw a lot of action after coming to Nova Scotia in 1899. In addition to being smashed during the Explosion, it was present during or following the wrecking of six vessels, including the relatively new SS *Bruce*, the first steel ship to ply the Cabot Strait between Newfoundland and Nova Scotia. On November 13, 1912, the tug collided with the *City of Sydney* (formerly Red Cross Line's SS *Rosalind*) in Sydney Harbour, resulting in the death of five men. (Two years later, the *City of Sydney* sank while coming into Halifax and has since become a popular dive site.)

In September 1909, the *Douglas H. Thomas* made a 475-mile trip from Sydney to Battle Harbour, NL, to take Associated Press correspondents to meet the SS *Roosevelt*, which was carrying Robert Peary back from his triumphal trip to the North Pole.[93] Today, Battle Harbour is a National Historic District, based on its two hundred–year significance in the Labrador fishery.

At the time of the Halifax Explosion, the *Douglas H. Thomas* was at the dry dock wharf with three other ships. Its deck was levelled and torn open, through which water poured and left the ship listing. Two or three men died, one of them fifteen-year-old Martin Moore, who was working with a repair crew. The wreck was towed to safety in Dartmouth and then to Liverpool, NS, where it was repaired. On the way to Sydney, it arrived in Halifax on April 27, 1918, where it was declared to have a "decidedly improved appearance, in fact more trim looking than ever before."[94] The tug's captain, Daniel McLaine, testified at the inquiry into the cause of the Halifax Explosion.

It continued to reliably serve the coal company until October 4, 1924, when it called at Ingonish Harbour to pick up a barge for towing to Louisbourg. In the narrow, shallow channel, the *Douglas H. Thomas* grounded and sank just ten minutes later. It seemed refloating the vessel and patching up the bottom would be a routine job, but they soon concluded the effort was not worth the cost.[95]

MORE REPAIRS FOR *MIDDLEHAM CASTLE*

By December 6, the *Middleham Castle* had just finished repairs at the dry dock and was at the wharf, planning to depart Halifax that day with a general cargo. The blast took off the smokestack and masts, smashed the bridge, and cleared away most of what was on the deck. This was a relatively new cargo ship, built in 1910 at Glasgow by William Hamilton and Co. for the Lancashire Shipping Company of Liverpool. It was 4,534 GRT, 380 feet long by 50 feet wide. The ship was powered by a single triple-expansion steam engine.

The *Middleham Castle* was taken to New York, departing on December 25, where it was repaired again. It lived to serve in the Second World War under the name *Everoja.* While travelling in convoy from Sydney, NS, carrying a load of wheat, it collided with the SS *South Wales* on September 26, 1941. Too badly needed to be put into the queue at the shipyard, the *Everoja* was patched up and sent on its way to Europe in another convoy. In a rendezvous with a German U-boat north of Newfoundland it met its end on or near November 6, 1941. It was just 80 miles from Belle Isle off Newfoundland's northern tip (not to be confused with Bell Island, near St. John's, where four ships were torpedoed while at anchor in the Second World War).[96]

J. A. MCKEE

The coal carrier *J. A. McKee* was also severely damaged in the explosion. As far as we know, there was just one death, Peter Paupin of West Arichat, NS. Because it was a Canadian merchant vessel waiting to go into the dry dock, many of the crew may have gone home, leaving only a skeleton crew aboard. It departed Halifax on January 1, 1918, to be repaired at New York.

RAGUS

The Acadia Sugar Refining Company's tug *Ragus*—sugar spelled backwards—was nearby when the explosion occurred. Pilot Mackey testified that the captain was one of the people he had warned of the impending explosion. Just a couple of weeks old when it was swept by the dragon's breath, it went down with all hands. It was a Nova Scotia–built vessel, constructed by the long-established firm of John McLean & Sons of Mahone Bay.

The vessels identified in this chapter had two things in common. They were severely damaged, some to the point of sinking, and they were all, with the exceptions of *Highflyer*'s whaler and *Niobe*'s pinnace, given a new life. Perhaps, in normal circumstances, some would have been considered too far gone to be repaired, but the times were extraordinary. There was an acute need for ships. The folklore associated with the Explosion is that the bottom of Halifax Harbour is strewn with the carcasses of many ships lost that day. That is not the case.

CHAPTER 7

THE DESTRUCTION ZONE

The primary area of destruction went well beyond the ships moored close to the explosion site. Along the shore and in the stream to the south lay the dockyard anchorage and the dockyard jetties, where many RCN assets were tied up, leaving, or arriving. Even vessels at the Deep Water Terminus and the waterfront did not escape. There are numerous stories of ships and boats sustaining at least some damage off the downtown area and in the Bedford Basin.

IMO IS FLUNG ASHORE

The *Imo* had virtually everything above the deck destroyed. On the deck, third officer Bjarne Birkeland was struck unconscious and was saved only because of his faithful dog, Ralph, an Airedale terrier. After the explosion, he remained unconscious on the deck into the night. Ralph, too, had taken the brunt of the explosion and was not in the best of shape, but in the chaos, he managed to find Birkeland and lay on top of him, keeping him from getting buried in the snow where he might have smothered and also providing enough warmth to keep his friend alive. Throughout the blizzard Ralph stuck to his post until a rescue team found him and his owner.

Birkeland was taken to HMS *Calgarian*, which dropped anchor in the stream at 10:00 A.M. on December 8, the day after the blizzard and forty-eight hours after the explosion. He and Ralph were transferred from *Calgarian* to *Highflyer*, but Birkeland had to go to hospital, and under quarantine rules

Ralph was not allowed ashore. What was to become of this faithful friend? An officer aboard *Highflyer* stepped forward with a solemn vow to love and care for the trusty dog, and soon Ralph became a part of the RN. Bjarne Birkeland remained in Halifax for six months, recuperating and testifying in the inquiry.

The only survivor from the *Imo*'s bridge was helmsman Johan Johansen. He was a crucial witness, but he spoke English with an accent and in the atmosphere of suspicion that had overtaken Halifax, he was immediately deemed a spy who somehow had contrived to cause the explosion. He and his shipmates were held aboard *Highflyer*, but he was not considered worthy of receiving medical treatment, despite serious injuries. The lawyer for the *Imo*'s owners, Charles Burchell, got him transferred to the Bellevue Hospital at Spring Garden Road and Queen Street, where he caused even more suspicion. He was caught trying to sneak out of the place when a nurse accosted him. He offered her money to go away, but that turned out to be a bad idea. They called the police, and he was marched off to jail. While poking through his belongings, they found a letter written in German and that settled it—until somebody pointed out that it was not German, but Norwegian.

Eventually, Burchell managed to secure Johansen's release. Burchell then swore an affidavit that he read during the inquiry, iterating the unreasonable

The Imo *aground on the Dartmouth shore, waiting to be salvaged.* (NS ARCHIVES)

and even cruel treatment doled out to Johansen, whose actions were simply a reaction to the way he had been treated and an attempt to ensure his own safety.[97]

An indication of the suspicious attitudes toward foreigners is revealed in a letter written by the navigator of HMCS *Canada*, Lieutenant Ernest Rankin, to his mother: "All the Germans and Austrians are being rounded up. It is surprising this was not done months ago."

Seven men from the *Imo*, including the captain and forty-year-old pilot William Hayes, perished. Hayes's body was recovered from the bridge of the *Imo* on December 9. He left his wife Gertrude and five children; the youngest was Charles, seven months. The blast and tsunami slung the ship across The Narrows and into shallow water on the Dartmouth shoreline, driving it ashore at the foot of Jamieson and Dawson Streets, just north of the Macdonald Bridge, where today the dilapidated jetty that serviced the Dockyard Annex is located. There it remained until being refloated in May 1918. It was patched up enough to be towed and departed Halifax on July 19 for Newport News, Virginia.

Soon, it had a new name—*Guvernören*—and a new occupation as a whale oil tanker. Four years later, while heading to the Falkland Islands at the end of November 1921 it struck a rock and was abandoned just 20 miles from its destination.

NIOBE'S FINAL POUNDING

The forlorn old *Niobe* was no longer HMS *Niobe* of the Channel Squadron, a glory of sleek black and buff, glistening brass, and bristling guns. Suffering the daily indignity of being arrayed like Noah's ark and occupied by a bunch of office workers, it had taken one final thrashing from the sea before being towed to the breakers in Philadelphia in 1922. With two of its four stacks destroyed, "it betokened a definite renunciation of open sea, a final decline into the senility of grey hulkdom."[98]

Despite its size, following the explosion, it had been bounced around and dislodged from its moorings, which had to be fixed post-haste because, forlorn or not, it was still the workplace of twelve hundred men who were essential to the war effort. More than twenty of their company had lost their lives.

HOVLAND RISES AND FALLS AGAIN

The *Hovland* was a regular visitor to Halifax and had been boarded on July 28, 1917, in mid-Atlantic by personnel from HMS *Changuinola* during a routine check. The ship was carrying a cargo of phosphates from Baltimore to Christiania (now called Oslo), Norway, via Halifax.

The *Hovland* was in the graving dock, with its crew remaining on board. Neutral seamen were not permitted free access to the city for fear there might be spies among them. Their ship's upper works sustained a severe pounding, losing its funnel and five crew members, including the chief engineer. The 325-foot-long ship jumped so violently under the force of the concussion and flooding of the drydock by the tsunami that the blocks upon which it was resting were forced up through the bottom of the vessel.

SS Hovland *in the dry dock, where it was when the explosion occurred.*
(MARITIME MUSEUM OF THE ATLANTIC)

Even though the *Hovland* got worked over while sitting in the dock during the explosion, the dock itself suffered only minor damage, most of it above ground. At first it was thought repair would cost millions of dollars, but the dock was back in operation after only two months. The machine shop building and the sugar refinery, both of which were destroyed, shielded the facility from catastrophic damage. Their destruction opened up a piece of prime real estate that enabled the beginning of a world-class shipbuilding industry in Halifax.

As the *Hovland* was conveniently located in the graving dock, temporary repairs were made, and it departed from Halifax to New York on February 9 for additional work, thus freeing up the graving dock for urgent repairs to other ships.

HILFORD HIGH AND DRY

Like many of the smaller vessels used in the harbour at the time, the *Hilford* was a wooden vessel. Alvin Stevens at Northwest Cove, Tancook Island, was the builder, completing it in 1908. Admiral Chambers reported that the *Hilford*, which the Port Convoy Office had chartered from the J. Foster Rood Co. of Halifax to provide transportation for his staff, had been put permanently out of action, which is not surprising, considering it ended up atop a pier, inside where the *Calonne* had been tied up.

SAMBRO SINKS THREE TIMES

The 55-foot-long shipyard tug *Sambro*, built by the Halifax Graving Dock Co. in 1915, sank in the explosion. Rated at 45 GRT, it is the first steel vessel listed in the shipyard's construction history. It was refloated ten years later in 1927, fitted with a diesel engine, and renamed *Erg*. It went back to work and on July 6, 1943, was run over and sunk in the basin by the Norwegian freighter *Norelg*, with the loss of nineteen men. It was later located and refloated to recover the

The tug Sambro, *after being recovered from the bottom of Halifax Harbour for the second time.* (NS ARCHIVES)

bodies, after which it was intentionally sunk, for the third time, on the eastern side of the basin near the magazine, in about 50 feet of water. A member of our dive group found it in the early part of the twenty-first century, and we all went to have a look at this little piece of history. He had the shipyard make a bronze plaque, which he installed on the remains of the *Sambro*.

CHANGUINOLA AND *HIGHFLYER*

Even though His Majesty's Ships *Changuinola* and *Highflyer* were anchored relatively close to one another out in the stream from the dockyard, the blast treated them differently. *Changuinola* suffered only minor damage, despite being in the path of significant falling debris. *Highflyer*, on the other hand, received considerable damage from the blast and from the fragments. The hull plating was split open on the starboard side and several buildings on the deck were destroyed, including the chart house, the wireless telegraphy cabin, and the captain's upper deck cabin. Parts of the bridge were knocked down, and most of the boats located on the deck were smashed, leaving just three. There were nine deaths reported, including those in the whaler, and about fifty sailors were injured.

While searching for the whaler, a group from *Highflyer* were hailed from the Dartmouth shore by a locomotive engineer. They rowed to the beach and the engineer said, "I have got one of your men on the footplate of my engine. I found him on the beach unconscious and I put him on the footplate with the furnace door open and his face in a bucket of hot water."[99] He was the only survivor from the whaler.

The galley of *Highflyer* served as a collection point for injured sailors.

SOMETHING NEW FOR *OLD COLONY*

By midday on December 6, it was clear that the city's hospitals and other medical facilities would become overwhelmed. A solution quickly presented itself in the use of an American passenger ship that had lots of unused space: the steamer *Old Colony*, launched on June 26, 1907, from the yard of William Cramp & Sons of Philadelphia. On November 12, 1917, the USN had acquired it from the Eastern Steamship Corporation, which provided service between Boston and Yarmouth, and sent the USS *Old Colony* to Great Britain for modifications to make it a minelayer for the RN. The ship had come to Halifax for boiler repairs and had received only minor damage on December 6. With its size and empty passenger cabins, the USN liaison officer Captain Hines volunteered the vessel for use as a hospital ship. Over the next days, operations were carried out with doctors and medical staff arriving from other ships, including the *Von Steuben* and *Tacoma*, and hospitals on shore.[100]

After sitting in line at the shipyard for a month, the *Old Colony* was moved to Evans's Wharf in Dartmouth to have its boilers re-tubed. That job was completed by the end of the following April. On May 3, it was out on sea trials and getting its compasses adjusted, docking at Pier 9 to await departure for the United Kingdom.

THE HORSE BOATS

The last ship tied in The Narrows was at Pier 9, the point where the basin opened. It was the *Calonne*, which lost fifteen of its ship's company. Along with the *Curaca*, at Pier 8, it was loading horses, which arrived at the docks of the Canadian Government Railways' Richmond Depot by train. Tracks on those two docks enabled the trains to get alongside the ships to move the animals aboard.

Horses and mules might sound like an unusual cargo, but they were a common and vital component of the war effort. Beasts of burden were essential in the First World War to keep the war machine grinding along. The use of automobiles was still in its infancy, and while trains had become an essential part of travel worldwide they did not provide the flexibility needed at the front. Trains might get horses to the front, but they could not do what horses did.

When Irving Stuttaford of Montréal joined the Canadian Militia as a gunner six months before the Halifax Explosion, he probably had no idea of the extent to which horses would become a part of his life. This was a war of wholesale human slaughter, fought with machine guns and artillery. Those heavy and ungainly artillery pieces needed to be constantly moved around in very rough terrain. In addition, they had an insatiable appetite for two consumables—projectiles and the propellants that sent them on their way toward their targets. Enter the noble horse, the only thing capable of moving the guns and ammunition to where they were required on the battlefield. That was just one of the jobs needed to keep the huge armies supplied and operating. The

France and Canada Steamship Company is reported to have shipped 200,000 horses to France throughout the war.[101] All told, it is estimated that 8 million horses and mules died in the war.

The animals were high maintenance, requiring shelter and regular care. Enormous amounts of hay and oats had to be shipped across the Atlantic to keep them fed. Harnesses and wagons were an important line item in shipping reports, as well as saddles for the cavalry units.

When the explosion came on December 6, the two horse ships, with their living cargoes, could not have been in a worse place.

CHAPTER 8

THE REAL DEATH SHIP

For Capt. E. Peck of the SS *Curaca*, the disaster launched what must have been the most disheartening period of his life. As a sailor, he was used to being far from his home at Bear River, NS, but he always had his ship to take him back. That ship was now severely smashed and perched on the bottom in shallow water on the other side of The Narrows, across from Pier 8, where it had been tied. The bow was buckled and the deck swept, but that was the least of his troubles. He would soon discover that of all the ships in the harbour, his had suffered the greatest losses of life.

RECORD DEATHS

In addition to the deaths of the animals, the *Curaca* lost forty-nine men, and the *Calonne* lost fifteen. Of those fatalities, twenty had their job description listed as "horseman." The *Curaca* was one of the ships closest to the *Mont Blanc* before it blew up. The inferno aboard had attracted a sizable crowd. The crews of ships were equally interested, and most of the *Curaca*'s stood at the stern of their ship, where the view was best. Edward McCrossan was among them. His testimony about the last minutes when the burning *Mont Blanc* drifted up to Pier 6 and grounded below what is now North Barrington Street is key to our understanding of those final seconds. McCrossan did not witness what happened next because he slipped below for a cigarette, thus becoming one of the handful of crewmen from the *Curaca* to have witnessed what happened moments before the explosion and survived. Smoking has killed a lot of people, but it saved McCrossan.

The Curaca *grounded at the entrance to Tufts Cove in Dartmouth.* (MARITIME MUSEUM OF THE ATLANTIC, MP 207.1.184)

By the time the *Merrimac* returned from dropping off the *Curaca*'s and *Calonne*'s survivors, the *Curaca* had sunk on the Dartmouth shore, after wallowing its way across The Narrows. Only the bow and a lonely wireless mast showed above the surface. It had been flipped 180 degrees and was facing out of the harbour, in a position it would not have been able to achieve under its own steam.

McCrossan's shipmates were virtually wiped out. For half of them, Captain Peck would not even have their bodies to identify. For the rest, he had the doleful duty of looking upon their broken remains—some not even out of their teens—and then having to write home to their families. He identified bodies as they turned up over a two-week period. Peck himself had pulled up two with the aid of a boat hook, and divers brought up fifteen more. By the end of the first week of January, twenty-two had been buried.[102] The gravesite trench was left open in the expectation that more would be found when the ship was salvaged. That proved to be the case, but before the bodies could be dealt with a complaint that coffins were visible caused some turmoil. An investigation showed that none were visible. The final burials were done, and the trench was closed.[103]

To complicate matters, we don't know whether the names of all those lost have been recorded, for the story of the *Curaca*, although a small part of the greater narrative of the Halifax Explosion, demonstrates the challenge of compiling a complete list of victims. In the chaos and grief of most disasters, rescue teams do their best to list the names of the lost, but those lists are rarely complete. Regardless, what they calculate ends up as the official record and many years after the calamity, researchers uncover the list in an archive and optimistically assume they have the complete details of the victims. However, if they have the misfortune to uncover a second source, the chances are good that the two will not agree, and they have some work ahead.

The *Halifax Morning Chronicle* reported on December 15, 2017, that the *Curaca* had fifty-five men aboard, of which seven survived. They were close.

CONTRADICTORY RECORDS

Relying solely on that information would make things simple, but I had access to four sources:

- the crew documents from the Board of Trade of the United Kingdom;
- the official list of all who died in the Explosion as compiled by the Nova Scotia Archives (NSA;)
- a monument containing the names of the *Curaca*'s dead, placed by the ship's owners in Fairview Lawn Cemetery;
- a monument to five of the victims from the Scottish island of Barra, also at Fairview Lawn.

They all sound official and reliable, but there is disagreement among the four.

In trying to reconcile these sources, the first thing I encountered was a transcription error in the records, a common quirk in such circumstances that often goes undiscovered. One record in the NSA database provides the name of a cook named Jen Yang. It says he was on the *Curaca*, but the handwritten form where his death was documented in 1917 says he was aboard the SS *Glasgow*. More research revealed that he was, in fact, aboard the *Curaca*, having signed on as cook on October 26, 1917. I did not find any evidence that an SS *Glasgow* was even in the harbour on December 6. An inauspicious start, but there are many such errors.

Including Jen Yang, the NSA list contains fifty-one names while the monument from the ship's owners lists forty-five. Four of the names on the monument list are not on the NSA list, and nine of the names on the NSA list are not on the monument list. In all, the two sources have only forty-one names in common. Although the second monument contains the names of five men from the island of Barra who were killed, the other two sources contain only four of those names.

In addition, there are numerous inconsistencies in the other information, such as where the men were from. One source says R. L. Pickering was from Liverpool, England, while another says he was from Sydney, NS. He was indeed living in Liverpool, but had been born in Sydney, New South Wales, Australia. The crew list says Sydney, NSW. In this case, where the cursive writing is not entirely clear, a transcriber in Nova Scotia can be forgiven for changing Sydney, NSW, to Sydney, NS. The boatswain is listed as P. McCann from Liverpool in one place and as T. McCann from Glasgow on the crew list.

The NSA list contains the names of eight sailors who died and were identified as being from the *Curaca*. The evidence is very thin, as the following examples illustrate. John Burns is described as a seventy-year-old fireman, responsible for shovelling coal into the furnaces in the boiler room. The physically demanding job carried out in hot, dusty conditions was the worst job aboard, especially for a seventy-year-old. On his handwritten death record, dated March 18, 1925, there is no mention of the *Curaca*, and he has a Halifax address. His body was not identified.

While most entries in the NSA database are supported by multiple sources, John McIvor's record has only one. There is no handwritten death record from the time. The same can be said for William Lockern and William West.

M. Neil's was one of six handwritten death records, numbers 1272 through 1277, created on February 27, 1918. The remains of the six were probably never found because they all say "Body not identified" and, for unknown reasons, they were documented nearly three months after the event. Mr. Neil is unique among the group in that the names of the other five are contained in the *Curaca*'s crew documents, while his is not.

R. A. Raeburn is a duplicate of Roy A. Auburn. Each record in the NSA database contains detailed information that matches the other record, including that they were both the chief steward aboard the *Curaca*. However, Auburn is in the crew documents but Raeburn is not.

J. Falls was indeed on the crew list, but it says clearly that on departure day he was not aboard. It would be interesting to know how the name turned up in Halifax and got included. It's tempting to argue that the crew documents got it wrong but, as with John McIvor, William Lockern, and William West, there is no handwritten death record, there is no mention of a body, and the single source is the same.

The document that I consider comes closest to the truth is *Curaca*'s crew list, which offers the following data:

- Between October 25 and October 30, forty-nine men signed on for the trip.
- Two did not show up by departure day, meaning forty-seven departed Glasgow in early November.
- Before Halifax, the *Curaca* went to Saint John, NB, where, between November 28 and 30, two men left the ship and another man deserted.
- One of the two who left the ship was the captain, M. Ward. He was from Sackville, NB.
- After Ward's departure, the chief officer, thirty-nine-year-old E. Peck, was promoted to captain. He was from Bear River, NS. The second and third officers were promoted to chief and second, and the bosun became third officer.
- Forty-four men were aboard when the ship arrived in Halifax and tied up at Pier 8.

- On December 4, two days before the explosion, twelve more men joined the ship. They were provided by a company in Montréal and would tend the horses on the way to Europe. Five had been born in Malta.
- That means fifty-six men were signed on when the explosion occurred.
- Seven survived, and were discharged from hospital between December 13 and January 9.
- All the horsemen, including their foreman and assistant foreman, died.

With a disaster like the loss of the *Curaca*'s crew, it is very difficult to find and/or identify all the living and the dead. With a disaster of the magnitude of the Halifax Explosion, the task is impossible. Two thousand deaths is the number we read most often. The NSA list contains 1,783 names. The Halifax Relief Commission at the time concluded that 1,963 died.[104] That is likely the bare minimum. For starters, there are at least three gravesites in Halifax that contain the bodies of unidentified victims. If they were never identified, then their names must not be in any list. In addition, there would have been many who were alone and had nobody to report they had disappeared. It was the height of the First World War. Halifax was the Canadian city most affected. Vast numbers of people were coming and going almost daily. There would have been homeless people. It is unclear if deaths on the ships were included in the count. There are many ways in which people who died would have been missed by those identifying and documenting the dead.

In the testimony of survivors from the *Stella Maris*, which had twenty-four men aboard, there are even wide variations in the number each person thought was aboard. On ships with more in their crews, the situation would have been worse and many would have been missed in the chaos of the aftermath and never reported. Another example of the uncertain count has to do with HMS *Highflyer*. John Griffith Armstrong writes in *The Halifax Explosion and the Royal Canadian Navy* about the complications of wartime censoring versus the public's right to know the truth about all these civilian deaths: "Journalists knew that some forty British seamen from *Highflyer* had died in the explosion."[105] However, the records in the NSA list only nine names from *Highflyer*. The captain's papers report the same number.

SHIP OR COMPANY	RIG	DEATHS
Calonne	Freighter	15
Curaca	Freighter	49
Glasgow	Freighter	1
Gloucestershire	Armed Merchant Cruiser	1
Hovland	Freighter	5
Imo	Freighter	6
Middleham Castle	Freighter	1
Mont Blanc	Freighter	1
Picton	Freighter	23
J. A. McKee	Coal Ship	1
USS *Old Colony*	Passenger Liner	1
Halifax Water Boat Co.	Water Tanker	1
HMS *Highflyer*	Warship	9
HMCS *Musquash*	Tug	5
HMCS *Niobe*	Warship	15
Niobe's pinnace	Steam Launch	7
HMCS *Stadacona*	Warship	1
Olearylea	Commercial	1
St. Bernard	Tern Schooner	3
Sawyer Bros.	Tern Schooner	1
Douglas H. Thomas	Tug	2
F. W. Roebling	Tug	1
Hilford	Tug	3
Ragus	Tug	5
Stella Maris	Tug	19
Wasp B	Tug	1
Naval Dept.	NA	5
Burns & Kelleher	Workboat	1
		184

The *Curaca* was only five years old and had been built by one of the world's leading builders. Joseph L. Thompson & Sons of Sunderland had integrated the latest technology such as a quadruple-expansion steam engine, the same type that powered the *Titanic*. As the name implies, it had a four-cylinder engine that used the steam four times, thereby increasing efficiency and burning less fuel. At 6,386 GRT, it was a respectable size for a merchant ship and had been built in 1912 for the New York and Pacific Steamship Company of London, a subsidiary line of W. R. Grace and Co. of New York. The *Curaca* was one of the first ships to go through the brand-new Panama Canal in 1914.

The company had been founded by William Russell Grace, who, as mayor of New York in 1885, accepted the Statue of Liberty from France on behalf of the US. By July 1918, they had eight ships in war service and had had another four sunk or captured.[106]

In the middle of April 1918, Rear Admiral Chambers, in his monthly report to the Admiralty about the state of affairs in the Port of Halifax, included this comment: "The 'CURACA,' one of the vessels sunk in the explosion, has just been raised. She is a terrible wreck, having sustained the full force of the explosion. It is difficult at present to see how she can again be made serviceable; every deck having been beaten in and every excrescence wrenched from its place." It took some doing to get the beleaguered ship ready to move, but on July 25, 1918, the *Curaca* left for New York, under tow. It was repaired and put back to work. In 1931, it was sold to Argonaut Steamship Line of Panama. In 1934, it was scrapped.

CHAPTER 9
SHIPS OF HALIFAX

Throughout history, peoples with easy access to bodies of water have had an advantage. They could put boats on the water and go places. The Mediterranean was a huge highway. Greece was a civilization of islands. The Nile irrigated Egypt, but it also made Egyptians mobile. Ships have been notable drivers of change, and by the time of the First World War, they had a lot of specialized uses, from carrying to killing.

SHIPS THAT DELIVERED THINGS

The *Imo* and *Mont Blanc* were commercial freight carriers. Their hulls were constructed from iron plates held together by rivets. Welding was in its infancy, and this was the accepted method of construction for ships, bridges, and other metal things requiring strength. Triple- or quadruple-expansion steam engines pushed them along, fuelled by coal. Some newer steamships were beginning to be fuelled with oil, but coal would be used for decades.

Most of what went on in Halifax Harbour in 1917 was associated with those precious freighters. They were life itself, enabling the Allies to keep fighting the war, transporting everything—from ammunition to vehicles to food—from North America to Europe. Ninety-one percent of the tonnage of British ships was reserved for war munitions, grain, and other government-controlled cargoes; 7 percent was reserved for cotton, canned goods, and other essential shipments. The remaining 2 percent was not restricted as to cargoes or rates.[107]

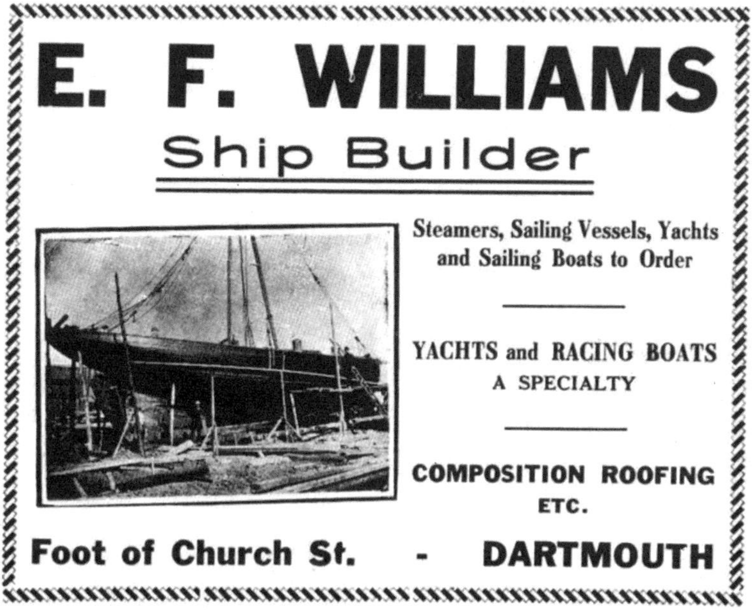

Edward F. Williams was the mayor of Dartmouth and a prominent shipbuilder.
(MCALPINE'S HALIFAX CITY DIRECTORY 1917)

Another type of cargo carrier contributed prominently to the war effort, using the time-honoured method of sail. The tern schooners were larger three-masted versions of the familiar schooner well known to Atlantic Canadians and New Englanders. Steamships had eclipsed sailing vessels over the past half century, but the U-boats had sunk so many steamers that sail experienced a major, albeit brief, renaissance. Even four- and five-masted schooners made a comeback. On December 6, like most days, there were tern schooners in the harbour. The *St. Bernard* was at Pier 6, *Herbert May* was tied at the Furness Withy Pier, and *J. Frank Seavey* was at the Plant Line Wharf. Another three dozen or so classic two-masted schooners were scattered along the waterfront.

In places like Essex in Massachusetts; Bath and Boothbay in Maine; and Shelburne, Liverpool, Lunenburg, and Parrsboro in Nova Scotia, tall graceful masts were reappearing. Liverpool builders McKean and Rawding were so confident that they built a tern on spec, launching it May 1, 1918, and advertising that it was "for sale to the first buyer."[108] Terns were even built in Halifax Harbour. On August 13, 1917, the 295-ton *Phileen*, newly launched from the shipyard of Edward F. Williams, the mayor of Dartmouth, departed Halifax en route to its new owners in St. John's. The registry closed on July 23, 1919, after the vessel was abandoned and lost on the Atlantic Ocean on May 15, 1919.

> **"About every trip of the steamer *LaHave* she takes a [load] of Oregon pine spars for shipyards in Lunenburg County. On her last trip she took several big sticks for a four-masted schooner and a three-master building at Chester Basin and on the previous trip she had a ton for Lunenburg. When she leaves today another lot will be taken for vessels building on the LaHave [River]."[109]**
> —*Halifax Herald*, January, 17, 1918.

The France and Canada Steamship Company saw wooden vessels as a logical alternative to the shortage of steel ships. In a twelve-month period up to December 1917, they amassed a fleet of fourteen four-, five-, and six-masted American wooden schooners, including the *Camilla May Page*, a four-master that had been at Halifax in the fall of 1917, and the seven-masted *Wyoming*, a 5,950-ton monster that was the largest schooner afloat, probably the biggest ever built.[110]

At 1,427 GRT, the most substantial sailing ship at Halifax on December 6, 1917, was the three-masted, forty-seven-year-old iron barque *Benmore*. Built on the Clyde in 1870 by John Reid and Co. of Port Glasgow, Scotland, it became the property of James Augustus Farquhar, a noted salvager, hard-hat diver, sealing master, and shipowner who is memorialized with a life-size statue in the Maritime Museum of the Atlantic.

Before the war, the *Benmore* had been used to transport supplies to Hudson Bay, under the ownership of the federal government. Then, it spent some time in Sydney while the government tried in vain to sell it. They engaged the *F. W. Roebling* to tow it to Halifax for an overhaul at the shipyard, after which it sat another year, waiting for a buyer. Farquhar, not one to miss an opportunity, purchased it and immediately sold it to the Americans, realizing a $10,000 profit.[111] At the end of January, 1918, it finally left Halifax for Liverpool, NS, where the new owners had additional work done. The *Benmore* was back in Halifax at the end of May, ready to depart for New York.

Schooners were easy pickings for U-boat captains, although they rarely wasted a torpedo on one. They usually dumped the crew into a boat, sent them on their way, pillaged the schooner of anything useful, and burned it or blew it up. On August 2, 1918, less than a month after it was registered and three months before the war's end, the 766-ton four-masted *Dornfontein*, built by Marine Construction of Saint John, NB, was burned off Brier Island in the Bay of Fundy—Canadian sovereign waters![112] The inquiry held on September 14 found Capt. Charles E. Dagnell to be "gravely negligent" in not destroying the ship's papers. He lost his master's certificate until the end of the war.

The *Dornfontein* was the first of twenty-four vessels, mostly fishing schooners, that U-156 sank or captured between Brier Island and the south coast of Newfoundland in the period August 2–26, 1918.[113] On August 21, a flotilla of four RCN vessels caught the sub on the surface. *Hochelaga* was well out in front. Rather than press the attack alone, the commanding officer, Lieutenant Robert D. Legate, decided to reunite with the flotilla, and U-156 escaped. Having the RCN's only opportunity for an engagement with the enemy end so feebly was too much for the leaders of the navy, who had achieved so little. *Hochelaga* was a converted yacht, smaller than U-156 and greatly outgunned. Engaging a sub that was capable of sinking a battleship would have been a glorious suicide for Legate and his crew. Regardless, he had to go. He was court martialled and dismissed from the RCN for failing to confront the enemy.[114]

SHIPS THAT CARRIED AND DELIVERED PEOPLE

The major transatlantic shipping lines such as Cunard and Allan tied up at the Deep Water Terminus, which opened in 1880 between the dockyard and the old waterfront off downtown Halifax, just north of where the casino is today. Ships had been increasing in size very quickly, needing deeper water

The destruction of this stone railway station attests to the force of the Halifax Explosion. (NS ARCHIVES)

and longer docking spaces. In addition, the arrival of the railways meant ships and trains needed to connect easily, so goods and people could get off a ship and onto a train for further travel to other parts of Canada. Otherwise, they would have to walk or take a carriage to the train station, and goods would have to be moved with horse and wagon.

When the railways were built, the tracks hugged the shore around the Bedford Basin into The Narrows, continuing all the way to the Deep Water Terminus. There, a grain elevator arose in 1882, and a splendid stone passenger station opened in 1878, below where the Macdonald Bridge comes ashore. The station became a victim of the Halifax Explosion.

In 1917, ships and trains met at the Deep Water Terminus and the Canadian Government Railways' Richmond Terminal, where the explosion occurred. The loss of that terminal pushed the timetable forward for using the new Ocean Terminals facilities that were under construction at the harbour entrance.

The main transporters of people were the troopships, the grandest and fastest craft on the ocean, the glamorous liners that took rich North Americans to Europe and returned to the US and Canada bursting with immigrants. Now, they were leaving Halifax laden with thousands of soldiers at a time to fuel the war's killing system—ships like Cunard's *Mauretania* and White Star Line's *Olympic*. Able to accommodate close to six thousand troops at a time—with nine hundred hammocks in what had been the first-class dining salon—the *Olympic* made ten round trips from Halifax to Liverpool between March and December 1916. It took two days just to get everybody aboard. On the return voyages it carried wounded soldiers and civilians back to Canada.[115] The crossing took a shade over five days; less time than it took to refuel. Many of these liners travelled without a naval escort as they were able to outrun just about anything afloat, including the assigned escort. The RN therefore decided such ships would be safer without an escort, which would only slow them down.

The less glamorous job of moving sailors around the harbour went to the smallest of RCN vessels, the duty boats that came in all shapes and sizes scurrying around with personnel, supplies, documents, and messages. For the general public, the Dartmouth Ferry Commission provided daily service between the Dartmouth and Halifax downtowns. There was another service called the North Ferry, run with smaller boats that crossed The Narrows where the two ships would collide.

In addition to the navy's duty boats, the army, which at that time was called the militia, had small vessels to support those crewing the forts and batteries that protected the outer parts of the harbour. The militia numbered around two thousand personnel manning guns and searchlights, providing engineering and telecommunication services, and guarding military facilities. To carry people and supplies to the islands and other difficult-to-access locations, there were five boats commanded by Lieutenant Donald Angus of the Canadian Army Service Corps. Typical of these was the steamboat *Alfreda*, 122578, built in 1907 at Tusket Wedge, NS, 44 feet long and 15 GRT. The others were *Beryl*, *Armstrong*, *Lighter*, and *Liberty*.[116]

In the harbour on December 6, there were also small coastal steamers, like the SS *Scotia*, built at Mahone Bay in 1907 and belonging to the Halifax

& Canso Steamship Co. Founded in 1902 by Halifax shipowners George S. Campbell Co. and William Stairs, Son and Morrow, it carried freight and passengers along the Eastern Shore between Halifax and the Strait of Canso. The wooden *Scotia*, 139 feet long and 268 NRT, survived the Halifax Explosion but burned at Drumhead, NS, on August 26, 1921, becoming a total loss. On the day of the Explosion, it was tied at the G. S. Campbell and Co. dock on the old waterfront. I dove on the wreck's remains in Drumhead on July 28, 2001.

SHIPS THAT PUSHED, PULLED, AND TOWED

The world wars were golden times for Halifax tugboat operators. As soon as steam power was invented and put to work pumping water out of mines, visionary men knew it had a future in watercraft. In March 1802, the Scotsman William Symington fitted the *Charlotte Dundas* with a 10-horsepower steam engine and a stern paddlewheel. It pulled two barges 20 miles along a canal. The benefit was obvious to Symington, but the canal's owners still banned his vessel from the canal for fear it would erode the banks of their waterway.

Steam-operated vessels were soon carrying passengers, towing barges and sailing ships in harbours, pulling them in to the dock, and helping them get underway. More than a century later, there were close to two dozen steam tugs busily engaged at Halifax with names like *Nereid*, *F. W. Roebling*, *Sambro*, *Boonton*, *Gladiator*, *Merrimac*, *Gopher*, *Douglas H. Thomas*, *Togo*, *Hilford*, *Maggie M.*, *Ragus*, *W. M. Weatherspoon*, *Stella Maris*, *Wasp B.*, *Delbert D.*, *Lily*, and the fifty-four-year-old *Goliah*, built of wood at Philadelphia in 1863. It would keep going until 1921. Unfortunately, its owner, William McFatridge, died in the explosion.

The record for longevity for a wooden tug involved in the explosion has to belong to the *Gladiator*, which lasted seventy-four years.

SHIPS THAT FACED THE ENEMY

The long history of warfare at sea began with men on ships trying to overpower one another, usually by ramming their ship into a vulnerable part of the enemy craft in the hope of sinking it. If that failed, they followed up by jumping aboard and stabbing or bludgeoning the opposing sailors to death. Gunpowder changed all that by enabling the ships to square off side by side and blast cannonballs at one another until one of them sank or surrendered.

The First World War, which in so many ways was a turning point in how wars were fought, changed naval history yet again. The goal was the same, but the tools were heftier, more sophisticated, and far more expensive. Destroyers, frigates, cruisers, and battleships were armoured with iron and steel, and they travelled much faster. Their huge guns could sink ships that were so far away they could barely be seen. The lowly torpedo boat could get lucky and sink a battleship, while submarines could lurk underwater, appear out of nowhere, destroy a vessel, and vanish.

By 1917, the Halifax defences were gearing toward detecting and neutralizing, or at least fending off, the U-boats. They succeeded in neutralizing none, essentially because there were not a lot to find. The RCN was responsible for patrolling the coast as well as protecting Halifax, but RN warships of all sizes operating in the western Atlantic came and went throughout the war. When the war started, the Canadian government, after dilly-dallying for years, scrambled to acquire vessels that could patrol the coastline and let the enemy know there was at least somebody out there looking for them. What would happen after an enemy was found was anybody's guess.

The only significant warship in the harbour on the day of the explosion was HMS *Highflyer*, a light cruiser, smaller than *Niobe*, anchored in the stream not far from the Naval Dockyard. On July 10, 1917, *Highflyer* provided the escort cover for convoy HS 1, the first significant convoy of commercial freighters, originating in Sydney, to sail from Canada to Britain.

Highflyer had a distinguished career, beginning at the start of 1900. Its high point was an engagement with the armed merchant cruiser *Kaiser Wilhelm der Grosse* off the coast of Africa. This had been a state-of-the-art liner, a bigger and faster vessel but not as heavily armed as *Highflyer*, which, after a two-hour battle, sent it to the bottom. Like all ships, naval ships like *Highflyer* carried small vessels for use in harbours. They had names like launch, cutter, barge, gig, whaler, and pinnace. Two types got destroyed in the explosion. The first was what might, on an ocean liner, be called a lifeboat. In the navy, they called them whalers. These were robust wooden rowboats powered by multiple sets of oars; the boats were often pointed at both ends for beaching bow- or stern-on. The other was a steam pinnace, what might in another context be called a cabin cruiser powered by steam.

In addition to using purpose-built warships to protect convoys, the RN had many armed merchant cruisers such as *Changuinola* and *Calgarian.*

Submarines established themselves as a major threat early in the war, when on September 5, 1914, U-21 fired a torpedo at HMS *Pathfinder* from a distance of 2,000 yards. It was the first ship to be destroyed by a self-propelled torpedo launched from a submarine. Detecting and avoiding submarines soon became a preoccupation for ships on the North Atlantic.

By 1917, ships travelled on a zigzag pattern to make it difficult for a sub to get in position to fire a torpedo and some, like *Changuinola*, deployed paravanes as a means of defence against submerged mines the subs might have deployed in the harbour's approaches. Paravanes looked like little rockets with short stubby wings. They ran just below the surface, held in position by a cable that ran at an angle off the sides from a ship's bow. As the ship moved forward, the cable attaching the paravane cut the moorings of any mine encountered, causing it to bob to the surface where those aboard the ship could safely destroy it, often simply with rifle fire.

Minesweeping was a major job of RCN vessels in keeping the sea lanes into ports like Halifax and Sydney safe to navigate. The cheapest and least risky way to sink an enemy ship is with a mine. A scant year before the Explosion, a mine sank the *Titanic*'s other sister ship, HMHS *Britannic* in the Aegean Sea. Mines were an ongoing ordeal because at any time, an enemy vessel could sneak in and anchor a cluster in the path of incoming and outgoing sea traffic. What was open and safe when the sun went down could be deadly when it rose again.

Two classes of wooden naval vessels were common in Halifax in the latter part of the war. Trawlers and drifters were developed from fishing boats used in the North Sea. Trawlers presented a classic fishing boat profile, high in bow and stern; they were tough, inexpensive, and seaworthy little craft that were indispensable in both world wars.

Expecting cruisers or destroyers when the word arrived of new ships finally coming their way in 1917 and 1918, the RCN ended up instead with the humble trawler and the even lowlier drifter. The trawlers' main job was minesweeping, but with their 12-pounder guns, they were also intended as an entry-level opponent for a surfaced submarine. In 1917, minesweepers were operating out of the Northwest Arm, where they could come and go when the submarine nets were closed. Their mobility was essential. So many vulnerable merchant ships were arriving and departing with crucial cargoes, the approaches to Halifax Harbour made for prime ground in which submarines might lay mines. Minesweepers worked in parallel pairs, towing between them an underwater sweep of serrated wire with cutters inserted at intervals designed to catch and cut the mooring line of a mine so that it came to the surface, where it could be destroyed.

The RCN acquired three batches of trawlers. All three classes of trawlers would have a QF-12 gun mounted forward, and those on patrol would carry depth charges to combat submarines. The first lot of seven working fishing trawlers was purchased in the US. With top speeds of 8 knots, they were put to work as minesweepers stationed out of Sydney and went into service in March 1917. They were named PV-I through PV-VII, the PV standing for "patrol vessel."

Coincident with that acquisition, the Canadian government engaged two companies, Polson Iron Works of Toronto and Canadian Vickers of Montréal, to each construct six vessels of a British design with the unlikely name of Battle class trawler. At 320 tons and with a top speed of 10 knots, the Polson boats included *Festubert*, which was in Halifax when the explosion took place. These were commissioned on November 13, 1917, just three weeks before the

TR class trawlers and drifters being fitted out at Vickers Montréal, November 6, 1917. (HALIFAX NAVAL MUSEUM)

Halifax Explosion. The others were plagued with construction delays caused by shortages of both materials and manpower.

For the final group, the Admiralty ordered sixty Castle class trawlers from Canadian shipyards. Called the TR series, these boats were lent to the RCN for patrolling Canada's east coast. Others were transferred to the US Navy. Some did not get put to use at all because the war was coming to an end by the time they arrived. Almost all were returned to the RN when the fighting ceased.

The smallest naval vessels, which comprised the bulk of the navy's "ships," were drifters, basically smaller trawlers. These small wooden craft were used for drift net fishing. As their name suggests, they used nets that were not anchored but drifted, catching fish, usually herring, as they went. When the German Navy started using submarines, the RN countered by using drifters dragging nets as an anti-submarine defence in approaches to harbours and ports. In January 1917, the RN ordered a hundred drifters from Canadian builders.

These vessels had wooden hulls 84 feet long with a beam of 19 feet. Their triple-expansion steam engines provided a maximum speed of 9 knots. Drifters were armed with one 6-pounder gun mounted forward and had a standard ship's company of twenty-three. Of the one hundred built, forty-two were transferred to the RCN and eighteen to the USN. They ended up doing a variety of jobs.

As they were delivered to Halifax, they went into the most westerly part of the Bedford Basin or into Dartmouth Cove, supplanting the normal occupants of the cove. That was where schooners and other vessels were stored for the winter. They had to go. Harbourmaster Francis Rudolf designated the Northwest Arm as the new storage location because Dartmouth Cove was needed for Admiralty craft and other naval assets. In the Arm, "a capable man" was designated to keep an eye on the vessels at $10 per ship.[117] On April 27, 1918, the last schooner to leave after the winter was the *Irene MB*, which was towed around from the Arm to Whitman's Wharf on the waterfront.[118]

Twenty-two trawlers and twenty-nine drifters were commissioned at Québec and sent on to the East Coast Patrol at Sydney and Halifax before the St. Lawrence River froze up for the winter of 1917, forcing the others to have to wait until spring for delivery.[119] After the war, many were sold to eager marine operators and fishers who, no doubt, got a good deal on an essentially new boat.

SHIPS THAT HARVESTED THE SEA

Besides merchant ships, navy ships, and tugs, there was another type of vessel in the harbour on that fateful day, boats whose crews made their living harvesting the sea. In those days, there were a lot of private docks on the old waterfront, most of which had schooners tied up. Halifax was not only a naval base and an important international port but also home to many fishing schooners and fish processors. On the day of the explosion, there were schooners tied up at the Commercial Wharf, Old Pier 2, and the wharves of merchants and agents such as Daniel Cronan, James Farquhar, T. A. S. DeWolf, A. M. Smith, Furness Withy, the Plant Line, Black and Flinn, S. M. Brookfield, Silver's, Mitchell's, Robin's, Whitman's, and many more.

Not all the schooners were in the city to sell their fish. Many were from tiny communities that did not rate a visit from a coastal steamer and had no rail service. The only way to get to Halifax for supplies, medical treatment, family visits, or any other business was on a schooner belonging to the merchant or a relative. This was the time of year when fishermen were getting ready for winter, which entailed a trip or two to Halifax or another centre to purchase supplies for themselves or their community.

Some schooners, especially the larger ones, were not unloading fish but were loading them instead, preparing for a trip to the Caribbean, where salt cod was a staple that had fed enslaved people on sugar plantations and was now consumed by their descendants. Rum, molasses, salt, and cane sugar had been the common freights on the return voyage. A load of fresh fruit for the vitamin C–deprived Maritimes might seem like a likely shipment, but the trip took too long for such perishable cargo. That market was cornered by Halifax firm Pickford & Black and other steamship operators. The war and the U-boats had significantly increased the risk of going to the historically important markets of Spain and Portugal, with their Catholic populations relying on fish for fast days. That pursuit had been reduced by 1917.

Even in peacetime, those trips across the Atlantic in winter were risky. My great uncle was in the crew of a large schooner heading to Spain with a load of salt cod when a hurricane engulfed them. Their ship got so severely stressed that it became unsafe to go on deck because the deck planks were opening and closing as the schooner pounded into the waves, presenting the risk of crushing a foot or even a leg. They were eventually picked up by a steamship heading to an African port, where they were discharged. It took six months to get back home. My sister-in-law's grandfather was lost on the 283-ton schooner *Inspiration* on January 20, 1922, while on a trip from St. John's to Lisbon, Portugal. He was swept overboard and never found. The ship had been built in 1917 at Conquerall Bank, NS. Many Atlantic Canadians have such events in their ancestries, but, sadly, most of the stories have been lost.

FISHING AND FREIGHTING SCHOONERS AND OTHER SAILING SHIPS THAT EXPERIENCED THE EXPLOSION INSIDE THE GATES

Most were tied at wharves or anchored off downtown Halifax. As far as we know, all except two survived.

OFFICIAL NUMBER	VESSEL NAME	PORT OF REGISTRY *(Nova Scotia, unless indicated otherwise)*	YEAR BUILT	PLACE OF CONSTRUCTION *(Nova Scotia, unless indicated otherwise)*	NET TONS	OWNER OR MANAGER *(Nova Scotia, unless indicated otherwise)*	LOCATION ON DEC. 6, 1917
130947	*Abacena*	Lunenburg	1912	Shelburne	88	Joseph Conrad, LaHave	Silver's Wharf
94632	*A. C. Greenwood*	Shelburne	1888	Shelburne	15	Ernest Mason, Tangier	Job's Wharf
138552	*Agnes D. McGlashen*	Lunenburg	1917	Mahone Bay	116	William Duff, Lunenburg	Silver's Wharf
100489	*Algoma*	Lunenburg	1892	Dublin Shore	56	Melford Bond, Chester	Silver's Wharf
103206	*Alice*	Liverpool	1896	Port Mouton	42	William Burke, Main-à-Dieu	Hendry's Wharf
77601	*Atlas*	Lunenburg	1878	LaHave	52	Simon Naas, Lunenburg	Silver's Wharf
63264	*Benmore*	Ottawa, ON	1870	Port Glasgow	1427	Minister of Railways and Canals of Canada	Anchored
112099	*Electro*	Lunenburg	1902	LaHave	88	Egerton Ritcey, Riverport	Robin's Wharf
88555	*G. C. Kelley*	Charlottetown, PEI	1885	Shelburne	99	Sampson Grady, Charlottetown, PEI	Lunatic Asylum Wharf
94944	*Gladys E. Whidden*	Liverpool	1905	Shelburne	197	Charles Lorway, Sydney	Black & Flinn's Wharf
121851	*Gladys B. Smith*	Halifax	1905	LaHave	100	Alexander Gunn, Sherbrooke	Farquhar's Wharf

116507	*Golden Rod*	Lunenburg	1904	LaHave	76	James H. Beaver, Pleasant Harbour	Black & Flinn's Wharf
121863	*Hazel*	St. John's, NL	1906	LaHave	71	John H. Clement, Burgeo NL	Farquhar's Wharf
203581	*Herbert May*	Portland, ME	1906	Phippsburg, ME	318	New York Shipping Exchange	Furness Withy's Wharf
138551	*Irene M Corkum*	Lunenburg	1917	Lunenburg	100	Leo Corkum, LaHave	Old Pier 2
100490	*Irene M. B.*	Lunenburg	1892	Mahone Bay	66	John Colford, Port Richmond	Northwest Arm
126584	*J. B. Young*	Lunenburg	1909	Lunenburg	100	John B. Young, Lunenburg	Old Pier 2
76742	*J. Frank Seavey*	Portsmouth, NH	1888	Bath, ME	336	B. F. Nealley	Plant Line Wharf
126915	*Lola B.*	Halifax	1910	Spry Bay	10	Cornelius Boutilier	DeWolf's Wharf
111721	*Maple Leaf*	Bridgetown	1901	Chester Basin	199	William Arenburg, Lunenburg	Central Wharf
122309	*Max C.*	Lunenburg	1907	Petite Rivière	46	Harris Croft, West Dublin	Smith's Wharf
121996	*Mildred G. Myers*	Lunenburg	1906	Lunenburg	55	Freeman Myers, Cole Harbour	Commercial Wharf
88402	*Mizpah*	Digby	1884	Freeport	53	Joseph E. Gaskill, Grand Manaan, NB	Black & Flinn's Wharf
122186	*M. O'Toole*	Arichat	1908	Louisbourg	32	John C. McDonald, Gabarus	DeWolf's Wharf
85665	*Nellie D.*	Halifax	1881	Lunenburg	12	Andrew Mason, Pope's Harbour	Cronan's Wharf
103800	*Nellie J. King*	Shelburne	1900	Shelburne	99	William Murray, Port Richmond	Roche's Wharf
138344	*Olga B. Kenny*	Halifax	1916	Sheet Harbour	50	Samuel H. Kenny, Sheet Harbour	Robin's Wharf

126107	*Minnie M. Mosher*	Lunenburg	1908	Mahone Bay	73	William Duff, Lunenburg	Farquhar's Wharf
131897	*Nellie Moulton*	St. John's, NL	1915	Pushthrough, NL	77	R. Moulton, St. John's, NL	Smith's Wharf
112090	*Noble H.*	Lunenburg	1902	Mahone Bay	95	Samuel R. Griffin, Goldboro	Old Pier 2
112329	*Silver Leaf*	Parrsboro	1903	Spencer's Island	283	Stewart T. Salter, Parrsboro	Anchored in Stream
NA	*Silver Thread*						Whitman's Wharf
107570	*St. Bernard*	Parrsboro	1901	Parrsboro	123	Sold to Demerara	Pier 6

CHAPTER 10

THE AFTERMATH

At first, many people assumed that the inevitable had finally happened: the Germans were bombing or shelling the city. Nobody had any idea of the scope of the disaster. All each individual thought they knew was that a bomb had dropped on the house or school or workplace they occupied. There was no television or radio to provide an update, let alone an internet bulletin. Nobody knew anything.

THE FIRST MINUTES AND HOURS

The response from the ravaged city was immediate. While some of the injured were opening their eyes in stunned confusion, there was already a meeting of senior civilian and military authorities. Admiral Chambers described it this way:

> The conference was a remarkable experience—held in the shattered town hall amidst splintered woodwork and floors covered with broken glass. In many cases those present had been at work since the explosion without even an opportunity to ascertain whether their nearest and dearest were in safety. Some showed traces of quick surgical attendance in the shape of plaster and bandages. I was much struck with the sane and business-like way in which the situation was faced. The difficulties were enormous, all telephonic communications were down and the roads blocked, but I left the building with the impression that order was already beginning to arise out of the chaos, and that what could be done would be done.[120]

The message that had cost CGR telegrapher Vince Coleman his life quickly propagated the news outside the city. Residents had felt the explosion at Truro, more than 60 miles away, and when the telegraph arrived, they sounded the town's emergency alarm. Within an hour, medical personnel and supplies were on the way. The same was true in the other direction from Halifax. The Dominion Atlantic Railway's lines carried the shocking news to Kentville in the Annapolis Valley, and the response was similar. That started a two-way movement of help coming in from and the injured going out to other parts of the province, which lasted for months. Support—emotional, practical, and financial—came quickly, from as far away as Australia and New Zealand.

Even the owners of the *Stephano*, Bowring Brothers, through the New York Newfoundland and Halifax Steamship Company, made at least two donations to the Halifax Relief Fund, as did the Cunard Steamship Company, the Royal Mail Steam Packet Company, and other marine organizations.[121]

THE AMERICANS

Upon hearing of the disaster, Massachusetts governor Samuel Walker McCall convened a meeting of state officials to draft a response. By 10:00 P.M. on the day of the disaster, a train departed Boston with medical supplies, clothing, and food, along with medical personnel and representatives of the American Red Cross. It arrived at Rockingham station on the morning of December 9. Next came the SS *Calvin Austin*, which tied up at Pickford & Black's Wharf on the twelfth, bearing about $300,000 worth of supplies and a crew of workmen. In the meantime, a second steamer, the SS *Northland*, was dispatched on December 10, carrying a fleet of ten trucks, each with a supply of gasoline and a driver. It was the beginning of an outpouring of support from all parts of Canada and the US.[122]

The *Calvin Austin,* named after the managing director of the Eastern Steamship Company, ran on a regular schedule between Boston and Saint John, NB.

The *Boston Transcript* newspaper reported:

> In its hundreds of voyages the ship *Calvin Austin* has never gone down the coast with a more important cargo than it carried from this port on Sunday, making all steam for Halifax.... Another ship, this time with all expenses of the voyage paid by the steamship company, will sail tomorrow.... Not until word comes from Nova Scotia that relief can be discontinued should we even think of the end of our efforts. The end is at present far distant.... The story is only now coming in, how Halifax itself has been fighting manfully for its own sufferers. But the gift of New England must be in proportion to no other standard than that of New England sympathy and of the stunned city's need.[123]

Late each autumn in Nova Scotia, a tall red spruce, the official tree of Nova Scotia, is cut down, loaded on a transport trailer, and trucked to Boston. Upon arrival, it is erected on the Boston Common, and shortly thereafter, a lighting ceremony takes place, with representatives of the City of Halifax in attendance. The tree is a traditional expression of appreciation from the City of Halifax for the overwhelming response to the disaster by the state of Massachusetts.

NEWSPAPER COVERAGE

Remarkably, the day after the explosion, with the city engulfed in a blizzard, the morning newspapers were on the street offering details of the disaster. With all the windows blown out and their buildings severely damaged, the staffs of the *Halifax Morning Chronicle* and *Daily Acadian Recorder* worked, as usual, through the night of the sixth and the nights following. On the seventh, the *Daily Acadian Recorder* managed to print just two sheets, for a total of four pages providing vital information to the overwhelmed citizens of the city and area—public service announcements, lists of the dead, living and missing, and, crucially, where to go for help. On the eighth they noted their paper was unable to provide a complete list of the dead "owing to the condition of the RECORDER building," which was located on Granville Street.

To compound the misery, the December 7 papers included the regular updates on Maritime casualties at the front in Europe. That day's reports included fourteen dead, two of which were from Halifax; four missing; three seriously ill; and four wounded.[124] There was also bad news for those wounded at the front and being returned to Canada. The reception hospital and clearing depot at Pier 2 was unusable, requiring hospital ships to divert to other ports in Eastern Canada. The most recent arrival was the Royal Mail Steam Packet Company steamer *Araguaya*, which had arrived on November 28. An anonymous American soldier who was involved in recovering bodies wrote this woeful account:

> The next scene was a heart-rending one. There was a trainload of Canadian veterans who had just returned from France, all of whom were wounded, and there could be seen many an armless sleeve and many a legless trousers in that pile of human debris. This train was on a siding awaiting orders to proceed with its load of crippled heroes to take them to their homes and loved ones, whom they had not seen for over two years when the explosion occurred. I don't believe ten out of the whole lot of them escaped. Having at least escaped death in France, they had to return to the door-way of their own country to be killed. They were so badly mutilated that in some cases the only means of identifying them was by the shoulder plates on their tunics with the word "Canada" on it.[125]

RESURRECTION

The cause of the destruction, suffering, and death was over. The explosives had all been consumed, and the *Mont Blanc*, which officials feared might be

One of the first milk bottles used in Nova Scotia, recovered from the harbour. (AUTHOR'S COLLECTION)

blocking The Narrows and posing a risk to navigation, ceased to be an entity.[126] It existed only in a piece of anchor shaft 3 miles to the west, on the other side of the Northwest Arm; in a pond 3 miles in the other direction on the outskirts of Dartmouth; and in a six- or seven-foot-long piece of riveted steel plating on the bottom of The Narrows near the site where it exploded. It was no longer a peril of any kind, which meant that the unharmed ships of the waiting convoy could depart as soon as an escort could be assembled. The disaster that was Halifax Harbour could not be allowed to slow the progress of the war—if we can call such a thing progress.

By December 14, committees had been organized to take care of the myriad needs. At the top was the Relief Committee. Below that were the Managing, Food, Clothing, Reconstruction, Emergency Shelter, Fuel, Transportation, Registration, Information, Medical, Financial, and Mortuary Committees.[127]

Reporting to the Central Food Committee, Charles N. Butcher, manager of the Scotia Pure Milk Co., was made milk superintendent. When they set up in business in 1901, there were forty-eight milkmen in Halifax. Each was basically a family business with a helper or two, delivering on a route using a horse and wagon, ladling milk from a container into a jug left on the customer's steps. The Scotia Pure Milk Co. was immediately in a different league from the neighbourhood milkmen. Under the leadership of Charles Butcher, they introduced bottled milk and had ambitious plans that included downtown facilities and a telephone. They located at 255–257 Barrington Street on land that is immediately north of Scotia Square. The phone number was St. Paul 189. In 1916, they got a second phone line, St. Paul 1014. It had taken fifteen years to justify the second line.

Admiral Chambers told a meeting attended by the prime minister and key officials from the port and the railway that the harbour was not blocked by the wreck of the *Mont Blanc*. Equally important, the only ships seriously damaged were in the inner harbour or The Narrows—*Calonne*, *Middleham Castle*, *Picton*, *Hovland*, *Curaca*, *Imo*, and *Mont Blanc*—meaning that all ships in the Bedford Basin, including the crucial convoy ships, had escaped damage. Finally (from the admiral's perspective), came the best news of all: while a convoy had been delayed because of damage to *Highflyer*, the essential repairs were almost done. The Admiralty had considered using an escort brought from Bermuda or using HMS *Calgarian*, which had arrived on December 8. They decided to wait until *Highflyer* was ready.

On Sunday, December 9, the cruiser HMS *Donegal* of the North America and West Indies fleet arrived and dropped its anchors off Jetty 1.[128] An hour later, the USS *Tacoma* departed Halifax, after doing its share in the recovery. Things were already moving ahead with regard to the port. Committees had been formed and plans had been made for reconstruction of docks and buildings. Even though the convoy scheduled for the next day would be delayed in its departure, orders were sent out to all ports to send ships to Halifax, and they would have convoy support as usual.

With *Highflyer* put back into shape and ready to resume the role of escort, a convoy of thirty merchant ships was ready to depart. There were twenty

UK-registered vessels, in addition to three American, three Norwegian, two French, one Spanish, and one Danish. Eleven had arrived in Halifax from Montréal and nine from New York, with others coming from Saint John, Baltimore, and Norfolk. They were set to go on the tenth but were delayed because of weather, a common occurrence at that time of year.

Late on the day of the eleventh, the escort ships *Highflyer* and *Knight Templar* departed from the harbour covering the first convoy to sail since the explosion, bound for London, England. By December 27, they were approaching the English coast, signalling their arrival to the relief escort ships. After passing Cornwall, *Highflyer* left the convoy, leaving *Knight Templar* with the relief escort ships, and proceeded to its home base at Devonport near Plymouth, tying up at noon on the 28th. On December 29, after passing the historic Eddystone Light, *Knight Templar* dispatched seven ships to France and kept eleven for escort to London, with the remainder going to other ports. *Knight Templar* tied up at the dock in London at 4:00 P.M. on December 31.

SHIPS OF THE DECEMBER 11, 1917, CONVOY[129]

SHIP	ARRIVAL DATE AT HALIFAX	ARRIVED FROM
Highflyer	November 12	Plymouth
Knight Templar	November 26	England
Alexander Kjelland	December 1	Baltimore
Algorteno	December 6	Norfolk
Ardgryfe	December 4	Montréal
Asuncion de Larrinaga	December 3	Saint John
Bayramento	November 22	Montréal
Borderer	December 1	Montréal
Chicago	November 29	New York
Clan McDougall	December 1	NA
Clara	December 6	New York

Clematis	December 4	Montréal
Corfe Castle	December 5	Montréal
Florence H.	December 1	New York
Franklin	December 3	New York
Indien	December 3	New York
Kanawha	November 25	Saint John
King Edward	December 6	Montréal
Knut Hamsun	November 22	Montréal
Levisa	December 6	New York
Maindy Abbey	November 25	Montréal
Mississippi	December 5	New York
Patroclus	November 30	Norfolk
Polyphemus	December 5	New York
Saint Bede	December 5	Montréal
Singapore	December 6	NA
Swainby	December 6	Baltimore
Trojan	December 6	Baltimore
Wagland	December 5	New York
War Monarch	November 29	Montréal
War Queen	November 30	Montréal
Yonne	December 3	Montréal

The Holland America liner *Nieuw Amsterdam*, with a cargo for Belgian Relief, was supposed to go with them but at the last minute the British informed the Netherlands Overseas Trust that they would not take responsibility for the ship. It had not been provided with a safe conduct distinguishing mark like *Imo* had, and was also carrying passengers. Given that the Germans had recently seized another Belgian Relief ship, SS *Helen*, the *Nieuw Amsterdam* was left behind.

On December 11, six other empty freighters recently arrived from Europe departed from Halifax: the Belgian ships *Gouverneur de Lantsheere*, *Ubien*, and *President Bunge* for New York; *Leopold II* for Baltimore; the Norwegian

Perhaps a crewmember of the Knight Templar *once used this cup. It was recovered in the area the ship frequented.* (AUTHOR'S COLLECTION)

Sommerstad for Baltimore; and the French *Eole* for Baltimore.[130] That was a total of thirty-six ships for the fourteen pilots to take out in one day, in addition to five arrivals.

Knight Templar was a commissioned escort ship, launched at the Charles Connell & Co. yard in Scotstoun, an area of Glasgow, on October 10, 1905, for the Knight Steamship Co. It was commissioned into the RN in May 1917. By then, the ship was owned by the Ocean Steamship Co., also known as the Blue Funnel Line. Its first convoy of which we are aware was from Liverpool to New York City, a three-week trip ending on September 20, 1917. Ten days later, *Knight Templar* left Norfolk, Virginia, with a convoy to Glasgow. That ended on October 21 and on November 15, it took a convoy to Halifax, arriving November 27 and tying up at the Deep Water Terminus docks just south of the dockyard.

The engineers immediately went to work pumping out the ballast tanks in preparation for receiving cargo. On November 28, ammunition, lumber, and steel billets began to go aboard, loading of which continued the next day. On the thirtieth, a harbour pilot arrived to direct three tugs as they moved *Knight Templar* to the grain elevator dock and grain commenced to pour into the ship's holds throughout the night. Under the watchful eye of the chief officer, the loading and balancing of the ship continued as the holds were filled. The job was over by the end of day on December 5, as though they knew they had been working to be finished before the dreadful morning of December 6.

The ship was moved to make way for another vessel—and not a moment too soon. It remained at Deepwater, however, and was somewhat sheltered when the blast came, but it still managed to rip out the posts that attached it to the wharf.

Three days after the departure of the first convoy, Captain Wilcox called a meeting of the captains of the next convoy aboard HMS *Changuinola* for a final briefing prior to departure. The next day, December 15, *Changuinola* weighed anchor at 2:20 P.M. and escorted seven more ships out of the harbour, passing through the outer net at 2:37 P.M. for the last time. It was the end of *Changuinola*'s only trip to Halifax during the war. No doubt, all aboard were glad to be on their way and grateful they and their ship had not taken the beating some had.

It was a fast convoy, consisting mostly of passenger liners carrying military personnel. The seven ships were White Star Line's *Adriatic*, Cunard Line's *Ascania*, White Star-Dominion's *Northland*, Allan Line's *Pretorian* and *Tunisian*, Atlantic Transport Line's *Manchuria*, and the oil tanker *Boxleaf* of the Leaf Line. Assisting *Changuinola* with the escort was *Cherryleaf*, a Royal Fleet auxiliary vessel, ordered in 1915 as one of six designed to work as escorts on Atlantic convoys, while also carrying cargoes of oil from the US to Britain. (A loaded oil tanker seems like an odd choice for a convoy escort.) The *Cherryleaf* was built at the same yard as the *Mont Blanc*.

The *Ascania* wrecked east of Port Aux Basques, NL, on June 13, 1918. Shortly thereafter, the company that had salvaged the ships damaged or sunk in the Halifax Explosion tried to raise the *Ascania* but was unsuccessful. On my first dive in Newfoundland, I visited the wreck in August 1990.

Five days after the second convoy departed Halifax, while travelling inward through the harbour to the basin aboard the troop ship SS *Orduña*, Kenneth Porter Kirkwood wrote:

> We have been slowly steaming up the harbour, and allowing a ghastly panorama of destruction to slide past our gaze. Far out on the rocks near the sea we saw the first wreck, a beached ship half-submerged [*Saranac*, which was not involved in the explosion]. Then we passed one after another until the Belgian Relief ship presented itself, and further up a remnant of a large boat we took to be the munitions ship [probably the *Curaca*]. Ships were sunk in the docks and only masts appeared through the debris. Railway cars lay upturned and wrecked along the shore. One freight car had either floated or been hurled to the opposite shore. On land buildings lay in ruins. Whole hillsides are devastated and denuded, and the straight intersecting roads alone indicate the blocks of houses that used to be. The spectacle is pitiful. There is very little snow here now but a damp mist hangs over the hills. The relief parties are still at work in the ruins looking for victims or helping refugees.
>
> We lay in Halifax, without being permitted to go ashore, for a couple of days, and then steamed silently out into the Atlantic. [131]

The *Orduña* had left New York on December 15, arriving in Halifax on the twentieth and departing for England on December 21. The previous May, the ship had carried the first members of the American Expeditionary Force, Base Hospital #4 group, to Liverpool, arriving May 18, 1917.[132] Cunard operated the ship on charter from the Pacific Steam Navigation Co.

On December 21, the third convoy following the explosion sailed with seven fast ships escorted by HMS *Calgarian*. Halifax was firmly back in the convoy business. And, there was good news for Belgian Relief. The German government had given safe conduct for *Nieuw Amsterdam* and it was already on its way to Rotterdam carrying ten thousand tons of grain, with the agreement of the War Trade Board, newly set up to control exports and imports, ration supplies to neutral countries, and conserve commodities and shipping facilities for the use of the United States and its allies.[133]

The Royal Mail Ship *Calgarian* was built for the Allan Line, founded by the Allans of Montréal as the Montréal Ocean Steamship Company. At 17,500 tons it could carry 1,700 passengers and 500 crew at more than 20 knots. At the time of launching, *Calgarian* was the newest and fastest vessel yet built for the Allan Line's principal routes from Liverpool to Québec and Montréal in summer, and Halifax and Saint John in winter. It went into service on May 8, 1914, five years after Canadian Pacific had quietly purchased the Allan Line.

However, Canadians travelling to and from the British Isles would have to make a sacrifice for the war effort and get by with older, slower vessels that *Calgarian* was built to replace. Just four months later, on September 15, 1914, the RN commandeered this fine new ship for conversion to an armed merchant cruiser. It would make many trips to Halifax but with its fancy interior stripped and carrying eight 6-inch guns, this state-of-the-art liner had made its last voyage as a passenger ship.

On its final trip, *Calgarian* left Halifax on February 15, 1918, with cargo and over six hundred aboard, including a party of Newfoundland Royal Naval Reserve sailors, but it would not reach its destination. Fourteen days later, off the coast of Ireland, three torpedoes vanquished the liner, with a loss of forty-eight lives.[134]

Operating in Halifax Harbour at the time of the explosion was the tug *Sir Hugh Allan*, named after the kingpin of the Allan Line. Along with Sir John A. Macdonald, he had been a key participant in the Pacific Scandal, one of Canada's notorious tales of political corruption.

Even though the city was in tatters and its citizens destitute and fearing for the future, the Port of Halifax was fulfilling its mission to the Allies. Ships were now moving in and out of the harbour without difficulty. Convoys were coming together. Neutral ships were being inspected.

REBUILDING

In the middle of the suffering and destruction, a recreational activity synonymous with Halifax and Dartmouth was down but not out. The Lorne Amateur Aquatic Club, wedged in between the sugar refinery wharf and Pier 6, was now gone. The long-time custodian and his wife were dead, and about thirty motorboats and a large number of racing sculls were destroyed.[135] The club's sport was competitive rowing, to this day a very popular activity on the lakes of the area and the Northwest Arm of the harbour. On January 24, 1918, the club's acting secretary, George W. Rhind, notified members of an upcoming meeting at the hall of the Union Protection Company, a firefighting firm, on February 6. They would eventually get new premises in 1922 at the foot of Russell Street, south of the graving dock. Their neighbours were the North Ferry, which had also been wiped out in the Explosion.

In addition to the human recoveries that would take lifetimes, there were two categories of infrastructure that had to be rebuilt. One was the city and the other was the harbour.

On January 19, 1918, the federal government began the work of rebuilding the city, when an order-in-council was passed appointing a three-man commission to be called the Halifax Relief Commission. It consisted of T. Sherman Rogers, KC, Halifax, as chairman; W. B. Wallace, judge of the County Court, Halifax; and F. L. Fowke, merchant of Oshawa, Ontario. Ralph P. Bell was the secretary. A subsequent act passed by the Nova Scotia Legislature on April 26, 1918, incorporated the Halifax Relief Commission and broadened its duties and powers.

The job would take many years to complete. One lasting monument to their efforts is Canada's first public housing project, the Hydrostone District, a neighbourhood of adjoining houses built of concrete blocks called hydrostone that was built near the explosion site. A Nova Scotia beach outside Eastern Passage was sacrificed to provide the sand for the blocks, which were moved to the harbour on a purpose-built railway. Cranes loaded the blocks onto barges for the trip up The Narrows. They then had to be carried up a steep hill to the

Obliterated in the explosion, the Lorne AA Club premises were built by the Royal Halifax Yacht Club, completed in 1870. By 1876, they were in financial difficulties, and the place was soon boarded up until the Lorne Club took it over in 1885. (NS ARCHIVES)

site. That called for the construction of a street, now called Devonshire Avenue that ran at an angle to lessen the grade for the horses and trucks tasked with getting the heavy stones to the top.

The commission administered a $30 million fund providing medical care, social welfare, compensation, and reconstruction for many thousands of people. By 1948, with that work completed, the commission became a pension board for the survivors. In 1976, with $1.5 million remaining and sixty-five disabled dependants, the Halifax Relief Commission's job was done, and its responsibilities were handed over to the Canada Pension Plan.

Overseeing the harbour cleanup was the Reid Wrecking and Towing Company, led by Tom Reid of Sarnia, ON, who was well known on the Great Lakes. Acting on instructions from the minister of marine in Ottawa, he left immediately for Halifax. It was winter and there was ice to contend with, so little could be done right away. In anticipation of the work ahead, he formed a company specifically for this job—the Maritime Wrecking Company. When navigation opened on the St. Lawrence River and the seaway, he brought the tug *Sarnia City* down, along with the barge *Maggie Marshall*, which was equipped for dredging.[136] John Randall had built the *Maggie Marshall* 141454, at Manistee, MI, in 1873. It was 150 feet long and rated at 570 GRT. On May 19, 1923, it wrecked off Cape Hogan, near Isle Madame, NS, at the northeast entrance to the Strait of Canso.

Other equipment was brought in, such as pumps, jacks, and pontoons used to raise sunken and disabled ships, and Reid was soon ready to go to work on the *Curaca*. It was resting forlornly on the bottom at the mouth of Tufts Cove, with the stern submerged in deep water and the bow visible in shallower water.

The project took about three weeks. Reid, working with diver Dave Beaudry of Sarnia and salvager J. P. Porter of Halifax, patched the worst holes in the hull and unloaded enough of the cargo of wheat, flour, lumber, and blank shells so they could start pumping, using the most powerful pumps available, up to 18 inches in diameter. With a pump in each hold and another in the engine room, they got the wreck sufficiently buoyant to tow down through The Narrows. It took five tugs to do that job. On April 19, 1918, they got the *Curaca* tied up at Deepwater Pier 4, where more patching was done until they could manage without the pumps. After more repairs, they transferred to Pier 2 and unloaded the rest of the cargo. Word soon got out and thousands of people started turning up to see the battered wreck.

Besides the bashing that ripped off all the deck buildings, masts, and funnel, the hull was broken and the whole vessel was bent amidships, such that there was a steep incline extending from forward to amidships with a matching incline running aft to amidships. The stern, which had been facing the *Mont Blanc*, was severely smashed in. Despite all that damage, it was considered worthwhile to spend the money to get the *Curaca* back in shape. Over the next three days, seventeen railway carloads of grain were removed and shipped to Québec. Two weeks of work still remained before all 130,000 bushels of grain were out and the *Curaca*'s remains could be prepped for towing to a shipyard. At that point the owners had spent $75,000.[137]

Bodies were still aboard, and they recovered four more. It was, of course, rumoured that some had been found in the grain that went to Québec. Some

The weak and wobbly Curaca, *barely afloat, is surrounded by support vessels as salvagers rush to stabilize the newly risen ship.* (MARITIME MUSEUM OF THE ATLANTIC [MP207.1.184.10])

of Captain Peck's crew members were missing in the weeks following the explosion; when their bodies were finally located, the remains were in such poor condition that they were beyond identification.

By mid-July, the *Curaca* had been patched up and reinforced to the point that it could withstand a long ocean tow. It departed from Old Pier 2 for New York on July 25 to be rebuilt.[138] It went back to work and survived until 1934, when it was broken up at Osaka.

The *Imo*, which had remained aground on the Dartmouth shore near the collision site since it had landed there on December 6, was refloated on April 23 and taken to Brookfield's Wharf. It was later moved to Silver's Wharf. Dubbed the "Death Ship," it also attracted great crowds and was probably the most photographed vessel of the Halifax Explosion.

About that time, one of G. S. Campbell's Halifax Towboat Company's tugs went back to work, having spent the winter being repaired at the Dartmouth yard of George Young. The *F. W. Roebling* had been badly damaged in the explosion and had lost its chief engineer. Just recovered from his injuries, Capt. Charles Mood was the only member of the original crew to be engaged on the vessel when it returned to the harbour on April 30.

By May 7, what had been the Acadia Sugar Refining Company's brand-new tug *Ragus* had been refloated and was back shuttling between the Dartmouth refinery and central wharf under the command of Capt. Crowell Newell of Clarks Harbour. It was soon discovered that Captain Newell's ambitions were not limited to commanding a small tug, however. By the end of July, he was working for the Royal Mail Steam Packet Company, one of the world's great shipping lines, and William Matthews had taken over the *Ragus*.[139]

FROM SHIP REPAIRER TO SHIPBUILDER: THE HALIFAX GRAVING DOCK COMPANY

The graving dock was a key piece of infrastructure in Halifax Harbour. Ships, like automobiles, need ongoing maintenance and repairs. At that time in Halifax, a ship in need of repair went through a triage process. The least complicated and most common option was to do fixes while the vessel was at anchor or tied to the dock. If that was not practical, then the ship would have to come out of the water. Smaller vessels up to 2,500 tons could come out at the Dartmouth Marine Railway. It had opened in 1859 as the Chebucto Marine Railway and had expanded several times by 1917.

There are marine railways in yards throughout Nova Scotia. They are the customary way to get small to medium-sized vessels onto dry land. As the name implies, the ship is pulled out on a track. To begin, a cradle wide enough to hold the ship is rolled down a pair of inclined railway tracks into the water until it is submerged. The vessel is floated into the cradle and secured. The cradle, attached to a cable on a winch, is then pulled out of the water, with the ship inside, similar to a pleasure boat coming out on a trailer.

The Dartmouth marine slips shut down in 2003, and the land was sold for condominiums. By then, the facility could handle a vessel up to 3,000 tons.

In the 1980s and '90s my friends and I did a few dives among the underwater tracks, which ran out into the harbour a surprising distance. I never did go out to the end of the rails because we were looking for old bottles and other bric-a-brac, and the pickings were best reasonably close to shore. It was certainly a spooky dive because it was a working yard, and there were often ships sitting on the tracks out of the water. But we did not have any close calls; we only went on Sunday afternoons when all was quiet.

The biggest ships went to the graving dock. Upon its completion in 1889, the Halifax Graving Dock was the largest such facility on the east coast of North America. It could handle the RN's biggest battleships, up to the advent of the Orion class dreadnoughts in 1911, at 581 feet long and drawing 31 feet. When the Halifax Graving Dock Company purchased the Chebucto Marine Railway Company in 1890, the combined facilities constituted one of North America's most modern ship repair yards.[140] The federal government purchased the graving dock from Samuel Brookfield and his partners in May 1918, first leasing and then selling the facility to a Montréal-based group of investors led by Roy Wolvin and Joseph Norcross, co-founders of Canada Steamship Lines and senior executives in the Collingwood Shipbuilding Company in Ontario. They established Halifax Shipyards Limited in the summer of 1918.

The destruction of the sugar refinery in the blast cleared the way for a series of four 500-foot-long building slips, a mould loft, and a plate shop to be built just north of the dry dock. These additions enabled construction of world-class steel-hulled ships. Canada was sorely in need of such a facility. A single wharf replaced the four piers that had previously existed, where the *Middleham Castle*, *Musquash*, *Douglas H. Thomas*, and *J. A. McKee* had taken such a pounding the previous winter.

The SS *Canadian Mariner* was the first steel-hulled ship launched at the Halifax Shipyard in September 1920. It was a 400-foot-long, 5,400-ton general cargo ship that was built for Canadian Government Merchant Marine Ltd. (A few china pieces bearing the C.G.M.M. moniker have been recovered in the harbour.) Its sister ship *Canadian Explorer*, along with the 7,200-ton *Canadian Cruiser* and *Canadian Constructor*, were launched the following year. They would remain the largest steel ships built in Canada until the end of the Second World War.

Today, the rebuilt and ultra-modern shipbuilding facility is owned by Irving Shipbuilding. The graving dock continues to pay its way. There is almost always a ship in there for repairs or upgrading.

At the time of the explosion, the Halifax Graving Dock Company owned the dry dock. Construction magnate Samuel Brookfield, who had built the sugar refinery, had also built the graving dock, and it was owned by S. M. Brookfield Limited. A graving dock could handle the biggest ships because they did not need to be hauled out of the water. Instead, a ship was pushed into the dock, which was a bit like a submerged bathtub open at one end. Once a ship was inside and secured with blocks and shores to keep it stable, the gates were closed and the water inside the dock was pumped out, leaving the ship's exterior fully accessible.

The company advertised the graving dock itself, which handled the largest ships, and four additional slipways where smaller vessels could be pulled out for repairs. The place was hopping, given the number of ships that were either being worked on or waiting their turn.

CHAPTER 11

FINDING SOMEONE TO BLAME

News travels fast, even without radio or internet. It was a relief that the enemy had not rained down the great calamity of December 6, but when Halifax residents learned that it had come from within, fear turned to disbelief and then to rage. Somebody had to pay!

INQUIRY

The federal minister of Marine and Fisheries, Charles Ballantyne, ordered a full investigation of the events of December 6, 1917, which took the form of a Wreck Commissioner's Court. It was led by a well-known Halifax jurist, the Honourable Arthur Drysdale. The inquiry convened on December 13, 1917, and wound up on January 31, 1918, with a month-long break in between, while Drysdale, a judge of the Supreme Court of Nova Scotia, dealt with other business. It took place in the courthouse on Spring Garden Road, which today is a National Historic Site. Drysdale released the ruling of the court on February 4, 1918.

The majority of marine inquiries have to do with the loss of a ship. They are convened under federal law to establish what happened and who was at fault. There is usually an assumption that somebody messed up. Depending on the nature of the blunder, there is often a penalty assessed upon guilty parties. Inquiry reports frequently contain recommendations on how to guard against similar mishaps in the future. In the case of the *Titanic*, for example, it was recommended that ships carry enough lifeboats for everybody aboard.

Because the Halifax Explosion inquiry involved the loss of at least one ship, Drysdale was assisted by two seamen, Dominion Wreck Commissioner Louis Demers and Capt. Walter Hose of the RCN.

The inquiry testimony record remains as part of the legal proceedings undertaken in the Exchequer Court of Canada by the owners of the two ships. In 1971, the Federal Court of Canada replaced the Exchequer Court of Canada.

With the *Imo*'s captain and pilot dead, all eyes were on the *Mont Blanc*'s pilot, Francis Mackey, and captain, Aimé Le Médec. Frederick Wyatt, the chief examining officer, who was supposed to know what was going on with every ship in the harbour, was also deemed to be complicit in a still-to-be determined crime.

Early on in the proceedings and following his questioning, Alfred Kayford, the third engineer from the *Calonne*, observed to a newspaper reporter, "All this inquiry seems to be after is to fix blame on some pilot or somebody for bringing on the collision. I should think they would have an inquiry to fix blame for the explosion."[141]

It was an important insight that nailed the weakness of the inquiry. In the first of thirteen rulings, the inquiry report stated that the explosion was "undoubtedly the result of a collision in the harbour of Halifax between the S. S. Mont Blanc and the S. S. Imo." In one respect that was true, but the collision was just a snippet in a longer time frame. The event really began when the *Mont Blanc* was loaded in New York. However, the inquiry became fixated on the final minutes and the blasts from each ship's steam whistle, as the lawyers for the two companies competed to place the blame on the other ship and those associated with it.

There was another challenge to be worked around. The witnesses were from all over the place. Reassembling them would be impossible and therefore, with minimal preparation, the proceedings had to commence. This was common with Wreck Commissioner's inquiries, and usually a hasty beginning was not a problem because the witnesses were few and the event being examined was straightforward. Not so in this case. With tens of thousands of people passionately interested in the outcome, there were many witnesses and opinion influencers. The events of December 6, with their horrifying results, had produced an atmosphere of extreme anguish throughout the city and a yearning for revenge.

Lawyers for the owners of the two ships that had collided figured prominently—the companies were suing one another and anxious to escape blame themselves. Because the captain and pilot of the *Imo* had died, it was deemed unseemly to dwell on how they might have been at fault. It was even institutionalized in a principle referred to as British fair play. But they still had Francis Mackey. He spent three days on the stand and was, by a wide margin, the person who took the most severe grilling of the inquiry. Mackey would go to his grave convinced that William Hayes, with whom he had worked for almost a quarter century and knew well, had not been giving the orders aboard the *Imo* that fateful morning. However, the man at the helm of the *Imo*, Johan Johansen, told the inquiry that pilot Hayes gave him all the orders and the captain did not speak other than to relay the pilot's instructions.[142]

Especially poignant was Charles Burchell's insistent reminding of how Mackey had failed the men who had died on the *Stella Maris* and the other boats and the stevedores on the docks whose last minutes were spent innocently gazing at the spectacle in front of them, for all were ignorant of the deadly cargo aboard the burning ship. Burchell pointed an accusing finger at Mackey, stating that these men were within earshot as he rowed away. While that may be debatable, ships carried megaphones for hailing one another. Pilot Renner testified that he and pilot Hayes used megaphones to communicate when they passed just minutes previously.[143] In his defence, Mackey noted that he told those aboard the *Hilford* and the *Ragus* the ship was about to blow up and to stay clear. Both vessels were lost, the *Ragus* sinking with all hands.

The thirteen points of the court's ruling squarely took aim at the men, ascribing illogical motivation and unprovable crimes to Mackey and Le Médec. The inquiry report called for Mackey's arrest so he could be charged with manslaughter. Having no jurisdiction over Le Médec, the commissioners recommended that he be taken to task by French authorities. Mackey and Le Médec were arrested when they exited the courthouse and clapped into jail.

There was an appeal.

> **"I have known [Pilot Mackey] for probably 25 or 30 years.... For many years while I was in the shipping business, the shipping trade, I was brought into direct intercourse with him and we always looked upon him as one of the best pilots, sober, industrious and attentive to his duties. We never had any reason to complain of his habits in any respect."**
> —James Hall, Chairman of Halifax Pilotage Commission[144]

On March 15, 1918, Justice Benjamin Russell, after carefully reviewing the evidence, determined there was no basis for the charges of manslaughter and criminal negligence. He ordered Mackey's release. He rendered the same judgment for Le Médec.

Public censure immediately rained down upon Justice Russell. He later explained his judgment: "To imagine any pilot in charge of a vessel loaded with explosives, as this was known to the pilot to have been, would expose himself and his associates to the risk of instantaneous death by the reckless omission of any precaution or the careless execution of any manoeuvre necessary to his own safety was irrational."[145]

That was not the end of it. Three days following Russell's ruling, the Attorney General of Nova Scotia, Orlando Daniels, gave notice that the government would appeal the verdict to the Nova Scotia Supreme Court. The Supreme Court justices ruled in agreement with Russell's judgment and refused the appeal.

On April 17, the third defendant, Commander Wyatt, was also found not guilty of manslaughter and criminal negligence in carrying out his duties as chief examining officer. The evidence was so thin that his lawyers did not even mount a defence, claiming simply that the prosecution had not put forth a convincing case against him. The jury agreed.

Was there nobody to blame? Close to two thousand people dead, untold suffering, widespread destruction, and a very dismal future for the city and its citizens, and it was nobody's fault? It was too much. The prosecution simply had to persevere. The next stop was the Supreme Court of Canada. Having carefully read the evidence, instead of simply concentrating on the *Mont Blanc*, they also considered the *Imo*'s actions. They ruled that both ships were equally to blame.

Still no villain! There was one final stop: the Privy Council in London.

The Privy Council looked at the situation with the two Halifax ships and asked a simple question: Why did they keep moving forward and not take any meaningful action until the last minute? For that reason, their lordships agreed with the Supreme Court of Canada. In the fifth of five statements of judgment, they noted, "On the case of both ships, it is clear that their navigators allowed them to approach within 400 feet of each other on practically opposite courses, thus incurring risk of collision, and indeed practically bringing about the collision, instead of reversing their engines and going astern, as our assessors advise us, they, as a matter of good seamanship could and should have done, long before the ships came so close together."[146]

Point twelve of the thirteen points in Judge Drysdale's findings recommended that pilot Edward Renner be censured for not complying with the rules of the road when he steered the SS *Clara* through The Narrows on the Halifax side, obliging the *Imo* to stay toward the Dartmouth side. He lost his licence and had to wait three years before getting it back on October 12, 1920.[147]

For Francis Mackey, a long and difficult road lay ahead. The treatment of Mackey is reminiscent of the old line from the Western movies, where the leader of the lynch mob declares, "Sure, we'll give him a fair trial—and *then* we'll hang him!" No matter what the courts might find, Francis Mackey would become the face of guilt in the public's mind, and remained so until he died on New Year's Eve, 1961.

In her book *Aftershock* (Nimbus, 2015), Janet Maybee makes a compelling case that, not only was Mackey innocent of wrongdoing, but also he was the victim of a plot by federal government officials to deflect their own culpability onto him. A simple example says it all. After the courts had found him not guilty of wrongdoing, and despite the recommendations of multiple industry groups, Marine and Fisheries Minister Charles Ballantyne flatly refused to reinstate Mackey's licence, as if on principle because those judges and justices were all wrong and Ballantyne was the guardian of the truth. It mattered not that Mackey was unable to earn a living, causing him and his family untold suffering. Only when another minister took over the Marine and Fisheries portfolio did Mackey finally have his certificate returned on February 14—Valentine's Day—1922.[148]

By then, he was so deeply in debt that it would be a long haul before he would ever be comfortable again. He had spent all his life savings and everything his wife's family might have donated, as well as what little he could earn by other jobs taking vessels to keep him afloat. Because he had a master's certificate, he was able to go up and down the coast.

Just by virtue of being a pilot, Francis Mackey was an easy target. The pilots were not especially esteemed by the Halifax population.

THE MEN WHO MOVED THE SHIPS

Any vessel over 50 tons was required to engage a pilot when entering or leaving Halifax Harbour. Exemptions were made for those regularly coming and going and whose masters could demonstrate their competence to the chief examining officer. With winds often approaching hurricane strength, stiff currents driven by two daily tide changes of 50 feet or more sloshing in and out of the Bay of Fundy, dramatic changes in water depths near the approaches, lurking reefs and shoals strewn about the harbour entrance, and thick fog hanging around sometimes for weeks, it is no place for a ship without an experienced local pilot on the bridge.

In the early days, pilots were not required by law. When Capt. Scory Barker of HMS *Tribune* allowed an overconfident sailing master to convince him that they did not need a pilot to take their 34-gun frigate into Halifax in late November 1797, he paid with the loss of his ship and some 240 lives, including his own. It was the greatest loss of life from a single shipwreck in the harbour's history.

In the beginning, pilots were untrained but experienced sailors with common sense (it was hoped) and intimate knowledge of the challenges presented by the harbour's makeup and environment. They lived in tiny villages clinging to the rocks: Purcells Cove, Herring Cove, and Portuguese Cove to the west and Devils Island to the east. They kept an eye on the horizon, and when a sail appeared, they took to their boats to head it off. With lots of competition, the strategy was to be the first to reach an incoming vessel. In 1826, a ship belonging to prominent shipowner Samuel Cunard ran aground, on the same shoal that snagged the *Tribune*, while being piloted by a nineteen-year-old from Portuguese Cove. A year later, an attempt was made to put some order to things with the creation of the Halifax Pilots Corporation.

When the SS *Humboldt* was lost in December 1853, it didn't take long to single out the pilot as the culprit. Short of coal while travelling from Southampton to New York, this nearly 300-foot paddlewheel steamer was approaching Halifax Harbour. A pilot went on board and, in dense fog, proceeded to strike a shoal called The Sisters, a tower of submerged rocks surrounded by deep water just outside Chebucto Head. It did not seem like a major grounding, so the captain backed the ship off, only to discover it was taking on water faster than the pumps could send it back. The captain headed for shallow water and grounded the vessel near Portuguese Cove, ensuring all lives were saved.

The *Saint John Morning News* declared, "To punish that pilot, then, ought to be the first wise thought of every man interested in the character and prosperity of Halifax."

It was a sentiment that would echo down through the years.

Just minutes after pilot William Flemming boarded the SS *Salerno* on July 3, 1905, the ship was immobile atop the Lichfield Shoal. Later, the Halifax tug *Togo* offered a price of $2,000 to pull the ensnared ship off the reef. The captain refused, confident he would get free when the tide rose. He miscalculated, and the *Salerno* sank in 90 feet of water.

At the subsequent inquiry, it was learned that forty-one-year-old Pilot Flemming had had his certificate rescinded in February 1902 for putting the Allan Line steamship *Grecian* ashore about 15 miles from where the *Salerno* was then grounded. He was reinstated in March 1905, but this was the final straw. His days of piloting were over.

Three years into the First World War and just four months before the Halifax Explosion, there was an uproar when a pilot botched the handling of HMHS *Letitia*, a hospital ship returning from Europe with 546 wounded soldiers aboard. *Letitia* was no stranger to the harbour. Along with *Araguaya*, the two ships worked full-time shuttling back and forth across the Atlantic, returning to Canada its injured from the fields and trenches of Europe.

The captain and his officers had been travelling through thick fog for several days, so they were relieved to have a local pilot to handle the final part of their trip. On the morning of August 1, 1917, the ship had been creeping along while entering the outer harbour when pilot Walter White came aboard, changed the ship's course and increased the speed. Ten minutes after he had boarded, *Letitia* plowed into the shore just inside Chebucto Head and hung precariously with its stern more than 120 feet above the bottom.

Naval vessels with names that only a bureaucrat could invent were put to work removing the wounded from the grounded hospital ship. PV-III, PV-IV, and PV-V soon had all the patients ashore in Halifax and the most severe ones in the hospital at Pier 2. The tugs *F. W. Roebling* and *Gladiator* were on hand along with one of Hendry's tugs, but they were unable to pull *Letitia* off the rocks. The tug *Gopher* was put to work towing the ship's nine lifeboats containing the crew to Halifax, where they were landed at the Market Wharf.

When asked if they had a pilot aboard, an officer replied, "Of course we had! You don't suppose we would have stopped here if we had been running the ship, do you? We would have been docked in Halifax long before this."[149]

On August 13 and 14, the inquiry took place at Halifax, before the Dominion Wreck Commissioner, Capt. L. A. Demers, assisted by the CXO, Cmdr. F. E. Wyatt, along with Cmdr. Charles White, and J. D. MacKenzie, RN, acting as nautical assessors. The stranding was attributed to the action of the pilot, in accepting, without verification, bearings given to him by another pilot aboard the pilot boat. That pilot was Edward Renner, who would lose his certificate for his handling of the SS *Clara* on the morning of December 6. The pilot boat was a schooner that carried a load of pilots to dispatch to arriving ships. They took turns standing the watch aboard the schooner, and at that time the pilot on watch was Renner, who simply responded to a question from

Pilot White as he was departing to board *Letitia*. That caused White to have an incorrect understanding of where *Letitia* was located in the fog. The inquiry did not find Renner at fault because he was simply passing on a position that the person navigating the schooner had incorrectly worked out.

It was reported that, in the fog, the pilot boat was 2 miles away from where it was believed to be, which caused Pilot White to handle the ship incorrectly. When *Letitia*'s captain expressed concern, White told him he had it under control, even though he had not confirmed the position Renner had given him. For that, the inquiry found him negligent.

It was within the captain's authority to override the pilot's command, but the captain was in a bind. There was fear that enemy submarines would mine the harbour approaches, and it was impossible to tell at any given time where the safe waters were. To the best of their ability, the minesweepers kept a channel open and kept the pilots informed, so an incoming captain was left with no choice but to rely on the pilot.

The loss of *Letitia* caused a lot of condemnation about the pilot system in Halifax. There was some feeling among mariners that the pilot station was too close to shore, that at other important ports like New York, the pilot went aboard much farther offshore. They had a reasonable point. It would give the pilot plenty of time to confirm bearings to pinpoint a ship's position, especially in foggy weather, as occurred in this case. But it also meant that the pilots would be occupied on each ship for a longer time. With only fourteen senior pilots and fifteen or more ships arriving per day,[150] moving the station further out to sea would have spread the Halifax pilots too thin.

In the inquiry report, the assessors made the following observation and recommendation:

> The court feels very keenly about this casualty and in order that a repetition may be impossible, and as a deterrent to any inclined to carelessness, it has to deal harshly with this pilot.
>
> Had it not been for this most objectionable custom of the pilots to take their possible position from another, the criminal courts would have been requested to deal with this case; but under the

> circumstances, having fully weighed every point, the court cancels the license of pilot Walter White, No. 24, and the Halifax Pilotage Commission is requested to see that the order of this court is carried out.
>
> The court suggests and recommends that a general and thorough inquiry should be made into the pilotage system in Halifax, in order to bring about a betterment so as to induce the confidence of the shipping public.[151]

On January 9, 1918, Walter White became captain of the little steamer *Strathlorne,* which was employed as a water boat, supplying water to steamers in the harbour.[152]

On April 28, 1873, in a letter to the *Halifax Morning Chronicle*, William Roche, one of the Commissioners of Pilots for the Port of Halifax at that time, wrote, "There are ninety pilots for the harbour of Halifax." In 1906, there were just nineteen pilots in Halifax. They brought in 1,155 ships for the year. Ten years later, in 1916, 1,624 vessels came in.[153] The next year, with the coming of the convoys, the number grew to 2,711, while the number of pilots was down to just fourteen. The average number of ships handled by each man had more than tripled. The Halifax Pilotage Commission had taken on eight apprentices but the apprenticeship was four years. Four of the apprentices had two years and four months service and the other four had four to six months each. The situation was so dire that James Hall, the chairman of the commission, told the inquiry they had even passed a by-law empowering the commission to employ competent shipmasters as pilots.[154] They were awaiting a response from Ottawa.

At the end of February 1918, the commission received the authority to proceed, and on September 1, 1918, they added six sea captains on temporary pilot licences. Three men left two months later with the end of the war, one departed on February 16, 1919, and the other two were finished on April 30, 1920.[155]

Becoming a Halifax pilot was a bit like becoming a lighthouse keeper. A father or uncle on the inside got you a position and you worked your way into what was considered a very well-paid job. Pilot Francis Mackey's granddaughter, Mona, put it bluntly: "You know, in those days you had to be born into a pilot's family to get taken on as a pilot."[156] The fewer pilots, the more money each man earned. There was no incentive for them to grow the organization. With the coming of war and the increase of harbour traffic through Halifax, they were making enormous amounts of money. It was claimed that some pilots were earning incomes that eclipsed those of the premier of Nova Scotia or judges of the Supreme Court.[157]

When questioned about it, Mackey told the inquiry that he averaged about $400 to $500 a month. When pushed, he admitted to making $1,000 in one month. At the time, the captain of the Canadian government ship *Lady Laurier* earned $1,320 in a year, as did the captain of the *Lansdowne*.[158] The fact that Francis Mackey, with his grade 8 education, even approached his income level must have rankled Judge Drysdale.

CONFLICT BETWEEN THE PILOTS AND THE NAVY

There was a poor relationship between the pilots and the navy. The job of the pilots had become complicated with the coming of war, and the complexity had increased with the implementation of the convoy system. Pilots were used to doing things their own way, and the navy's need for information meant they had additional work at a time when their numbers were dwindling and ship traffic was significantly growing.

When he was the CXO, Commander Wyatt was frustrated by the situation. Not only had the pilotage commission allowed the pilot population to get dangerously low, but they were also not cooperating with the navy. Wyatt was responsible for the movement of merchant ships. To do that, he needed to know everything about them at all times—when they arrived, what they were carrying, where they berthed, when they were scheduled to leave. The pilots were the essential asset in his information network because whenever a ship came or went, a pilot was in the picture. Nobody knew better the situation on a given ship than its pilot.

In the office of the Halifax Pilotage Commission on Bedford Row, there were just two employees. James Creighton, an accountant by training, was called the secretary. He ran the office, did the billing, and kept the books. His one staff member was a fifteen-year-old clerk named Edward Beazley. He answered the phone, took orders from ships' agents to schedule pilots for outbound ships and for moves within the harbour, called the pilots at home when there was a job, maintained the docket on a chalkboard for all to see, updated the pilots' card each time a pilot returned from bringing a ship in the harbour, delivered the invoices to the ships' agents, and did whatever other tasks James Creighton assigned.

> **"We have made a rule that every pilot bringing a ship in Halifax must report to the pilotage office after bringing the vessel in, but some of them neglect to do that."**
> —Francis Rudolf, Harbourmaster and Pilotage Commissioner[159]

In addition, there was a weekly rotation of pilots to ensure one was on duty at the office for emergencies.

In May 1917, the navy had instructed the pilotage commission that they were to advise the CXO of all ship movements on a daily basis. Beazley prepared the report and at 4:00 P.M. each day he called the Examination Office with the list of movements for that day. If it was a particularly busy day, he called twice. There would often be the names of fifteen to twenty movements to report on. Beazley rhymed off the names of the ships, some of which had foreign names like *Asuncion de Larrinaga*, *Kanawha,* and *Marie Z. Michalinos*, which he must have had trouble pronouncing. He complained that the person on the other end never asked him to repeat anything or to slow down, and as this continued, he started to suspect they weren't writing it down, either. Did they really need him to call? He did not like the task so, in teenager fashion, he started skipping some days and after six or seven weeks, he just stopped. He didn't bother to tell Creighton and would later claim nobody called the office to find out what was going on.[160]

Testimony at the Halifax Explosion inquiry on January 24, 1918, revealed that the mysterious person on the phone from the Examination Service was the CXO himself, Acting Commander Wyatt. It was the last straw. Four days later, on January 28, 1917, with the inquiry still in process, and before a report was released, the navy relieved Frederick Evan Wyatt of his duty as CXO and replaced him with Lieut. Russell Barber.[161]

They were glad for the opportunity to get rid of Wyatt. He had become CXO with the support and best wishes of Admiral Kingsmill and was a popular officer within the navy and in Halifax society. The relationship soon soured, however, over issues in Wyatt's personal life. In January 1909, he had married Madeline Izod in England and soon became a father. Early in 1913, he abandoned his family. With the coming of war, the RN assigned him to Halifax, where he was soon in a relationship with Dorothy Brookfield, the niece of Samuel Brookfield, owner of the dockyard and other Halifax businesses.

In July 1916, Wyatt and his wife divorced, freeing him to marry Dorothy on February 1, 1917. Not long after that, he stopped support payments to Madeline, an indiscretion that soon found its way to Kingsmill's attention, thanks to the efforts of Madeline's solicitors and the Admiralty. It was 1917. Divorce was bad enough—and extremely rare—but stiffing his family was just "not on."[162]

His story made for good gossip, which affected his relationship within the small navy community. When he testified at the inquiry, he spoke at length about his inability to get the pilots to co-operate, how he was unsupported by his boss, and how he feared he was being made a scapegoat for the disaster.

At the inquiry, he produced three letters on the subject of pilots' lack of cooperation that he had sent to Captain Martin (see appendix A). Martin, who would have known all about Wyatt's personal life, told the inquiry that he had no recollection of such letters and later reported they were not to be found in the files. By then, Wyatt had been replaced as CXO and would soon be thrown out of the navy. Not having a record of those letters was convenient for everybody—except Wyatt.

The Examination Service staff were getting by because pilots would often drop by the *Niobe* on the way to the basin to get a ship, as Hayes had done

"We got very irregular reports from the pilots these last months.... It got me in to no end of trouble, not knowing where ships were, and I made it a point on one particular day, one morning at 9 to come down to the pilot's office and ask them to keep up that rule in order to keep me out of trouble, if for nothing else—to hold hard to the rule." —Roland Iceton, Examination Service[163]

on his way to the *Imo* on the afternoon of December 5. The duty man would take the opportunity to ask what other ships were scheduled to depart that day and who the pilot was. If the pilot did not inform them that he was taking a ship outbound from the basin, the examining staff had no other way of knowing it was about to happen. In many cases, they would find out when they saw the ship coming through The Narrows. Occasionally, they still called the pilotage office.

It's hard to believe that this important procedure was handled in such a slipshod manner. A major part of the problem was the lack of strong management. The pilots were used to having authority and giving orders, not taking them. Only a senior pilot could command the respect required and understand the challenges the pilots faced. It was not an easy job—irregular hours in all weather, getting from the rolling deck of the pilot boat onto a rope ladder strung down the side of a steel ship and then climbing aboard—in the dark, in rain and snow, giving crucial life-and-death instructions to people who did not understand English. And if they took a ship out of the harbour and were unable to get off, then what? They were on the way to England, or New York, or Montréal.

James Creighton, the pilot commission secretary, was an accountant by trade, so his interest was in taking care of the financial aspects of the business. With the fifteen-year-old as his staff to manage the work of fourteen pilots and eight apprentices, the organization had neither the insight nor the foresight it required. The pilots were managing themselves. They had to. Moving ships was their business, not doing paperwork. Their overseers were a board of volunteer commissioners that met monthly, chaired by James Hall.[164]

When asked by the inquiry for the name of the fifteen-year-old clerk, Mr. Hall was unable to give his name. There were two people working in the office and the commission chairman could only name one of them!

Did all this have a direct influence on the events of December 6? Yes. The people in charge of traffic control in the harbour did not know the *Imo* would be coming through The Narrows that morning. In questioning Wyatt at the inquiry, Charles Burchell asked why he didn't use the guard ship as a means of tracking ship departures instead of banging his head against the wall with the pilots. Wyatt was at a loss to answer.[165]

CHAPTER 12

GETTING TO THE BOTTOM OF THE STORY

In 1987, I got certified as a scuba diver. Unlike 75 percent of the people who take up this unique sport, I stuck with it, and in 1989, I did my first dive in Halifax Harbour. Since then, I have done more than twelve hundred dives in the harbour, all in pursuit of a good time. During that period, I have worn out at least eight suits and countless pairs of mitts, and spent thousands of dollars on air fills.

With a record like that, people ask me if I was a commercial diver or in the navy. No, and no. It's just a hobby. My first harbour dive was in the north end of The Narrows, where the *Imo* struggled to get away from the Dartmouth shore. Today, it's one of the busiest parts of the harbour. It wasn't long before I had the largest ships that come into the harbour passing over me during a dive. That wasn't intentional; they have a habit of sneaking up.

THE VIEW FROM BELOW

My buddy came up from my first harbour dive with a dinner plate that was more than a hundred years old. In the centre was the crest of the Canadian Pacific Railway. It had come off a Canadian Pacific steamship and was an important piece of Canadiana. That plate, a wonderfully historic artifact, caught my imagination. On my next dive I was in 80 feet of water in the middle of The Narrows. I came out with some very exciting artifacts, mostly bottles and crocks from the mid- to late 1800s. From the writing embossed or printed on them, such as "The Original Ship Brand Chutney Bombay" and "J A Sharwood Calcutta and London," it appeared they had all come from ships, probably during wartime, from the days of the British in India. A soda pop bottle embossed "British and Foreign Mineral Water Co Ltd Glasgow" had me thinking of steamships being built on the River Clyde in Scotland.

Soon, I had bottles from RN strongholds like Malta, Gibraltar, and Bermuda. No doubt, bottle divers in those places have beauties from Felix J. Quinn and James Roue of Halifax because Halifax and the RN were synonymous for almost two centuries. Halifax was one of just four imperial fortresses of the RN, with the others being Bermuda, Gibraltar, and Malta. RN ships travelled between those harbours, and the sailors tossed stuff overboard.

Eventually, I was exploring all over Halifax Harbour. In my many harbour dives I have amassed a collection of more than two thousand bottles and crocks, all researched and documented in a database. I also have a respectable collection of chinaware from shipping lines like Cunard, White Star, Allan, and others. All I need now is a museum interested in having all those articles.

My attention inevitably turned to the Halifax Explosion, the defining event in the history of our storied harbour. I have spent many hours in my boat studying the shoreline to identify where significant points like the sugar refinery and Lorne Club were located and to understand how the Explosion affected the waters and the bottom of The Narrows. Observing while underwater is a drawn-out process. You don't get to cast your gaze far and wide to take it all in. You cast your eyes down, mostly, because your range of vision is so limited that there is little to see when you look ahead.

Good visibility on every dive is every diver's dream. In the harbour, it's hit and miss; one day it's great and on another it's terrible. You rarely get to take in a scene while remaining still, the way you would on land. All the gear limits your ability to turn your head. It's easier to turn your body as you would if you had a stiff neck, while being careful not to stir up the silt on the bottom.

Because of the inability to take in a wide area, when you're diving a site like a shipwreck, you have to methodically build a map in your mind as you swim around. It's a bit like trying to remember the pattern on a Persian carpet while crawling around on it with your eyes down and wearing blinders. It is very easy to get disoriented when moving because you have few if any points of reference, and you're always in motion.

COLD, DARK, AND CHAOTIC

Almost all the diving my buddies and I did in The Narrows was between October and May, when the pleasure craft had been put away. That means tolerating cold water below and cold air above. It definitely takes some getting used to, but it's not as bad as it sounds, and there are a few tricks you learn to stay comfortable.

Diving in that area also means contending with ships and boats of all sizes. Container ships come and go daily and ore carriers weekly. The Coast Guard and navy are in there all the time doing training. When a container ship travels through the area accompanied by two or three tugs it dominates the place, but it is not the danger that harbour divers fear most—their presence is obvious. The real worry is the sailboats, which glide silently above. It's possible to surface and have one run over you because you can't hear it. As long as you don't come up, you're okay!

Currents are another challenge while diving in The Narrows. A vast amount of water passes through there four times a day as the tides change, so it is virtually always in motion—in, out, in, out every twenty-four hours. The tides are very complex; they rise and fall a different amount and at a slightly different time each cycle, so they are never the same from one day to the next. Sometimes, the current is so strong you can't swim against it. Like the other challenges, it has to be managed. Still, you are never as close to instant death as you are when driving on an undivided highway.

Another consideration for divers is water depth. The Bedford Basin was once an ancient lake and The Narrows are an ancient riverbed. The basin, significantly deeper than The Narrows, goes down to 240 feet, which is three times as deep as 75 percent of the harbour. To find water that deep, you need to go 15 miles out past the harbour boundary. If we consider The Narrows to be the area between the two harbour bridges, perhaps it is shallowest under the Macdonald Bridge. The tides in the harbour are a maximum of about 6 feet, so if you dive in exactly the same place each day for a week you will descend to a different maximum depth each day. If somebody points to a spot and asks, "How deep is it right there?" the answer will always be, "It depends on the tide." So, we always talk in approximations when referring to depth. It's around a minimum of 60 feet deep under the Macdonald Bridge.

Generally speaking, the bottom of The Narrows undulates, so as you swim along you are usually gently rising or descending between 60 and 90 feet. The explosion took place in an area that rapidly dropped from shore to around 60 feet deep. For most of The Narrows, the shoreline drops off quickly, as if it were a big ditch dug by an excavator. There are no shallow spots anywhere that would endanger ships of the size common during the First World War. The massive ships that travel through The Narrows today need additional care more because of their length than the amount of water they draw. There is one hefty turn that a pilot must plan for long before getting to it. It occurs just before a ship enters the basin—the same turn that caused the *Imo* problems when coming out of the basin.

THE HARBOUR BOTTOM TODAY

I am often asked what I have seen from the Explosion. It's a difficult question to answer because I have observed trainloads of what I'll call wreckage—material that for one reason or another has ended up on the bottom of the harbour. In some respects, it all looks the same—corroded, twisted, broken, tangled—making its origin difficult to identify. There's rusty iron, pitted aluminum, green bronze. There is rope and cable and netting to be avoided. There are beer and pop cans as well as broken and intact bottles and crocks originating from before the founding of Halifax up to yesterday. There are broken dishes everywhere, even an occasional intact treasure from a nineteenth-century RN ship, sometimes even with the ship's name. Its finder goes to sleep contented that night. Everywhere there is ash from burnt coal, the same stuff the *Stella Maris* crew was dumping. They weren't the only ones doing it.

There is very little organic material down there. If it's something that once lived, there is something else that will consume it and get life from it, the same as we do. Those creatures are not as fussy about freshness as we are, so it all gets gobbled up. And, there are lots of living things on the bottom: scallops, lobsters, crabs, anemones, mussels, barnacles, even oysters. For that reason, or in spite of it, of the hundreds of dives I've done in The Narrows, I don't recall a single conversation in the boat after the dive where somebody said they saw something that might have been from the Explosion.

After going skyward in the explosion of its cargo, the *Mont Blanc* rained back down to earth in many pieces, no doubt killing some and giving others the knowledge they had, as the saying goes, dodged a bullet. Today, you can see the stern gun, bent and buckled, on display at a street corner in a residential area of Dartmouth. It is perhaps a mile from where it landed in a shallow lake. There are similar artifacts all over the city, including the shaft from one of the ship's anchors, also in a residential area, near the Northwest Arm. Lots of that sort of material ended up on the bottom of the harbour, but who can separate it from other similar objects that ended up there?

THE HATED SILT

In the last few years, while diving in the harbour and especially in The Narrows, I have remained on the lookout for anything that might be from that shocking event. But what am I looking for? How would I know if I found something? The bottom of the harbour is full of rusty junk, and it has been more than a century since the Explosion. I'm sure I've glided over many pieces of the *Mont Blanc* and other unfortunate vessels and never knew it because of another complication with searching the harbour bottom. It is covered with a deep blanket of silt, the product of millions of years of decaying organic material like leaves, grass, trees, and seaweed, not to mention all the rivers, rain, and melting snow that have deposited dissolved matter on the ocean floor. It is characteristic of all sheltered areas and finding a bit of hard bottom where debris has not been swallowed up is the exception rather than the rule. That means 98 percent of the basin, Northwest Arm, Eastern Passage, and the inner and outer harbour give up next to nothing.

Perhaps 25 percent of The Narrows is the exception. Those strong tides that I mentioned keep some parts of The Narrows bottom swept, as happens with other constricted areas of the harbour. But you can stand on the Halifax waterfront and look across to Dartmouth over the expanse of water that has been frequented by tens of thousands of vessels over the centuries, or look left toward The Narrows or right toward the outer islands and consider the thousands of tons that have been thrown or dumped into just the inner harbour. A scuba diver looking for anything out there would be on a fool's errand. We have just scratched, not the surface, but I suppose the top of the bottom. The substantial depths of Halifax Harbour have meant that wholesale dredging to deepen it has been rare, making Halifax unique among the important harbours. I have heard stories of required dredging in a few places in the harbour and how the workers had to be discouraged from sifting through the diggings as it was slowing the work.

THE LEGENDARY CRATER

I recall swimming along somewhere in the centre of The Narrows across a bland and pretty much flat area when I came to a bank that dropped precipitously by 20 feet or more. I absently followed the drop and continued on my way as I searched for old bottles, which meant I was doing a lot of twisting and turning to make sure I covered the most ground possible with the greatest efficiency given the limited time I had. A few minutes later I came to a slope leading up. *I must be in that underwater riverbed*, I thought, assuming I was at the other side of the depression, but as I swam upward, I did a routine compass check to ensure I was on my westerly heading, leading from the Dartmouth shore where I had entered, toward the Halifax side. I had gotten off course, not unusual, and was heading south instead, parallel to the shoreline. That meant it was not the underwater riverbed I had come upon but a hole.

I decided it was time to turn around and work my way back to the Dartmouth shore. As I changed direction, I noted the bank had a gentle turn, so I followed it for a while back through where I had first encountered it. I soon found the depression in the bottom was basically round, a bit like a huge, shallow bowl, maybe a saucer. Instantly, I thought of the Explosion and started wondering if I had found the legendary crater that some believe was created when the blast occurred.

After some cursory research following the dive, I realized that I had not been in the area of the Explosion. It was a natural depression in the bottom, a significant one that marked the deepest place in The Narrows, at 105 feet. Now that I understand exactly where the actual explosion occurred, I am of the opinion that we will never know if a crater was blasted into the bottom, which was cleaned up after the war and partly filled in to create a parking lot.

A CHUNK OF THE *MONT BLANC*

However, that dive did turn up an artifact that I'm pretty sure is from the *Mont Blanc*. As I was heading back on that dive, with the explosion very much in mind, I ran across what I thought was a flat rock. But as I went past, I decided it was worth a closer look. It turned out to be a piece of iron plating about 7 feet long by perhaps 4 feet wide, bent and twisted, especially on the edges. The edges are ragged and bent inward, indicating a great deal of stress. It sits alone on a flat, bland bottom with nothing else like it in the area. The absence of any other pieces of metal in the vicinity eliminates the possibility it's from a complete wreck and makes me believe instead it's a random piece that must have been a part of the hull or deck of the exploding *Mont Blanc*.

The area of that dive was interesting for another reason: the lack of artifacts. The first dives I experienced in The Narrows were at the extreme north end, where The Narrows and the basin meet, an area with a fairly consistent density. We did a lot of diving there over several years and found a lot of bottles and dishes from steamships. After we moved on, other divers continued to score good finds in the area. The Maritime Museum of the Atlantic even sponsored a dive day, providing a boat so a group of us could explore farther afield. One of the museum staff likened the area to a large midden field. (The term pertains to old sites where early civilizations dumped their garbage. Such places are valuable for researching how ancient people lived.)

Everybody was curious as to where all this stuff had come from, considering there were no docks in the basin and, therefore, there was no apparent reason for the level of ship traffic these finds would indicate. They must have been from the convoy ships. As time went on, we started working our way to the south, where we found the remains of the two railway bridges that spanned the harbour in the 1880s. We continued deeper into The Narrows in the direction of the explosion site. Eventually everything had thinned out, and there was nothing there to find. In fact, when I ran across that metal piece I mention above, I was on one of several dives I did while exploring whether there was any point in going farther south. By then, we were diving from boats, so we did a thorough sweep and decided there was nothing to be found in that direction.

Instead, we went to the other end of The Narrows, where the second bridge, the Macdonald, is located. We even obtained permission to dive at the dockyard, so it was a rare privilege for weekend recreational divers like us to dive under the warships. We didn't find much at the dockyard because it had all been dredged and rebuilt during and after the Second World War, but offshore, we were back to happy hunting. Soon, we were working our way north toward the explosion site and eventually the same thing happened. The pickings petered out.

It's as if the blast went down and out from the Halifax shoreline where the *Mont Blanc* had drifted, pushing everything in a semicircle away from the blast site and the detritus got sent, like a leaf blower moving leaves, north toward the McKay Bridge, east across to the Dartmouth shore, and south toward the

Macdonald Bridge. On the Dartmouth shore, across from the blast site and in shallow water, the pickings were respectable.

All this diving happened over a period of at least twenty years, so I am making no pretensions that we were on some kind of journey of discovery about the Explosion. We were just enjoying our hobby, and I am giving a very unscientific analysis of what might have happened, after having lots of time to think about it. It is a fact that in the area out from where the blast occurred, we recovered few if any artifacts from the period before the First World War.

DREDGE SPOILS

The cleanup after the Halifax Explosion included some dredging to remove debris from the wrecked docks and to deepen the area for reconstruction of the wharves and shipyard. Directly across The Narrows from the blast site is an area consisting of ridges of gravel close to and running parallel to the shore. I first encountered it when I did the dive in which I found what I am calling the *Mont Blanc* piece. Expecting to find the usual eclectic assortment of artifacts, I was surprised to encounter absolutely nothing except sterile piles of gravel. I concluded that those berms must be from dredging. With the depth of The Narrows, there is no reason to dredge nearby other than as part of the cleanup from the Explosion. There is a second area of dredge spoils near the shore, under the Macdonald Bridge.

WRECKS

Across from the blast site at the entrance to Tufts Cove stands Nova Scotia Power's imposing thermal generating station. It was built in 1965 and 1,000 feet of shoreline was filled in to make room. There is a small wreck on each side of the power station. They both have wooden hulls and are near the shore in fairly shallow water. It is difficult to ascertain if they are from the Explosion, but I think it's likely, considering where they are located. In such a sheltered spot, I can think of no other reason why they would be there unless they were thrust against the shore when the tsunami hit. Getting up close to the power station can be intimidating enough in a boat but doubly so when you're in the water. There is a huge intake drawing in cooling water for the equipment and another one sending it back, sometimes with a roar of whitewater. It's no place to be exploring underwater.

ST. BERNARD ANCHOR

Across The Narrows from the explosion site is a small, shallow cove called Tufts Cove. The *Curaca* grounded nearby when it got shoved across The Narrows from Pier 8, where it was tied. The water depth in that area goes from about 80 feet at mid-channel, and then the bottom slopes up at a forty-five-degree angle to less than 10 feet at the cove's entrance. A boater who might venture into the cove would probably be spooked by white rocks that suddenly appear beneath the water's surface, frighteningly close to the bottom of the boat. The problem with rocks in shallow water is that there might be one sticking up a foot or two higher than the others, close enough to snag a propeller or destroy the drive train of a boat's engine.

As my little boat slowly proceeded over those rocks one day a few years ago, the water suddenly became deeper again, and I found myself wondering why those rocks were there, neatly arranged, appearing suddenly, giving me a scare, and then disappearing again as the boat moved into the cove.

After some research, I concluded that they had held the foundation of the railway bridge that the Intercolonial Railway had built across that part of Tufts Cove in the 1880s, so trains could pick up sugar from the new refinery near the site of today's Woodside Ferry terminal. That bridge started on the Halifax side of The Narrows at Pier 9, where the *Calonne* had been tied, and crossed to Dartmouth in a long arc that landed not far from the MacKay Bridge and

This anchor, believed to have come from the St. Bernard, *lies in 15 feet of water in Tufts Cove.* (AUTHOR'S COLLECTION)

then passed through the woods, across Tufts Cove, through the area where the power station now stands, and then along the shore toward Eastern Passage.

On May 13, 2021, I was scuba diving in that deeper area when I came across two pieces of wreckage that appear to be from a wooden vessel. There are two pieces lying in line. One is 10 feet by 3 feet, and the other is 13 feet by 3 feet. Between them are several short pieces of wooden planking arranged in a straight line, implying that they had originally been a single piece 23 feet long that perhaps had been broken by an impact. The planks are long and straight and about 3 inches thick. They are held together by iron pins or spikes going down through them from edge to edge.

I swam around to see if there was anything interesting. There was. I found an anchor, obviously old, about 6 feet long, corroded, but still reasonably sound. Such clues are often an indication there is a wreck in the area. I looked around for more evidence but found none. There was just some planking from the side or deck of a good-sized wooden ship and an anchor. That puzzled me because, while these items are in 15 feet of water, the way into the cove is less than that—10 feet at high tide, 3 or 4 at low. A vessel of the size this wreckage seemed to be from would not have been able to enter the cove. Because I was across The Narrows from where the Halifax Explosion occurred, I started wondering if these items might be associated with the event.

I returned the next day, anchored my boat in the same area, donned my dive gear, and entered the water. Intending to take some measurements of the anchor, I moved across the bottom, in the direction of the wreckage. About halfway there, I encountered a piece of iron machinery, too corroded to identify. I thought it might have been a windlass, an iron-geared machine used to raise and lower an anchor. It was one of the few pieces of iron on a wooden ship.

My measurements showed the anchor to be 6 feet long. The distance between the tips of the two flukes is 41 inches. I could not get the measuring tape under the shank but estimate it to be 5 or 6 inches in diameter. Each fluke is triangular shaped, like an arrowhead, and 14 inches long by 12 inches wide. Four feet of chain are attached to a ring at the top of the shank. The chain is well corroded; I picked up what looked like the end going into the silt and the link came off in my hand. Then, I noticed something strange. The chain runs along the shank, not away from the anchor as it would if a vessel were moored to it. And, the anchor is not set; the flukes are flat on the bottom and the stock is lying on the bottom.

If a vessel had been attached to it, one of the flukes would be dug into the bottom, in the attitude of an anchor holding a ship. And the final anomaly: the anchor is oriented on a path leading into the cove, with the ring end on the inner side, in water decreasing in depth. If a ship were attached to the anchor, that ship would be in water less than 6 feet deep because, even though the anchor is in 15 feet of water, it's in a hole that tapers upward until the water is no deeper than 5 or 6 feet on a high tide. There is just not enough room for a ship. In the absence of any other explanation, the anchor looks like it was dropped there and landed on the bottom more or less in a heap, not in the orderly fashion in which a functioning anchor sits, dug into the bottom.

To make sure there was no wreck in the cove, I scouted around, rowing my boat and checking an occasional deeper spot using scuba. All I found was one more piece of wreckage, a wooden knee that could have come from a ship

Above, the anchor from HMCS Protecteur, *the same type that the author found in Tufts Cove* (AUTHOR'S COLLECTION)*; below, the author checks out two other large anchors in the murky waters of Tufts Cove.* (SEAN MCMULLEN)

of the type I had in mind. I found it in silt at a depth of 6 feet, about 50 feet from the anchor. I also found a couple of small pieces of corroded iron that were difficult to identify. Both the wood and the anchor I found are of the size a vessel such as the *St. Bernard* would have used.

The presence of the anchor and the other bits of iron and scraps of wood makes it appear they are all related. The *St. Bernard* had been tied to the north side of Pier 6. On the other side of the pier was the grounded bow of the burning *Mont Blanc*. The force of the explosion could have taken the *St. Bernard*'s bow as a unit, complete with decking, anchor(s), windlass, and other pieces of the schooner, and sent it into the air, spreading it across The Narrows and beyond, at least as far as Tufts Cove. One of the deck guns from the *Mont Blanc* went at least three times that distance, soaring far past where that anchor lies.

CURACA ANCHOR

A year later, on May 21, 2022, I went diving in the general area where the *Curaca* had lain for more than four months. I intended to search for a wreck found near the location of the power station at Tufts Cove a few years previously. At the time, it did not occur to me the wreck might be a product of the Explosion, but in the process of researching for this book, I decided it needed another look. I anchored deep in the cove because it was windy, and I would be leaving my boat unattended. That meant I faced a long swim in the shallow water against hefty currents pushing into the cove.

The long fight against the current consumed a lot of air. I soon realized I would not make it to the area of the wreck and was stopped in 10–12 feet of water, considering my options, when something caught my attention: rust, a sure sign of wreckage. It turned out not to be the debris field of a shipwreck; it was an anchor from a sizable ship, covered in heavy marine growth. Of the dozens of anchors I have seen underwater, it was my only encounter with a stockless anchor of the type used on large steel ships. The shank, which includes most of the length, is 10 feet long. Looking at it endwise it is not circular, like a broom handle, but square, like an 8 × 8 post, with the four sides totalling 34 inches at midpoint. The two flukes total 4 feet—meaning the anchor is 4 feet wide—and each fluke is 43 inches high. It's a sizable anchor from a decent-sized ship, lying in 10 feet of water.

The next day, when I returned to measure and place a marker buoy on the anchor I had discovered, I noticed a second one. It was lying next to the first, oriented the same way. The water is too shallow for the *Curaca*, which ended up a couple of hundred feet away, but the tsunami could have carried it in, bashed it around enough to lose its anchors, and carried it back out, where it sank, nearby.

My dream is that one day they will be raised and placed on the waterfront as a memorial to the seamen who died in the Explosion. If they are indeed from the *Curaca*, they are from the ship that sustained the greatest number of deaths.

Like the other anchor I located in Tufts Cove, those anchors are not in water deep enough for the ship they would have belonged to and are not in a location where such a ship, or any ship for that matter, would have anchored. They are a matched pair, lying neatly next to one another. I believe they are from the *Curaca*, but the evidence is circumstantial, not definitive.

ORDNANCE

We know that ammunition was aboard many of the ships on December 6. It would have been needed for deck guns, which were found on most of the convoy ships. The *Picton* carried many tons of explosives in its cargo, and the *Musquash* was an armed tug so it had ammunition that got thrown overboard to get it away from flames in the two ships. I don't recall seeing any significant collections of ammunition in the area, but it's so common that I could easily have just ignored it. In different parts of the harbour, I have seen a variety of ordnance types, including depth charges, artillery shells, and airplane bombs all the way down to handguns and shotgun shells. Certainly, some of it would have been associated with the Explosion.

There is another compelling area of live ammunition off Pier 20 at the Ocean Terminals. Based on its location, it could have come from the *Picton*. After being towed into Eastern Passage, the ship was moved to one of the new Ocean Terminals docks. By then, Pier 20, which is near Georges Island, was completed to a state where it could accommodate a ship. While diving in the area early in the twenty-first century, several of us came up with empty brass shells. We were puzzled about finding ammunition at that location because it has always been used for passenger ships. Off the north end of the pier there were a lot of live shells in about 40 feet of water and about a ship's width from the dock. It's easy to imagine a vessel tied there and cargo, including the ammunition, being thrown in a panic over the outer side.

We noted that the detonators were still in them, so those shells had not been fired, even though they were empty. It was a mystery until we found a few with the projectiles still in them—iron projectiles instead of lead. They had rusted away. The brass shell casings are a foot long by 2.5 inches at the base. After close to a century in salt water, the remaining projectiles had become rusty and puffed-up, looking a bit like a mushroom growing on the end of the shell. Thinking about them now, I wonder if they were not ammunition at all but the volatile cartridges used in creating a smokescreen that was such a problem for the ship and the nervous folks nearby. Otherwise, why would they have been cast overboard?

CHAPTER 13

THE DANGEROUS CITY

New traffic regulations for the Port of Halifax had come into effect well in advance of the Halifax Explosion, on May 15, 1915. Section 5, "Regulations for Harbour Traffic, Small Yachts and Pleasure Craft," ends with this chilling reminder: "It should be noted that when vessels are outside the harbour limits, they are in the zone of fire from the forts." In other words, as soon as they passed Point Pleasant, where all the sailboats go! Surely, owners of pleasure craft would never have expected to be subject to such a caution when they acquired their boats.

Nor did homeowners like the O'Briens of 12 Lucknow Street, in the city's South End, imagine such an event. On March 1, 1915, a 12-pound projectile struck their house and exploded, causing significant damage. It also caused an uproar in the neighbourhood when people assumed a German attack was happening. Fortunately, nobody was in the house at the time. And it was just friendly fire! The battery at Ives Pont on McNabs Island had fired on, of all things, a government boat—an error in communications. The warning shot had missed, as it was supposed to, but it ricocheted off the water and struck the house 2 miles away.[166]

THE ROAD TO DISASTER

A harbour, by definition, should not be dangerous; it's a place you go to for safety. Halifax is a great harbour, but despite all its military advantages, the City of Halifax had a problem. The civilian population was vulnerable. The

RN ships Tribune, Crescent, Psyche, Pallas, Niobe, Proserpine, *and* Indefatigable *at anchor in October 1901. The Royal Navy Anchorage was at the entrance to The Narrows and often created an obstruction for other vessels heading in or out.* (TOM LYNSKEY)

vast, secure part of the harbour where all the ships could safely gather was the innermost part, and though it was far away from the main population centre, getting there meant that everything entering and leaving Halifax had to travel close to where most people lived. Not only that, but the escort warships anchored practically within shouting distance of the neighbourhoods, and the merchant ships entering the harbour had to work their way around those. Many of the merchant ships carried explosives.

By June 1915, Canada was shipping 1,000 tons of ammunition per week, and the rate was rapidly increasing.[167] On December 6, 1917, just one ship, the *Picton*, was carrying 1,500 tons. Even passenger liners carried ammunition during wartime. The Germans claimed that was why they sank the *Lusitania*, a four-stack Cunard liner on May 7, 1915, killing approximately seven hundred people, including more than one hundred Americans, at a time when the US was neutral.

Having explosive cargoes not only on the harbour but also on residential land had been brought up in the past. The reassuring, oblique, perhaps unspoken response was always, "It will be okay. You can trust us." There had been some close calls, but remedying the threat would have been a formidable undertaking, and nobody ever anticipated a disaster of the scale that occurred in 1917. The Naval Dockyard was built in the 1750s, outside the town. By 1917, the dockyard and its instruments of death had become surrounded by houses, roads, railway tracks, shops, schools, and churches—everything that makes up a neighbourhood. It was too late: the dockyard had become part of the city. And it still is, now more than ever.

There was a time when even the City of Halifax kept a cache of explosives, as the citizens discovered near midnight on August 13, 1857. The Richmond powder magazine blew up without warning, shattering windows throughout the city, destroying several dozen buildings, and scaring the daylights out of everybody. In an editorial written from the time, the *Acadian Recorder* declared, "Perhaps a more desolating catastrophe has never occurred in Halifax. It is infinitely more serious than a fire; for, without a moment's warning or the least time for preparation lives were lost, and thousands of pounds of property destroyed." (That potential preparation time went to waste on December 6, 1917, when fire attracted onlookers, and they died as a result.)

The paper wasted no time in assigning blame. "There responsibility in this matter, to a very great extent, rests upon the City Council. Year after year they have been petitioned and entreated to remove this magazine, to which they have always lent a deaf ear; and, besides, we learn, it was not looked after of late. They now see the result of culpable neglect."

An ominous note followed: "Painful as the circumstances are, we may be thankful the Government magazines did not ignite, for if they had, the entire city would have been destroyed.... We earnestly hope the experience we have had will be a lesson in future, and that steps will be taken on the part of the military authorities to remove the two other magazines without delay."[168]

That didn't happen, as Lieutenant Baddeley of *Niobe* was well aware when he had to send a contingent of workers to move artillery shells belonging to the militia away from the fires just minutes after the explosion. And, still in the future was the harebrained scheme of mining Halifax Harbour off the downtown near Georges Island—during peacetime!

The *Mont Blanc* and *Picton* were not the first ships to put the people of Halifax on edge. In an incident eerily similar to the Halifax Explosion, on July 17, 1899, a ship owned by Standard Oil Co. was tied at the Imperial Oil Co. tank terminal, on the south side of the Bedford Basin, where the Ceres Container Terminal is located now. In the ten tanks of the nine-year-old SS *Maverick* were 10,000 barrels of refined oil, probably kerosene. Between the decks were 2,500 cases—each containing two 5-gallon cans—of White Rose brand lamp oil, an essential household consumable in the days before widespread electrical service. Pumps were unloading oil from the ship up a hill through an 8-inch copper pipe. Around 4:00 P.M., the pipe burst, gushing oil back down the hill and into the ship. It quickly got to the furnaces and, in an instant, tongues of fire appeared from below. Before long, the 5-gallon cans between the decks started exploding.

Men in rowboats were sent to smash the tanker's lower portholes to let water aboard. They cut the lines to keep the fire from destroying the docks and nearby buildings, and let the blazing ship drift into the basin, where the fire could burn itself out. Fear of an explosion was realized when one of the storage tanks aboard the ship blew up with a roar, sending a mass of burning oil heavenward. For a moment it looked as if it would cover the area and annihilate all present, but the huge red ball consumed most of the oil on its way up.

As the outgoing tide moved the ship from the land, there was concern it might be carried into The Narrows, a giant torch to ignite the Richmond Terminals and spread across the city. Instead, it grounded on a reef 200 feet offshore and started to list. As the ship rolled, great clouds of hissing steam went up as the red-hot side and deck struck the cold water. At the same time, oil poured out onto the water and sheets of fire flowed across its surface in a widening circle, which one reporter described as a "burning mountain rising from the bosom of the Basin."[169]

It was still burning at midnight. A Halifax newspaper reported, "What was up to yesterday afternoon a fine looking and well fitted steamer is now a mass of twisted iron, fit only for the junk shop."[170]

Just as they would be wrong about the *Curaca*, they were wrong about the *Maverick*. The next spring, for a fee of $20,000, local salvage captain James Farquhar, whom we have already met, salvaged the wreck and remaining cargo.[171] The ship was rebuilt and carried on for another fifteen years.

On September 10, 1915, history repeated itself on a smaller scale at the same location. The 98-ton schooner *Hiawatha*, built at Lunenburg in 1906, had just loaded at the Imperial Oil Wharf with 400 barrels of gasoline and 100 barrels of oil. While they awaited good weather to depart for Newfoundland, fumes had built up in the galley. When the cook lit the stove, it exploded, quickly igniting the cargo. Three of the five-man crew died and another broke a leg. Only one escaped uninjured.[172]

On December 6, 1917, perhaps the most important asset fighting the fires in the destruction zone was the navy's tug *W. H. Lee*. Ironically, it went out in a blaze of glory on the night of January 29, 1922, but not before giving the authorities a good scare that it might send the new Ocean Terminals docks up in flames. The *Lee*, with 80 tons of newly loaded coal aboard, had been tied at Pier 25 next to two large steamers when a fire started in the stern and the old wooden tug was quickly ablaze. The fire department arrived on the scene, along with the *Weatherspoon*. As with the *Mont Blanc*, four streams of water were of no use. In desperation, Captain Weston nudged the *Weatherspoon* alongside and got a line attached. In the same way that the *Lee*, on December 6, had towed the burning *Musquash* stern-first away from the shipyard wharf and extinguished the fire aboard, the *Weatherspoon* now pulled the flaming *Lee* away stern first from the valuable new ships, docks, and sheds. The *Gladiator* arrived in the nick of time, and together they managed to get it into the stream, where it burned through the night and finally sank.

With the coming of the Second World War, more dangerous traffic continued to pass through the harbour. On April 10, 1942, the SS *Trongate*, with ten thousand cases of ammunition and two hundred drums of toluene aboard, caught fire in the harbour, directly off downtown Halifax and Dartmouth. Fortunately, there were quick-acting navy officers on the scene and swift measures followed. Guns aboard HMCS *Chedabucto*, loaded with 4-inch diameter non-explosive practice rounds, fired into the waterline of the *Trongate*. The

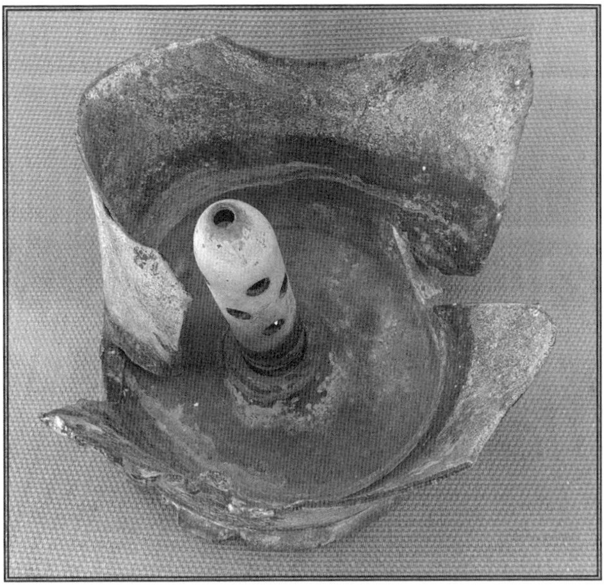

All that remains of a 6-inch artillery shell blown up in the magazine explosion. Next to it on the harbour floor was a series of live anti-aircraft rounds. Their neat arrangement indicated they had been in a wooden box that shipworms had eaten away. (AUTHOR'S COLLECTION)

burning ship sank where it was anchored before serious damage could occur to the surrounding area.

In the 1920s, a vast unpopulated area on the eastern shore of the Bedford Basin had finally been developed for the storage of naval ordnance. At the end of the Second World War, ships from the third largest navy in the world—the RCN—were unloading so much ammunition at the magazine that they ran out of space. With explosives everywhere, the inevitable fire started. In the early evening of July 18, 1945, there was an explosion, not on the same scale as 1917 but enough to get everybody's attention. More explosions ensued. At dusk, Naval Headquarters broadcasted a recommendation to evacuate the surrounding area.

It didn't take long for the nervous locals to get moving. In an hour, there was a traffic lineup 10 miles long, snaking south toward Halifax as people crowded into the area of the Common, Citadel Hill, parks, gravel pits, parking lots, anywhere they could get to spend the night. Explosions around 4:00 A.M. knocked down some people within range and broke windows in houses. By 6:00 P.M. people were allowed to return to their homes. Army sappers then got to work to recover any unexploded ammunition before the 85-foot-wide by 65-foot-deep crater could be filled in.[173]

Although nothing like the Explosion of 1917, the incident is still referred to by many Haligonians as the second Halifax Explosion. That storage area is still there, and thousands of automobiles pass it on daily commutes. Radio reports regularly refer to how heavy or light the traffic is on Magazine Hill. Nobody gives it a thought. I suspect many commuters think first that the "magazine" referred to in the name has something to do with those paper things people used to read.

Nor do they think about nuclear submarines that come into the harbour every so often. It's hard to believe that the nuclear age has been with us for nearly a century. During that time, Halifax Harbour has seen many nuclear-powered submarines, often carrying nuclear missiles. Even though Canada is an avowed non-nuclear nation when it comes to weapons, our two most important allies have the bomb. Every so often, an American or British nuclear submarine quietly arrives and ties up at the Fleet Diving jetty in Eastern Passage. Inquiries by the media invariably receive a "no comment" response.

Trust us.

CHAPTER 14
MOVING ON

The First World War has been recognized as a turning point in world history. Long-standing institutions like monarchies had fallen. It was the end of some empires, the beginning of the end for others. The great Communism experiment had started. Everywhere, there was change.

The First World War had brought the Halifax Explosion, still recognized as an event of epic proportions and up to that time the most destructive explosion of its type outside of Europe. Because it happened in wartime and during a trying period for the Allies, the inquiry did not cast its net very widely. Whether that was by design or because of the mindset of the person convening it, we have no way of knowing. Yes, it was a terrible disaster, some may say, but people were dying by the thousands elsewhere and the sooner we could stop the war, the better. What really mattered was getting the convoys moving again.

As mentioned, the inquiry was less interested in getting at the facts and more interested in assessing blame. They went after two groups, the Halifax Pilotage Commission and the RCN. Change came to both.

THE PILOTS

For the pilots it began in early February 1918, when a Royal Commission into the Halifax pilotage system began under Thomas Robb of Montréal. By March 13, the report was in the hands of Charles Ballantyne, the minister of Marine and Fisheries. The federal government took over administration of the pilot system and appointed Capt. H. St. George Lindsay, a former superintendent of pilots at Québec, to run things. The system of equal shares of the revenue that had been so lucrative was discontinued, and pilots were placed on a salary.[174]

Mackey, the pilot on the *Mont Blanc* on December 6, 1917, did not get his licence back until February 1922, when Ballantyne was gone and a new minister took over at Marine and Fisheries. In the public's mind, though, it was Mackey who was to blame for the Explosion. He retired in 1938 and died on December 31, 1961.

The public demanded more. The dockyard management was replaced. CXO Frederick Wyatt, already relieved from his job, was discharged from the navy on May 3, 1918, his "services no longer required."[175] He left Canada to settle in Boston. Among his many jobs, he became chief officer aboard the *Cacique*, owned by W. R. Grace, the company that had owned the *Curaca*.[176]

And, of course, changes were made to the way ships moved in the harbour. If they were going out, the examining officer was notified to hold all ships outside the gates until those outbound were away. Then, he had to pause for clearance to let any waiting ships enter. Those with explosives were sent to a special anchorage outside the gates until cleared to enter. Munitions ships were held at the Examination Anchorage until orders were received to let them through the gates.

The changes didn't eliminate the risks, however. On February 21, 1918, pilot Walter Brackett was taking the Cunard liner RMS *Carmania* out of the Bedford Basin, with the captain standing beside him. At nearly 20,000 GRT and a length of 630 feet, it was an imposing, powerful ship. Under a tight schedule, they weighed anchor and sped across the basin toward The Narrows. When they were about to enter the gap, Bracket suddenly exclaimed that the signal from *Niobe* was "against us." In other words, they were denied entry into The Narrows. He ordered that the ship be stopped.

The captain, Arthur Rostron of RMS *Carpathia* and *Titanic* fame overrode him, as was his prerogative. They were committed and had to proceed. There wasn't enough room to stop or turn the ship. He told Brackett they would proceed slowly. Brackett explained he would be arrested. Rostron insisted there must be an error, and Brackett could explain it afterwards. Out went the ship. Rostron and the *Carmania* went through the gates and over the horizon, while

Brackett was charged and convicted of wilfully disobeying and neglecting to observe a signal from an examining officer.[177]

THE NAVAL SHUFFLE

The navy, it was asserted, had been doing a sloppy job of handling ship movements in the harbour. As the argument went, when the *Mont Blanc* showed up with its deadly cargo, the Examination Service should have raised the alarm. In response, a red flag should have been flown from the *Mont Blanc*'s masthead, the ship should not have entered the harbour until a clear pathway from the gates to the anchorage had been established, and no ships should have been moving in the other direction.

> **"Red flags mean, all the world over, a ship is working munitions out of her hatches into barges, or from one hatch to another alongside a wharf; or actually working stuff into a barge, she flies a red flag and when the barge is shut off and the holds closed the flag comes down."**
> —Commander Frederick Pasco, acting captain superintendent of HMC Dockyard.[178]

It sounds reasonable in retrospect, but that would have caused serious disruption in the harbour, and the red flag, in Frederick Pasco's words, "would be suicidal—giving information to enemy agents."[179] And should that have been the process for all dangerous cargoes in Halifax during a war, even though it was not the process in similar ports? Requiring extra precaution because a ship had explosives aboard would have been similar to those signs some new parents put in the rear windows of their cars: "Baby on Board," as though the person reading them is required to take special precautions to keep somebody's baby safe. They're doing that anyway; it's one of the requirements of owning a driver's licence!

W. A. Henry, Crown Counsel at the inquiry, noted, "The harbour regulations were sufficient, in my opinion, to safeguard the port, in view of rules of the road designed to prevent collisions, and I cannot see why regulations should have been framed based upon the assumption that the rules of the road would be infringed. The officials charged with the carrying out of the regulations were not, I consider, to blame for not taking precautions not required by the regulations."[180]

Then, there was the matter of the pilots. By coming up the wrong side of the channel, the *Clara* limited the *Imo*'s options. For that, Pilot Renner lost his certificate for three years. If there had not been a collision and explosion, he would not have lost it at all. Besides that, the *Imo* may have been travelling too fast. The *Imo*'s captain, known to be irascible, was running late and was impatient to get out of the harbour.

The inquiry expected those steering the *Mont Blanc* to somehow read the minds of those aboard the *Imo* and cancel the results of their unusual ship handling. The only way to do that would have been to go to the left as soon as they saw that the *Imo* seemed to be wanting their lane. That would have meant passing starboard-to-starboard, which was what Pilot Renner had done. So, the inquiry decided they should have done what the inquiry had punished Renner for, only sooner. Then, when Le Médec and Mackey were left with no other choice but to do that very thing, they were deemed to have caused the collision and explosion.

Another of the many problems with the inquiry was in taking the position that dying absolved From and Hayes from any blame. It was the same with the worst shipwreck in Nova Scotia history—the SS *Atlantic* disaster—when 550 people died because of the incompetence of the second officer. He died in the disaster. Deeming it unseemly to speak ill of the dead, the inquiry ended up with vague generalities as to the cause and penalized otherwise innocent officers.

The Halifax Explosion inquiry's exceedingly brief report started with what may perhaps seem obvious: "The explosion on the S.S. Mont Blanc on December 6 was undoubtedly the result of a collision in the harbour of Halifax between the S.S. Mont Blanc and the S.S. Imo." The court then concluded that whoever caused the collision caused the explosion, and the effort of the inquiry went into digging up all the things and people that contributed to the collision. In the process, the findings essentially ignored a simple insight provided by the senior RCN officer in Halifax and the first naval officer to testify at the inquiry, acting captain superintendent Frederick Pasco. He made this observation: "I don't expect a ship to blow up because she has had a collision."[181]

However, the *Mont Blanc* did just that. Was Pasco naive? He also did not expect a ship to be carrying the lethal combination of materials the *Mont Blanc* was carrying. In wartime, many ships carried explosives. And many ships carried flammable materials. But the *Mont Blanc* was jam-packed with both—and they were crammed so tightly together that sparks from a minor collision found something nearby to ignite and the ensuing flame found something nearby to detonate.

However, all those questions about special handling of the *Mont Blanc* were still valid because of the lethal combination of materials aboard, a mixture with which the CXO was familiar. He testified that three days before the ship's arrival he became aware there were flammables and explosives aboard. When asked what action he took, he answered that he took no action because he did not feel any was necessary.[182] Even Pasco must have been shocked to hear that.

Avoidable disasters often come about not because of an event but because of a series of events, and we normally blame the first one. Using that logic, the first event, and therefore the cause of the Halifax Explosion, was the loading of explosive materials and flammable materials in proximity on a ship. The failure of the inquiry is that its members started their considerations partway through the series of events instead of starting at the beginning—the loading of the *Mont Blanc*.

A lot of lawyers, journalists, and pundits levelled much criticism about pilot error, the fact that the *Mont Blanc* did not fly a red flag, the strange way the *Imo* was handled, the location of the SS *Clara* in The Narrows, the fact that the *Imo* was permitted to leave while the *Mont Blanc* was incoming. All these circumstances and more may have contributed to the collision but that does not change a simple fact. The fault lies with the people who decided the *Mont Blanc* would be loaded with two materials that should never have been put so close together under any circumstances.

Joseph Scanlon notes, "She had been checked out by the Royal Navy in New York, and checked again by the examining officer in Halifax. She had no need to come into harbour other than for safety against possible enemy attack. In the view of the port authorities, the threat to the city was less than the risk of losing a ship loaded with badly needed ammunition. Halifax was deliberately put at risk."[183]

Were those who loaded the *Mont Blanc* incompetent? Probably not. They were just hoping for the best. It happens a lot in wartime.

COURAGE, HEROES, AND MEDALS

On the water that day, like every day in Halifax, navy men and civilians worked alongside one another, often doing the same job. Some vessels were owned by the navy and were crewed by navy sailors, while others were owned by companies and individuals under charter, complete with crew, to a navy. Navy sailors and civilian sailors alike risked their lives and died. Only navy sailors got medals.

Who decides who gets a medal is a subject fraught with incomprehensible emotions, motivations, and circumstances. Not many medals were handed out after the Halifax Explosion, though there were many examples of courage that never caught the attention of those with authority to recommend individuals for special recognition.

The cases of the men who went to the burning *Mont Blanc* are puzzling. The comedian Woody Allen once famously said that "ninety percent of success in life is just showing up." Three vessels—*Niobe*'s pinnace, the whaler from HMS *Highflyer*, and the *Stella Maris*—showed up at the *Mont Blanc* in the final minutes before it blew up. We know next to nothing about what transpired in those brief moments, but there were more than thirty men on the scene, and only four medals were later bestowed—three to the highest ranked people.

Two men from the pinnace received the Albert Medal for gallantry in life-saving at sea. But they did not save anybody. By giving them medals, there is an assumption that those two did something beyond what the other five did. What was it? Nobody in the boat survived to tell their story. Were the medals awarded because they, as Woody Allen would say, showed up? If that was the reason, why did only the senior ranked men aboard the boat receive them?

Of those who went in the pinnace, the Government of Canada website states, "They first attempted to tow the burning ship, which had been abandoned by its crew, away from populated areas. When that effort failed, they tried to fight the fire."[184] That is completely untrue and would be laughable if it did not so glibly dismiss the efforts of the *Stella Maris* men, the ones who did fight the fire briefly before concluding it was a waste of time and who were preparing to attempt the tow.

The case of the two men rescuing the divers is straightforward. They went above and beyond the call, exposing themselves to extreme danger, putting forth extraordinary effort and saving two lives, for which they received medals. The two RN men on the *Musquash* also risked their lives and they received medals. Good on them.

In the case of the whaler, the Albert Medal in gold was awarded to Lieutenant-Commander Triggs for life-saving at sea. What did Triggs do that was so far beyond what others in his boat did that he should deserve the medal? Yes, it took courage, but it required no more than was required of the men rowing the boat. The words of another naval officer are telling: "Unlike the hands sent from the *Niobe*, the *Highflyer*'s party knew the nature of the cargo they were approaching, and Commander Triggs was posthumously awarded the Albert Medal."[185] He is, in essence, saying that these brave men knew what they were going into and they died. Therefore, their commanding officer deserved a medal. Equally puzzling is the case of the only survivor from the whaler. William Becker also received a medal—for surviving, it would appear.

Despite claims that those in at least one of the three boats knew about the *Mont Blanc*'s cargo, subsequent research has indicated that nobody in the three boats knew anything about the cargo.[186]

BORROWED SHIPS GET RETURNED

Eight months after the Explosion, on August 29, the *Knight Templar* was back in Halifax after sailing with HMS *Cumberland* and a destroyer to escort a convoy from Plymouth. It then headed to Sydney to pick up another convoy bound for London. On November 10, the *Knight Templar* was part of the escort force for a convoy departing Baltimore for London. The next day the war ended.

After completing the convoy and spending some time in London, the ship went to Liverpool and the guns and other property of the RN were removed. On December 31, 1918, HMS *Knight Templar* was declared—to use another naval term that has drifted into the language—out of commission, but it still had a long life ahead before finally being scrapped in 1954.

Changuinola was at Liverpool when the war ended. It never returned to Halifax, but two days after the Armistice, it departed for Saint John, NB, still a warship. It arrived on November 23 to take on a general cargo and was back in Liverpool on December 17. Over the next two weeks, guns and ammunition were removed. It entered the Langton Dry Dock on December 30, where it remained until January 13 while being converted back to a merchant ship. RN sailors started leaving on the fourteenth, and on the sixteenth came the official notification that the ship was to be paid off. It ceased to be HMS *Changuinola.*

Named after a city in Panama, *Changuinola* served in the RN from December 1914 to January 1919. It spent most of those four years at sea in a war zone. Yet, the closest it came to being destroyed was on a calm, sunny morning while peacefully anchored in a harbour that had provided sanctuary to RN ships for close to two hundred years. Who would have believed it?

SS *Changuinola* went back to its owners Elders & Fyffes and continued as a run-of-the-mill freighter, until it was broken up in 1933.

APPENDIX A

LETTERS FROM CHIEF EXAMINING OFFICER TO CAPTAIN SUPERINTENDENT, HMC DOCKYARD[187]

June 21, 1917
R. 103
Captain Superintendent
H.M.C. Dockyard

Submitted for your consideration that my orders given to the pilots re movements of shipping into and out of the ports (as contained in my W.P.O. 6 and W.P.M. 8 of the 4th May last), are not being carried out, reports coming in very occasionally and spasmodically and making it difficult to trace shipping movements in the port and impossible to regulate sailings.

COMMANDER R.N.R.

August 1, 1917
R. 104
Captain Superintendent
H.M.C. Dockyard
N.A.P. Aug. 1st. 1917

Submitted for your earnest consideration that some action re W.A.P. of June 21st last in connection with pilots not carrying out orders re arriving and sailing of vessels. At present no reports are being sent in by the pilots and there is absolutely no means of controlling shipping unless these orders are carried out.

COMMANDER R.N.R.

September 5, 1917
R. 105
Captain Superintendent
H.M.C. Dockyard

With reference to my W.A.P. of June 21st and Aug. 1st, it is submitted for your earnest consideration that some action, if not already taken, may be immediately taken. I understand that, under the Defence of the Realm regulations, the competent naval authority i.e. yourself, has the power to punish these pilots for breaches of orders.

Under existing circumstances, it is impossible to berth vessels properly in the stream, and vessels are continually sailing without any reference to myself, such as contained in my orders to the pilots and regardless of whether the net defences are open or not, on many occasions having to drop anchor on arriving at these defences until they have been opened at the proper hour. Under these conditions it is not possible to regulate the traffic in the harbour, and it is submitted that I cannot in this regard accept the responsibility of any accident occurring.

COMMANDER R.N.R.

APPENDIX B

SHIPS IN OR NEAR HALIFAX HARBOUR DECEMBER 6, 1917

What follows is an assimilated record of some, but not necessarily all, the ships that were in Halifax Harbour and experienced the explosion and its aftermath. The physical details of the ships provided here are for that time period. Ships regularly changed hands and were renamed, modified, and registered in other places, complicating the process of documenting them. The ship's official number stayed with a British-registered ship as long as it was owned somewhere in the British Empire. "Registration closed…" does not mean the vessel no longer existed; it meant that it was no longer British-registered.

STEAMSHIPS THAT ARRIVED ON DECEMBER 6, AFTER THE EXPLOSION

They remained outside the gates during the blizzard. As far as we know, all except *Clara* arrived after the explosion, but would have heard and seen the blast. They had their own challenges to face, spending the night in an exposed anchorage in the outer part of the harbour while getting pummelled by a blizzard.

Name, Number; Arrival; Departure; Type; Builder, Location, Year; Length / Tonnage; Fate

A. E. Ames 114449; from Toronto, December 6, shortly after explosion; steel freighter; Northumberland Shipbuilding, Howdon-on-Tyne, UK, 1903; 246 feet / 1,637 GRT; at Examination Anchorage during storm; damaged when *Northern King* dragged its anchor and they collided; sunk by mine off Sardinia, 1940.

Iroquois 124067; from Port Arthur, TX, December 6; to Norfolk, VA, December 15 towing a six-masted oil barge, *Navahoe*; steel tanker; Harland & Wolff, Belfast, 1907; 476 feet / 9,202 GRT; the "horse and cart" as the two ships were called, made sixteen voyages between Port Arthur and Halifax, averaging 10 knots, delivering 290,000 tons of oil; from 1930 to 1936 acted as an oil storage facility in Venezuela; was towed out and scuttled in 400 fathoms.

King Edward 120671; from Montréal, December 6; to England with December 11 convoy; steel freighter; R. Stephenson & Son, Newcastle, 1906; 355 feet / 4,357 GRT; broken up in Italy 1932.

Levisa 214484; from New York, 1:15 P.M. December 6; to Bordeaux, with December 11 convoy; steel freighter; Detroit Shipbuilding, Wyandotte, MI, 1916; 251 feet / 2,118 GRT.

Manchester Hero 135366; from Montréal 1:30 P.M. December 6; to England December 16; steel freighter; Northumberland Shipbuilding, Howdon-on-Tyne, UK, 1916; 400 feet / 5,738 GRT; sold to a company in Genoa, 1939. Torpedoed and sunk September 3, 1941, by HMS *Utmost.*

Northern King 130420; from Montréal, December 6; to New York, December 16; steel freighter; Globe Iron Works, Cleveland, OH, 1888; 299.5 feet / 2,476 deadweight tons; US Shipping Board acquired it in 1917, had it cut in two at Buffalo, to fit through the Welland Canal, towed to Montréal, and put back together; scrapped in Italy 1926.

Northern Wave 130437; from Montréal, December 6; to New York, December 16; steel freighter; Globe Iron Works, Cleveland, 1889; 299.5 feet / 2,476 deadweight tons; US Shipping Board acquired it in 1917, had it cut in two at Buffalo, to fit through the Welland Canal, towed to Montréal, and put back together; scrapped at Genoa, 1926.

North Wind 130419; from Montréal, December 6; to New York, December 16; steel freighter; Globe Iron Works, Cleveland, 1888; 299.5 feet / 2,476 deadweight tons; US Shipping Board acquired it in 1917, had it cut in two at Buffalo, to fit through the Welland Canal, towed to Montréal, and put back together; stranded July 1, 1926, in Georgian Bay and later slipped into deep water.

Saranac From Montréal, December 6; to New York, May 28, 1918; steel Great Lakes freighter; Globe Iron Works, Cleveland, 1890; 307 feet / 2,669 GRT; US Shipping Board; cut in two by Buffalo Dry Dock Co., towed to Lauzon, QC, rejoined by Davie Shipbuilding & Repairing; at Examination Anchorage during the storm; ran ashore on McNabs Island; sank March 13, 1920, 100 miles off Georgia, US; nineteen lives lost.

Singapore 123729; arrived December 6; to England with December 11 convoy; steel freighter; Archibald McMillan & Son, Dumbarton, UK, 1906; 364 feet / 4,262 GRT; broken up Port Glasgow, UK, 1938.

Swainby 135603. From Baltimore, December 6; to England with December 11 convoy; steel freighter; Ropner & Sons, Stockton-on-Tees, UK, 1917; 390 feet / 5,811 GRT; torpedoed and sank by U-13 April 17, 1940, north of Great Britain.

Tacoma From UK early afternoon December 6; departed December 9; USN cruiser; some 50 miles away when explosion occurred; Union Iron Works, Mare Island, CA, 1903; 309 feet / 3,200 tons displacement.

Trojan 120837; from Baltimore, December 6; to England with December 11 convoy; steel freighter; William Pickersgill & Sons, Sunderland, UK,

1905; 375 feet / 4,017 GRT; under German ownership, torpedoed by HMS *Truant* and sunk October 23, 1941; thirty-five survivors picked up by a nearby freighter.

Von Steuben Arrived December 6; departed December 10; American troop transport; AG Vulcan, Stettin, GER; 1901; 637 feet / 11,476 GRT; scrapped in 1923.

OTHER VESSELS OUTSIDE THE GATES NEARBY WHEN THE EXPLOSION OCCURRED

Acadien 112239; about 15 miles away, inbound to Halifax; wooden coastal steamer; Thompson Shipbuilding, Saint John, 1904; 183 feet / 1,011 GRT.

Baleine 129916, minesweeping the harbour approaches; fishing vessel; Dunkirk, FR, 1907; 159 feet / 418 GRT; wrecked off Isle Madame, Cape Breton, September 30, 1921.

Lady Evelyn 109680; patrolling outside the harbour; steel auxiliary patrol ship; John Jones & Sons, Tranmere, UK, 1901; 189 feet / 483 deadweight tons; scrapped in Bedwell Bay, BC, in 1936.

PV-VII Minesweeping the harbour approaches; fishing trawler; built at Noank, CT, as the *Rowland H. Wilcox*; 132 feet / 247 tons.

CONVOY SHIPS THAT ARRIVED BEFORE DECEMBER 6 AND EXPERIENCED THE EXPLOSION INSIDE THE GATES

Name, Number; Arrival; Departure; Type; Builder, Location, Year; Length / Tonnage; Fate

Alexander Kjelland From Baltimore, December 1; bound for England; steel freighter; registered at Bergen, NOR; sank in 1951.

Ardgryfe 127551; from Montréal, December 4; to England with December 11 convoy; steel freighter; Russell Co., Port Glasgow, UK, 1909; 400 feet / 4,897 GRT.

Asuncion de Larrinaga 115311; from Saint John, December 3; to England December 11; steel freighter; Russell & Co., Port Glasgow, UK, 1902; 370 feet / 4,142 GRT; broken up in Japan in 1933.

Bayramento 139196; from Montréal, November 22; to Europe with the December 11 convoy; steel freighter; Palmer's Co. Ltd., Newcastle, 1900; 452 feet / 7,017 GRT.

Borderer 119188; from Montréal, December 1; to England with the December 11 convoy; steel freighter; Russell & Co., Port Glasgow, UK, 1904; 375 feet / 4,872 GRT; converted to tanker; in 1939, under German ownership, scuttled in the Gulf of Mexico October 23 to avoid capture by HMS *Caradoc* and HMCS *Saguenay*.

Buckleigh 140320; from Montréal, December 3; to Europe December 16; steel freighter; Archibald McMillan & Son, Dumbarton, UK, 1904; 400 feet / 4,920 GRT; registered in 1923 at Genoa; renamed *Delia*; sunk by submarine HMS *Turbulent* in Mediterranean April 16, 1942; one of nine Italian merchant ships sunk by *Turbulent* and its Victoria Cross–winning captain John Linton, credited with sinking a cruiser, a destroyer, a U-boat, and twenty-eight supply ships.

Cairncross 133522; from Montréal, November 30; to Europe December 11; steel freighter; W. Doxford & Sons, Sunderland, UK, 1913; 370 feet / 4,016 GRT; sunk by U-62 May 28, 1918, 110 miles NNW of the Azores; no casualties.

Calonne 110121; from Saint John, December 5; to Saint John January 10, 1918; steel freighter; Short Brothers, Sunderland, UK, 1899; 370 feet / 4,019 GRT; broken up at Genoa, in March 1929.

Cherryleaf 140278; from Montréal, December 4; to Europe December 15; Royal Fleet Auxiliary oil tanker; Sir Raylton Dixon & Co., Middlesbrough, UK, 1917; 405 feet / 5,934 GRT.

Chicago 139314; from New York, November 29; to England December 11 in convoy; steel freighter; Earle's Shipbuilding and Engineering Co., Hull, UK, 1917; 445 feet / 7,709 GRT; torpedoed and sank by UB-17 on July 8, 1918.

Clan MacDougall 119184; arrived December 1; left in convoy December 11 for England; steel freighter; Wm. Doxford & Sons, Sunderland, UK, 1904; 385 feet / 4,710 GRT; torpedoed by UB-49 March 15, 1918.

Clematis 109887; from Montréal, December 4; to Europe December 11; steel freighter; Tyne Iron Shipbuilding Co., Willington Quay, UK, 1898; 345 feet / 3,406 GRT; broken up at Savona, IT, in 1930.

Clara From New York, December 6; to Europe December 11; steel freighter; Russell & Co., Port Glasgow, UK, 1903; 332 feet / 3,932 GRT; sank in a hurricane near Cuba in 1926.

Corfe Castle 114773, from Montréal, December 5; to Europe with the December 11 convoy; steel freighter; Barclay, Curle & Co., Glasgow, 1901; 402 feet / 4,592 GRT; broken up at Lübeck, GER, in 1933.

Corinthian 111257; from Montréal, November 29; to England December 16; passenger liner of the Allan Line; Workman, Clark & Co., Belfast, 1900; 430 feet / 7,333 GRT; on December 14, 1918, ran aground off Brier Island, NS, in the Bay of Fundy, travelling from Saint John, to Glasgow; a total loss.

Curaca 135178; from Montréal, December 3; departed for New York, under tow July 25, 1918; steel freighter; Joseph L. Thompson & Sons, Sunderland, UK, 1912; 403 feet / 6,386 GRT; repaired and put back to work; broken up at Osaka, JA, 1934.

Eole From Rotterdam, December 5; to Baltimore, December 11; steel freighter; Joseph T. Eltringham & Co., North Shields, UK, 1916; 330 feet /

3,143 GRT; RN sailor Frank Baker wrote in his diary December 6 they had to put down a riot among the crew aboard ship that afternoon; sank off the coast of Spain 1921.

Florence H. 215643; from New York, December 1; to Le Havre December 11; steel freighter; Great Lakes Engineering Works, Ecorse, MI, 1917; 372 feet / 3,819 GRT; exploded and burned near Quiberon, FR, night of April 17, 1918, with some forty deaths.

Franklin 213624; from New York, December 3; to Europe December 11; steel freighter; New York Shipbuilding Co., Camden, NJ, 1915; 368.5 feet / 5,226 GRT; wrecked 1945 near Cape Elizabeth, ME.

Gouverneur de Lantsherre 26663; from Rotterdam, November 30; to New York, December 11; steel freighter; A. Rodger & Co., Port Glasgow, UK, 1905; 360 feet / 4,147 GRT; broken up in 1934.

Graciana 118054; from St. John's, NL, November 30; to St. John's and Liverpool, UK, December 12; steel freighter; Charles Connell & Co., Scotstoun, 1903; 361 feet / 3,536 GRT; broken up in Turkey 1932.

Hovland 110524; from Baltimore, November 7; to New York, February 9, 1918; steel freighter; J. L. Thompson & Sons, Sunderland, UK, 1898; 325 feet / 2,996 GRT; struck rudder on The Sisters shoal on the way in; in dry dock when the explosion struck; wrecked in 1923 off Algiers.

Imo 93837; from Rotterdam, December 3; to Newport News, VA, July 19, 1918 for repairs; steel freighter; Harland & Wolff, Belfast, as *Runic*, for the White Star Line, 1889; 431 feet / 5,043 GRT; wrecked in the Falkland Islands in November 1921.

Indien From New York, to England December 11; steel freighter; Flensburger Schiffbau-Gesellschaft, Flensburg, GER, 1902; 390 feet / 4,199 GRT.

J. A. McKee 125442; from Sydney, NS, November 26; to New York, January 1, 1918; Great Lakes coal carrier; Swan Hunter & Wigham Richardson, Newcastle-on-Tyne, UK, 1908; 248 feet / 2,158 GRT; wrecked March 30, 1940, near Louisbourg.

Kanawha 102122; from Saint John, November 25; to London, in convoy December 11; steel freighter; Alexander Stephen & Son, Govan, UK, 1893; 370 feet / 3,884 GRT; broken up at La Spezia, 1923.

Knut Hamsun From Montréal, November 22; to Europe with the December 11 convoy; steel freighter; Burmeister & Wain, Copenhagen, 1907; 310 feet / 2,728 GRT; ran aground March 16, 1931, and was wrecked.

Kong Foo From Norway December 2; to New York, December 7; steel freighter; 1,902 NRT.

Lake Manitoba 113497; from Montréal, December 3; to England December 16; Canadian Pacific passenger liner; C. S. Swan & Hunter, Wallsend-on-Tyne, UK, 1901; 470 feet / 9,674 GRT; gutted by fire at Montréal August 26, 1918, and was scuttled; raised and repaired; renamed *Iver Heath* of Bishop Navigation Co., Montréal; broken up 1924.

Maindy Abbey 106961; from Montréal, November 25; to France December 11; steel freighter; Furness Withy & Co., West Hartlepool, UK, 1897; 340 feet / 3,743 GRT.

Manchester Corporation 108844; from Montréal, November 30; to England December 16; steel freighter; Furness Withy & Co., West Hartlepool, UK, 1899; 430.5 feet / 5,397 GRT; scrapped at Barrow, UK, 1929.

Marie Z. Michalinos From Norfolk, VA November 26; to Europe with the December 11 convoy; steel freighter; W. Gray and Co., West Hartlepool, UK, 1902; 332 feet / 2,864 GRT; broken up at Rosyth, UK, 1936.

Middleham Castle 128049; from England November 24; to New York, on Christmas Day; steel freighter; William Hamilton & Co., Port Glasgow, UK, 1910; 380 feet / 4,534 GRT; torpedoed and sunk 1941.

Mississippi From New York, December 5; to France with the December 11 convoy; steel freighter; Chantier Naval de Normandie, FR, 1912; 410 feet / 6,403 GRT.

Mobila From New York, November 29; returned to New York December 8 because of leaky tanks; steel freighter; Armstrong Mitchell & Co., Newcastle, 1886; 308 feet /1,909 GRT.

Mont Blanc From New York, December 5; blew up at Halifax; steel freighter; Sir Raylton Dixon and Co., Middlesbrough, UK, 1899; 320 feet / 3,279 GRT.

Nieuw Amsterdam From New York, November 26; to Rotterdam, December 16; passenger liner; Harland & Wolff, Belfast, 1906; 600 feet / 14,278 GRT, broken up in Japan in 1932.

Noruega Arrived Halifax, December 5; departed for New York, December 7; steel freighter; Fevigs Jernskibsbyggeri, Grimstad, NOR, 1909; 332 feet / 3,627 GRT; as SS *Brisbane* was damaged in air attack June 8, 1938, at Denia, ES, during the Spanish Civil War, and was beached and scrapped.

Patroclus 105395; from Montréal, November 30; to England with the December 11 convoy; steel freighter; Workman, Clark & Co., Belfast, 1896; 422 feet / 5,312 GRT.

Picton 123165; from Montréal, November 25; to Sydney, NS, August 14, 1918; steel freighter; Richardson, Duck & Co., Thornaby-on-Tees, UK, 1906; 378 feet / 5,083 GRT renamed *Herta Engeline Fritzen*, *Picton*; wrecked October 26, 1941, off the Hook of Holland.

Polyphemus 120945; from New York, December 5; to Europe by convoy December 11; steel freighter; Armstrong, Whitworth & Co., Thornaby-on-Tees, UK, 1906; 392 feet / 4,968 GRT, broken up at Osaka, JA, 1930.

Pomeranian 85193; from Montréal, December 4; to Europe with December 11 convoy; passenger liner of the Allan Line; Earle's Shipbuilding Co., Hull, UK, 1882; 381 feet / 4,241 GRT; torpedoed and sunk April 15, 1918.

Saint Bede 131408; from Montréal, December 5; convoy to Europe December 11; steel freighter; Russell & Co., Port Glasgow, UK, 1911; 405 feet / 4940 GRT.

Strathearn 121282; from Newport News, VA, November 29; to England December 16; steel freighter; Grangemouth & Greenock Dockyard Co., Greenock, UK, 1906; 370 feet / 4,419 GRT; bombed and sunk in the Irish Sea, September 7, 1941.

Sygna From Norway December 4; to the US December 10; steel freighter; Sir Raylton Dixon & Co., Middlesbrough, UK, 1907; 360 feet / 3,881 GRT; broken up at Bombay (Mumbai), 1955.

Wagland From New York, December 5; to Europe with the December 11 convoy; steel freighter; Fujinagata Dockyard Co., Osaka, JA, 1916; 272 feet / 1,902 GRT.

War Monarch 140361; from Montréal, November 29; to England with the December 11 convoy; steel freighter; Union Iron Works, Alameda, CA, 1917; 410 feet / 7,887 GRT; torpedoed by UB-57 in the English Channel February 14, 1918.

War Queen 140346; from Montréal, November 30; to England with the December 11 convoy; steel freighter; Kawasaki Dockyard Co., Kobe, JA, 1917; 385 feet / 5,870 GRT.

War Soldier 140379; from Montréal, November 29; to England December 16; steel freighter; Kawasaki Dockyard Co., Kobe, JA, 1917; 415 feet / 7,521 GRT.

Yonne 129522; from Montréal, December 3; to Europe December 11; steel freighter; A. McMillan & Son, Dumbarton, UK, 1910; 377 feet / 4,385 GRT; registration closed 1928.

RCN SHIPS THAT EXPERIENCED THE EXPLOSION INSIDE THE GATES

Name, Number; Location; Type; Builder, Location, Year; Length / Tonnage; Fate

Acadia 133535; Narrows entrance SE corner of basin; guard ship; Swan Hunter NE Ltd., Newcastle, 1913; 170 feet / 849 GRT, with armament and configured as patrol ship 1,067 tons displacement; still afloat.

CD-9 Narrows; wooden drifter; Canadian Vickers, Montréal, 1917; 84 feet / 99 GRT.

CD-14 Taking injured to *Old Colony*; wooden drifter; Canadian Vickers, Montréal, 1917; 84 feet / 99 GRT.

CD-73 Went to burning *Mont Blanc* to offer assistance; wooden drifter; Canadian Vickers, Montréal, 1917; 84 feet / 99 GRT.

Canada 116870; dockyard Jetty 2; patrol ship; Vickers, Sons and Maxim, Barrow-in-Furness, UK, 1904; 206 feet / 411 GRT, displaced 556 tons; paid off 1919 and sank 50 nautical miles south of Miami, in 1926.

Cartier 129745; dockyard Jetty 3; hydrographic survey ship served in both world wars, used as armed patrol ship; Swan Hunter & Wigham Richardson, Newcastle, 1911; 164 feet / 556 GRT; paid off 1945, scuttled off Sydney, NS, 1957.

CC1 & CC2 Jetty 1; submarines; Seattle, 1914; sold for scrap 1920.

Festubert near Jetty 1; Battle class steel trawler; Polson Iron Works, Toronto, 1917; 130 feet / 320 tons displacement; gate vessel in Halifax, during the Second World War; scuttled off Burgeo, NL, 1971.

Grilse Jetty 2; yacht *Winchester* repurposed as patrol ship; Yarrows & Co., Glasgow, 1912; 202 feet / 292 tons displacement; sold 1922; lost in a hurricane 1938.

Gulnare 97071; Narrows entrance SW corner of Basin; guard ship; Charles Connell & Co., Glasgow, 1893; 137 feet / 262 GRT; became a lightship in 1925; broken up around 1948.

Hochelaga 138074; Jetty 4; private yacht *Waterus* converted to auxiliary patrol ship; Hawthorn & Co., Leith, UK, 1900; 193 feet / 628 GRT; sold in 1923 and became Pictou-to-Charlottetown ferry; last seen laid up in Cyprus 1953.

Margaret 135668; Jetty 2; customs patrol vessel repurposed as auxiliary patrol ship; John I. Thorneycroft & Co., Southampton, 1914; 182 feet / 756 GRT: returned to customs work, chasing rum-runners during Prohibition; sold to Brazil 1932.

Niobe Hospital wharf north of Jetty 4; heavy cruiser; Vickers, Barrow-in-Furness, UK, 1897; 462.5 feet /11,177 tons displacement; scrapped at Philadelphia, 1922.

PV-V Jetty 3 awaiting a refit; herring trawler converted to minesweeper; Essex, MA, 1911; 155.6 feet / 323 tons displacement.

RN SHIPS THAT EXPERIENCED THE EXPLOSION INSIDE THE GATES

Name, Number; Location; Type; Builder, Location, Year; Length / Tonnage; Fate

Changuinola 134701; anchored in stream off dockyard; armed merchant cruiser; Swan Hunter & Wigham Richardson, Wallsend-on-Tyne, UK, 1912; 410 feet / 5,978 GRT; broken up 1933.

Highflyer Anchored in stream off dockyard; light cruiser; Fairfield Shipbuilding & Engineering, Govan, UK, 1899; 372 feet / 5,650 tons displacement; paid off 1921.

Knight Templar 120900; commissioned escort ship; Deepwater Pier 3; Charles Connell & Co., Glasgow, 1905; 470 feet / 7,175 GRT; broken up at Hamburg, 1954.

UNITED STATES GOVERNMENT SHIPS THAT EXPERIENCED THE EXPLOSION INSIDE THE GATES

Name / Number /Location / Type / Builder & Location, Year / Length / Tonnage / Fate

USCGS *Morrill* Dartmouth Cove; US Coast Guard cutter; Pusey & Jones, Wilmington, 1889; 145 feet / 288 tons displacement; decommissioned and sold 1928.

USS *Old Colony* 204528; Nova Scotia Hospital Dock, Dartmouth; passenger liner Eastern Steamship Corp.; William Cramp & Sons, Philadelphia, 1907; 375 feet / 4,779 GRT.

LOCAL STEAMSHIPS THAT EXPERIENCED THE EXPLOSION INSIDE THE GATES

Name, Number; Location; Type; Builder, Location, Year; Length / Tonnage; Fate

Chebucto 108683; lay-up dock for repairs; steel harbour ferry; John Shearer & Son, Glasgow, 1897; 125 feet / 578 GRT; sold to Loudee Steel Corp. Montréal, 1951, after fifty-two years of service.

Dartmouth 90889; ferry terminal; wooden side-wheeler harbour ferry; Burrell-Johnson Iron Co., Yarmouth, NS, 1888; 136 feet / 311 GRT; scrapped at Dartmouth 1935.

Elaine 111156; steel coastal steamer; Newburgh, NY, 1888; 113 feet / 272 deadweight tons; provided service between Campbellton, NB, and Gaspé, QC.

Halifax 129590; ferry track mid-crossing; steel harbour ferry; Napier & Miller, Old Kilpatrick on the Clyde, UK, 1911; 125 feet / 295 GRT; sold to the Dartmouth Scrapyard, 1956.

Mackay-Bennett 89965; docked south of Deep Water Terminus; cable repair ship; Fairfield Shipbuilding and Engineering, Govan, UK, 1888; 259 feet / 1,731 GRT; famous as one of two Halifax cable ships sent to recover bodies from *Titanic*; scrapped at Plymouth, UK, 1965.

Minia 56762; docked south of *Mackay-Bennett*; cable repair ship; London & Glasgow Engineering & Iron Shipbuilding Co., Govan, UK, 1867; 328.5 feet / 2,061 GRT; involved in recovery of bodies from the *Titanic* in 1912; broken up 1921 in the Netherlands.

Scotia 122423, wooden coastal steamer; tied up for the winter at downtown wharf of G. S. Campbell Co.; Abraham Ernst, Mahone Bay, NS, 1907; 139 feet / 376 GRT; burned and sank at Drum Head, NS, August 1921.

Tyrian 60459; Smith's Wharf; cable ship; Robert Duncan & Co., Glasgow, 1869; 238 feet / 1,039 GRT.

LOCAL TUGS AND DUTY BOATS THAT EXPERIENCED THE EXPLOSION INSIDE THE GATES

Name, Number; Location; Type; Builder, Location, Year; Length / Tonnage; Fate

Boonton 131211; Jetty 4; wooden tug; Philadelphia, 1871; 75 feet / 115 GRT; register closed 1938, when *Boonton* was sixty-seven years old.

Cruizer 104606; Farquhar's Wharf; iron tug; William Hamilton & Co., Port Glasgow, UK, 1895; 150 feet / 380 GRT; register closed 1953.

Delbert D 126806; wooden tug; Meteghan River, NS, 1910; 61 feet / 44 GRT; registry closed in 1919.

Despatch Boat Dockyard; 45 feet long.

Douglas H. Thomas 101291; shipyard wharf; steel tug; Bethlehem Steel Sparrows Point Yard, MD, 1892; 117 feet / 212 GRT; sank in Ingonish Harbour, NS, in 1924.

F. W. Roebling 113782; Campbell's Wharf; wooden tug; Milford, DE, 1890; 102 feet / 162 GRT; registry closed 1938.

Gladiator 61393; Campbell's Wharf; wooden tug; Brooklyn, 1864; 74 feet / 70 GRT; registry closed 1938, when *Gladiator* was seventy-four years old.

Goliah 75819; wooden tug; McFatridge's Wharf; Philadelphia, 1863; 88 feet / 147 GRT; involved with wreck of SS *Atlantic* 1873, registry closed 1921.

Gopher 131308; dockyard; steel tug; Garston Graving Dock & Shipbuilding Co., near Liverpool, UK, 1910; 100 feet / 198 GRT; scrapped at Davie Shipyard Sorel, 1961.

Hilford 122426; Pier 9; wooden launch; Alvin Stevens, Northwest Cove, Tancook Island, NS, 1908; 65 feet / 38 GRT; wrecked in the explosion; registration closed 1920.

Jutland Basin; motor duty boat of the metalworking firm Burns & Kelleher.

Lily Tug; Eastern Passage, NS.

Maggie M. 94752; downtown wharf; wooden tug; Portland, NB, 1888; 68 feet / 66 GRT; registry closed 1938.

Merrimac 74264; mid-basin; wooden tug; Quebec, 1876; 73 feet / 86 GRT.

Mouton 130629; downtown wharf; wooden tug; Liverpool, NS, 1913; 82 feet / 53 GRT.

Musquash 131307; shipyard wharf; steel tug; Garston Graving Dock & Shipbuilding Co. near Liverpool, UK, 1910; 100 feet / 198 GRT; sank August 4 1921, after colliding with a barge it was towing in heavy seas near Louisbourg; crew survived.

Nereid 133751; anchored near Jetty 4, gate vessel; Waterborough, NB, 1912; 53.5 feet / 40 GRT; registry closed 1938.

Olearylee 131209; downtown wharf; wooden steamer; Liverpool, NS, 1905; 77 feet / 76 GRT.

Ragus 138348; shipyard wharf; new wooden tug; John McLean & Sons, Mahone Bay, NS, 1917; 72 feet / 78 GRT; sank with all hands—five deaths; refloated and repaired, registry closed 1948.

Sambro 134463; steel tug; Halifax Graving Dock Co., 1915; 55 feet / 45 GRT; sank in Explosion, refloated ten years later, equipped with diesel engine, renamed *Erg*; cut down July 6, 1943, and sunk in Basin by Norwegian ship *Norelg*, with loss of nineteen men.

Sir Hugh Allan 130534; downtown wharf; steel tug; Vickers, Barrow-in-Furness, UK, 1911; 130 feet / 354 GRT; sank close to shore Sorel, 1972; raised and scrapped the next year.

Speedy II 104920; harbour gate; examination vessel; Henry Robb Ltd., Leith Docks, Edinburgh, 1896; 115 feet / 252 GRT; sold in 1920 and was for a while the ferry between Rivière-du-Loup and Tadoussac, QC; registry closed 1938.

Stella Maris 117528; Pier 6; wooden tug; Samuda Dockyard, London, 1882; 126 feet / 229 GRT; sustained greatest number deaths of local sailors of any vessel, crushed by ice and destroyed off Newfoundland's northeast coast March 14, 1925.

Togo 116741; south of Jetty 1; wooden tug; Halifax, 1904; 80 feet / 97 GRT.

Trusty 107118; wooden launch; LaHave, NS, 1898; 77 feet /58 GRT; used as despatch boat for guard ships in the basin. In the Explosion, it was pierced by a large plate from the *Mont Blanc*, which struck and cut off a portion of the cook's foot. Registry closed 1938.

Wasp B. 126902; shipyard wharf; wooden tug; Mahone Bay, NS, 1910; 43 feet / 19 GRT; registry closed 1938.

W. H. Lee 134548; Jetty 4; wooden derrick tug; USA, 1898: 129 feet / 317 GRT; burned night of January 29, 1922.

W. M. Weatherspoon 94697; Hendry's Wharf; wooden tug; Digby, NS, 1890; 70 feet / 59 GRT; registry closed 1938.

Wilfred C 103713; harbour gate; wooden gate vessel; Yarmouth, NS, 1897; 80 feet / 99 GRT; registry closed 1938.

VESSELS THAT PROBABLY EXPERIENCED THE EXPLOSION BUT HAVE NOT BEEN CONFIRMED

Name, Number; Type; Builder, Location, Year; Length / Tonnage; Fate

Amphitrite 112121; wooden wrecking tug; Clarence A. Larder, Mahone Bay, NS, 1903; 111 feet / 149 GRT; arrived December 5 towing disabled schooner *Herbert May* to Furness Withy Wharf. Halifax was *Amphitrite*'s home base; likely it was still in harbour the next day when the Explosion occurred.

Batiscan 131314; steel coal carrier; Shorts Brothers, Sunderland, UK, 1911; 375 feet / 4,836 GRT; arrived Halifax, December 4 with no notification of departure date; lost off southwestern Nova Scotia with all hands March 15, 1918—forty-one deaths.

Beaverton 125440; steel freighter; Robert Stephenson & Co., Hebburn-on-Tyne, UK, 1908; 249 feet / 1,012 GRT; entered harbour on an unspecified date, departed with January 11 convoy.

Coastal Drifters 13, 26, 27, 53, 74 are mentioned in records with indications they may have been in the harbour December 6, 1917.

Davis McNab 130589; wooden boat; Mahone Bay, NS, 1912; 68.5 feet / 53 GRT; owned by McNab Resort Co., Halifax; in 1917, businessman Arthur J. Davis ran park & "pleasure grounds," complete with soda pop bottling plant on the island; name of vessel and ownership indicate A. J. Davis probably owned the boat to support his business.

Glasgow 102662; steel freighter; W. B. Thompson & Co., Dundee, 1894; 240 feet / 1,068 GRT; clue it might have been in harbour on December 6, 1917, is a death record for assistant cook Tam Laung, stating he was from SS *Glasgow*.

Lansdowne 90604; wooden RCN auxiliary patrol ship; Maccan, NS, 1884; 189 feet / 680 GRT; John Armstrong quotes log of HMCS *Lady Evelyn* sighting *Lansdowne* entering harbour December 5.

Sawyer Brothers American tern schooner; Milbridge, ME, 1906; 121 feet / 347 NRT; record states twenty-three-year-old seaman Andrew Peterson of the *Sawyer Brothers* died in Explosion.

Viking 117314; wooden sealing ship; Nylands, Arendal, NOR, 1881; 154 feet / 586 GRT; supposedly arrived Halifax, December 5, 5:00 P.M., too late to go through gates, may have entered after *Clara* and *Mont Blanc*; in 1931, among ice floes off northern Newfoundland, blew up and sank; twenty-eight lives lost.

ACKNOWLEDGEMENTS

Roger Marsters, Maritime Museum of the Atlantic, for making the museum's resources available and taking a museum display apart on two occasions so I could have access to the inquiry report.

Amber Laurie, Maritime Museum of the Atlantic, for access to the museum's photograph collection, locating key images, giving me access to the library, being available for questions.

Ellen McLaren, Maritime Museum of the Atlantic, for letting me loose aboard the CSS *Acadia*.

Derek Harrison, Maritime Museum of the Atlantic, for taking me to hidden places on the *Acadia* and sharing his vast knowledge of steamships.

Jennifer Gamble, Naval Museum of Halifax, for making the museum's resources available and providing some key images.

Lisa McNiven, Naval Museum of Halifax, for patiently and cheerily giving me access to the museum's photograph collection and locating important images.

Staff at the Nova Scotia Archives for answering many questions, locating many resources, and helping in a variety of ways.

Sean McMullen for accompanying me on dives with his video camera to document several Explosion sites.

Gilles Paquet for lending me his chart collection for eighteen months.

Colin Millar for assistance with the history of piloting in Halifax.

Tom Lynskey for lending me several rare publications from the period and providing images.

BIBLIOGRAPHY

Armour, Charles A., and Thomas Lackey. *Sailing Ships of the Maritimes.* Toronto: McGraw-Hill Ryerson Limited, 1975.

Armstrong, John Griffith. *The Halifax Explosion and the Royal Canadian Navy.* Vancouver: UBC Press, 2002.

Atlantic Geoscience Centre. *Geological Interpretation of a SWATH Bathymetric Image of Halifax Harbour.* Geological Survey of Canada: GF962p, August 1994.

Baddeley, Allan. *Blackwood's Magazine.* Vol. 229. Edinburgh: William Blackwood & Sons, 1931.

Baird, Donal M. *Under Tow: A History of Tugs and Towing.* St. Catharines, ON: Vanwell Publishing, 2003.

Bird, Michael J. *The Town That Died.* Halifax: Nimbus Publishing, 1995.

Baker, Frank. "Diary: October 9, 1917, to January 14, 1918." Dartmouth Heritage Museum.

Boileau, John. *Halifax & the Royal Canadian Navy.* Halifax: Nimbus Publishing, 2010.

Brannen, Bruce. *The Halifax Explosion: SS* Stella Maris *and the Cape Island Connection.* Ottawa: Privately published, 2017.

Burke, David. "Is a Mystery Shipwreck Connected to the Halifax Explosion?" CBC News, December 1, 2017, cbc.ca/news/canada/nova-scotia/mystery-ship-schooner-halifax-explosion-1.4413822.

Calow, Keith. "Rough Justice: The Court Martial of Lieutenant Robert Douglas Legate." *The Northern Mariner* 15, no. 4 (October 2005): 1–17.

The Canadian Almanac and Miscellaneous Directory for the Year 1915. Toronto: The Copp, Clark Company, 1914.

Chambers, Bertram. *Naval Review* 8, no. 3 (1920): 445–57, halifaxexplosion.net/chambersarticle.pdf.

Chaulk, Bob. *Time in a Bottle: Historic Halifax Harbour from the Bottom Up*. Lawrencetown Beach, NS: Pottersfield Press, 2002.

Doner, Mary Frances. *The Salvager: The Life of Captain Tom Reid on the Great Lakes*. Minneapolis: Ross and Haines, 1958.

Erhard, Nancy. *First in Its Class: The Story of the Royal Nova Scotia Yacht Squadron*. Halifax: Nimbus Publishing, 1986.

Farquhar, James A. *Farquhar's Luck*. Halifax: Petheric Press, 1980.

Fifty-First Annual Report of the Department of Marine and Fisheries for the Fiscal Year 1917–18—Marine. Ottawa: J. De LaBroquerie Taché, 1918.

Foster, J. A. *Heart of Oak: A Pictorial History of the Royal Canadian Navy*. Toronto: Methuen, 1985.

Garnett, Herbert N. "Draft report of experience aboard HMS *Highflyer* during the Halifax Explosion," personal papers.

Gray, David R. "Carrying Canadian Troops: The Story of RMS *Olympic* as a First World War Troopship." *Canadian Military History* 11, no. 1 (2002).

———. "*Olympic* Trooping in the First World War," *The Titanic Commutator* 30, no. 175 (2006): 139–54.

Greene, B. M., ed. *Who's Who in Canada 1927.* Toronto: International Press Limited, 1927.

Halliburton, G. Burton. *What's Brewing? Oland 1867–1971 A History.* Tantallon, NS: Four East Publications, 1994.

Harding, Marguerite. *Through the Gates.* Bridgewater, NS: H&B Langille's Print, 1999.

Henneberry, Allan P. *Wreck Diving Tales: Diving Nova Scotia's Shipwrecks.* New York: iUniverse, 2008.

Huntington, Melvin S. "Melvin S. Huntington Diaries." Louisbourg Collection. Cape Breton Regional Library, 2014, cbrl.ca/services/local-history-resources/louisbourg-diaries/.

International Marine Engineering, vol. 19 (May 1914). New York: Aldrich Publishing Co. Simmons-Boardman Pub. Co, library.si.edu/digital-library/book/internationalma191914newy.

Johnston, William, William G. P. Rawling, Richard H. Gimblett, and John MacFarlane. *The Seabound Coast: The Official History of the Royal Canadian Navy, 1867–1939,* vol. 1. Toronto: Dundurn Press, 2010.

Jones, Charles H. *1919 Signal Letters of British Ships.* London: Spottiswoode, Ballantyne & Co., 1919.

Kemp, Peter. *The Oxford Companion to Ships and the Sea.* Oxford: Oxford University Press, 1988.

Lawrence, Hal. *Tales of the North Atlantic.* Toronto: McClelland and Stewart, 1985.

Lilley, Terence Dawson. "Operations of the Tenth Cruiser Squadron." Doctoral thesis, University of Greenwich, 2012.

Macbeth, Jack. *Ready, Aye Ready: An Illustrated History of the Royal Canadian Navy.* Toronto: Key Porter Books, 1989.

Macpherson, Ken, and John Burgess. *The Ships of Canada's Naval Forces 1910–1981*. Toronto: Collins Publishers, 1981.

Maybee, Janet. *Aftershock: The Halifax Explosion and the Persecution of Pilot Francis Mackey*. Halifax: Nimbus Publishing, 2015.

Metson, Graham, ed. *The Halifax Explosion, December 6, 1917*. Toronto: McGraw-Hill Ryerson, 1978.

Mills, John M. *Canadian Coastal and Inland Steam Vessels 1809–1830*. Providence, RI: Steamship Historical Society of America, 1979.

Ministry of Transport. *Statement of Shipping Casualties Resulting in Total Loss in St. Lawrence River and Gulf, and on the Atlantic Coast from 1896 Up to Date*. Marine Investigations and Wrecks, April, 1998.

O'Leary, Wayne M. *The Tancook Schooners: An Island and Its Boats*. Montréal & Kingston: McGill-Queen's University Press, 1994.

Parker, John P. *Sails of the Maritimes*. Aylesbury: Hazell, Watson & Viney, 1960.

Parsons, Robert C. *In Peril on the Sea: Shipwrecks of Nova Scotia*. Lawrencetown Beach, NS: Pottersfield Press, 2000.

Payzant, Joan, and Lewis Payzant. *Like a Weaver's Shuttle: A History of the Halifax-Dartmouth Ferries*. Halifax: Nimbus Publishing, 1979.

Peary, Robert E. *The North Pole*. US: Frederick A. Stokes, 1910, hellenicaworld.com/History/RobertEPeary/en/TheNorthPole.html.

Pickford & Black Shipping Register Book #856. Nova Scotia Archives, MG7 vol. 48, Creighton and Marshall, Halifax.

Protection of Shipping Leaving Canadian Ports—Arrivals at and Sailings from Halifax, NS, for Convoy. Library and Archives Canada RG24, vol. 3774, File number: 1048-48-8, File part: 1.

"Record of Proceedings in the Exchequer Court of Canada in Admiralty, The Nova Scotia Admiralty District; Compagnie générale transatlantique and The Ship 'Imo'"; "Action for Damages by Collision." Halifax, January 10, 1918.

Ruffman, Alan, and Colin D. Howell, eds. *Ground Zero: A Reassessment of the 1917 Explosion in Halifax Harbour*. Halifax: Nimbus Publishing and Gorsebrook Research Institute for Atlantic Canada Studies at Saint Mary's University, 1994.

Sarty, Roger. "Incident on Lucknow Street: Defenders and the Defended in Halifax, 1915," *Canadian Military History* 10, no. 2 (2001).

Scanlon, Joseph. *Catastrophe: Stories and Lessons from the Halifax Explosion*. Waterloo: Wilfrid Laurier University Press, 2020.

———. "Source of Threat and Source of Assistance: The Maritime Aspect of the 1917 Halifax Explosion." *The Northern Mariner* 10, no. 4 (October 2000): 39–50.

"Sessional Papers of the Dominion of Canada," vol. 13, Seventh Session of the Twelfth Parliament, 1917.

75th Anniversary: Naval Service of Canada. Halifax: The 75th Anniversary Publishing Company, 1985.

Smith, Marilyn Gurney. *The King's Yard: An Illustrated History of the Halifax Dockyard*. Halifax: Nimbus Publishing, 1985.

Soucoup, Dan. *Explosion in Halifax Harbour 1917*. Halifax: Nimbus Publishing, 2017.

Tulloch, Tom. "The Halifax Graving Dock and the 1917 Explosion." *Argonauta* 36, no. 1 (Winter 2019): 6–22.

White, James F. E. "The Garrison Response to the Halifax Disaster, 6 December, 1917." March 31, 2014. Halifax Defence Complex, Parks Canada, hmhps.ca/pdf/The-Garrison-Response-to-the-Halifax-Disaster_James_White_Preliminary_Report_2014-04-09.pdf.

Zemel, Joel. *Scapegoat: The Extraordinary Legal Proceedings Following the 1917 Halifax Explosion.* Halifax: New World Publishing (Canada), 2012.

NEWSPAPERS

Daily Acadian Recorder

Halifax Daily Echo

Halifax Daily Mail

Halifax Herald

Halifax Morning Chronicle

WEBSITES

Halifaxexplosion.net.

"Royal Navy Log Books—Ship Histories," Naval-History.net, naval-history.net/OWShips-LogBooksWW1.htm.

"Scottish Built Ships," Caledonian Maritime Research Trust, clydeships.co.uk.

"Sunderland Built Ships," Shipping and Shipbuilding Research Trust, sunderlandships.com.

"Tyne Built Ships," Shipping and Shipbuilding Research Trust, tynebuiltships.co.uk.

Wreck Site, wrecksite.eu.

ENDNOTES

INTRODUCTION

1 Canada's biggest avoidable disaster in terms of lives lost was the Halifax Explosion. The second was the result of a collision between the steamships *Empress of Ireland* and *Storstad* in the St. Lawrence River on May 29, 1914. The third was the wreck of the SS *Atlantic* near Halifax on April 1, 1873.

CHAPTER 1

2 T. Joseph Scanlon, *Catastrophe: Stories and Lessons from the Halifax Explosion* (Waterloo: Wilfrid Laurier University Press, 2020), 17.

3 William Johnston, William G. P. Rawling, Richard H. Gimblett, and John MacFarlane, *The Seabound Coast: The Official History of the Royal Canadian Navy, 1867–1939*, vol. 1 (Toronto: Dundurn Press, 2010), 295.

4 John Griffith Armstrong, *The Halifax Explosion and the Royal Canadian Navy* (Vancouver: UBC Press, 2002), 20.

5 Nancy Erhard, *First in Its Class: The History of the Royal Nova Scotia Yacht Squadron* (Halifax: Nimbus Publishing, 1986), 15.

CHAPTER 2

6 Log of HMS *Victorian* and NSA convoy records.

7 Armstrong, *The Halifax Explosion and the Royal Canadian Navy*, 32.

8 Johnston et al., *The Seabound Coast*, 534.

9 John D. Grainger, *The Maritime Blockade of Germany in the Great War: The Northern Patrol, 1914–1918* (Navy Records Society, 2003).

10 Alan Ruffman and Colin D. Howell, eds. *Ground Zero: A Reassessment of the 1917 Explosion in Halifax Harbour* (Halifax: Nimbus Publishing and Gorsebrook Research Institute for Atlantic Canada Studies at Saint Mary's University, 1994), 35.

11 *Halifax Herald*, December 27, 1917, 4.

12 Johnston et al., *The Seabound Coast*, 221–22.

13 Ibid., 389.

14 Ibid., 453.

15 Jack MacBeth, *Ready, Aye Ready: An Illustrated History of the Royal Canadian Navy* (Toronto: Key Porter Books, 1989),13.

16 *Halifax Morning Chronicle*, December 3, 1917.

17 *Pickford & Black Shipping Register Book #856*, Creighton and Marshall, Halifax.

18 Johnston et al., *The Seabound Coast*, 461.

19 *Protection of Shipping Leaving Canadian Ports—Arrivals at and Sailings from Halifax, NS for Convoy*, Library and Archives Canada RG24, vol. 3774, file number 1048-48-8, file part 1.

20 Bertram Chambers, "Halifax Explosion," *Naval Review* 8, no. 3 (1920): 445–57, halifaxexplosion.net/chambersarticle.pdf.

21 Johnston et al., *The Seabound Coast*, 500.

22 Ibid., 125.

23 Ibid., 158.

24 Ibid., 167.

25 Ibid., 219.

26 J. A. Foster, *Heart of Oak: A Pictorial History of the Royal Canadian Navy* (Toronto: Methuen, 1985), 14.

27 MacBeth, *Ready, Aye Ready*, 12.

28 *Fifty-First Annual Report of the Department of Marine and Fisheries for the Fiscal Year 1917-18—Marine*. Ottawa: J. de Labroquerie Taché, 1918.

29 Johnston et al., *The Seabound Coast*, 396.

30 Ibid., 266.

31 Janet Maybee, *Aftershock: The Halifax Explosion and the Persecution of Pilot Francis Mackey* (Halifax: Nimbus Publishing, 2015), 16.

32 Johnston et al., *The Seabound Coast*, 318.

33 John Boileau, *Halifax & the Royal Canadian Navy* (Halifax: Nimbus Publishing, 2010), 11.

CHAPTER 3

34 David R. Gray, "*Olympic* Trooping in the First World War," *The Titanic Commutator* 30, no. 175 (2006): 154.

35 *Halifax Morning Chronicle*, July 20, 1918.

36 *Pickford & Black*, Aug 4–9, 1917.

37 Log of HMS *Changuinola.*

38 Ruffman and Howell, *Ground Zero*, 378.

39 Record of Proceedings in the Exchequer Court of Canada in Admiralty, The Nova Scotia Admiralty District; Compagnie générale transatlantique and The Ship "Imo"; Action for Damages by Collision, Halifax, January 10, 1918, 721–24.

40 Gary Sheffield, "The Battle of the Atlantic: the U-boat Peril," BBC History, March 30, 2011, bbc.co.uk/history/worldwars/wwtwo/battle_atlantic_01.shtml.

41 "Record of Proceedings," 693–4.

42 Janet Maybee, Library and Archives Canada podcast, *Francis Mackey and the Halifax Explosion.*

43 *Berwick Register*, February 6, 1918.

CHAPTER 4

44 "Record of Proceedings," 483.

45 "Record of Proceedings," 47.

46 Ruffman and Howell, *Ground Zero*, 472.

47 Ibid., 385.

48 Ibid., 383.

49 "Record of Proceedings," 89.

50 Ibid., 745

51 Ibid., 648.

52 Ibid., 475.

53 Ibid., 739.

54 Ibid., 656.

55 *Blackwood's Magazine* quoted in *Halifax Evening Mail*, December 5, 1931.

56 Ibid.

57 "Record of Proceedings," 373

58 Marilyn Gurney Smith, *The King's Yard: An Illustrated History of the Halifax Dockyard* (Halifax: Nimbus Publishing, 1985), 40.

59 Ruffman and Howell, *Ground Zero*, 307.

CHAPTER 5

60 Ruffman and Howell, *Ground Zero*, 317.

61 *Acadian Recorder*, December 10, 1917.

62 "Record of Proceedings," 334.

63 *Blackwood's Magazine* quoted in *Halifax Evening Mail* December 5, 1931.

64 Herbert N. Garnett, report of experience aboard HMS *Highflyer* during the Halifax Explosion. Courtesy Maritime Museum of the Atlantic, Halifax.

65 *Midland Free Press* (Ontario), December 20, 1917.

66 Ruffman and Howell, *Ground Zero*, 332–34.

67 Joan Payzant and Lewis Payzant, *Like a Weaver's Shuttle* (Halifax: Nimbus Publishing, 1979), 196.

68 Ibid., 196.

69 Ruffman and Howell, *Ground Zero*, 341.

70 The work of Archibald MacMechan quoted in Graham Metson, *The Halifax Explosion, December 6, 1917* (Toronto: McGraw-Hill Ryerson, 1978), 24.

71 *Blackwood's Magazine* quoted in *Halifax Evening Mail* December 5, 1931.

72 The diary is at the Dartmouth Heritage Museum in Dartmouth, NS. Although a witness at the inquiry states the *Acadia* replaced the *Gulnare* as guard ship, the diary of *Acadia* crewman Frank Baker states that the *Acadia* replaced the *Berthier* on December 4, 1917. I was unable to find any information about a ship called *Berthier*, including in *Lloyd's Registry of Ships*. Baker identifies the *Gulnare* as a previous guard ship and even provides details of moving the telephone cable on December 16.

73 Armstrong, *The Halifax Explosion and the Royal Canadian Navy*, 18.

74 James F. E. White, PhD, "Appendix B: 'My Experience in the Halifax Disaster,'" *The Garrison Response to the Halifax Disaster, 6 December, 1917*, March 31, 2014, Halifax Defence Complex, Parks Canada. hmhps.ca/pdf/The-Garrison-Response-to-the-Halifax-Disaster_James_White_Preliminary_Report_2014-04-09.pdf.

75 Log of HMS *Calgarian*, naval-history.net/OWShips-WW1-08-HMS_Calgarian.htm.

76 *Halifax Morning Chronicle*, December 16, 1917.

CHAPTER 6

77 Joel Zemel, *Scapegoat: The Extraordinary Legal Proceedings Following the 1917 Halifax Explosion* (Halifax: New World Publishing, Canada, 2012) 70.

78 "Record of Proceedings," 467.

79 Quoted in Bruce Brannen, *The Halifax Explosion: SS* Stella Maris *and the Cape Island Connection* (Ottawa: Privately published, 2017), 20.

80 *Halifax Evening Mail*, December 10, 1917.

81 *Halifax Morning Chronicle*, December 11, 1917.

82 Scanlon, *Catastrophe*, 133.

83 Atlantic Geoscience Centre, *Geological Interpretation of a SWATH Bathymetric Image of Halifax Harbour* (Geological Survey of Canada: GF962p, August 1994).

84 David Burke, "Is a Mystery Shipwreck Connected to the Halifax Explosion?" CBC News, December 1, 2017, cbc.ca/news/canada/nova-scotia/mystery-ship-schooner-halifax-explosion-1.4413822

85 Scanlon, *Catastrophe*, 56.

86 Erhard, *First in Its Class*, 55.

87 *Halifax Morning Chronicle*, December 12, 1917.

88 *Halifax Evening Mail*, December 12, 1917.

89 *Halifax Morning Chronicle*, April 27, 1918.

90 Armstrong, *The Halifax Explosion and the Royal Canadian Navy*, 65.

91 *Halifax Morning Chronicle*, April 30, 1918.

92 Robert C. Parsons, *In Peril on the Sea* (Lawrencetown Beach, NS: Pottersfield Press, 2000), 89.

93 Robert E. Peary, *The North Pole* (US: Frederick A. Stokes, 1910), hellenicaworld.com/History/RobertEPeary/en/TheNorthPole.html.

94 *Halifax Herald*, April 29, 1918.

95 Parsons, *In Peril on the Sea*, 105.

96 shipsnostalgia.com/media/ss-middleham-castle.

CHAPTER 7

97 *Halifax Morning Chronicle*, December 14, 1917.

98 *Blackwood's Magazine* quoted in *Halifax Evening Mail* December 5, 1931.

99 Herbert N. Garnett, "Draft report of experience aboard HMS *Highflyer* during the Halifax Explosion," found among his personal papers and presumed to have been submitted as his official report.

100 NavaSource Online: Section Patrol Craft Photo Archive, navsource.org/archives/12/171254.htm.

101 "France and Canada Steamship Coporation," Marine Link, n.d., marinelink.com/history/francecanada-steamship-corporation

CHAPTER 8

102 *Halifax Herald*, January 7, 1918.

103 Ibid., May 6, 1918.

104 Graham Metson, *The Halifax Explosion, December 6, 1917* (Toronto: McGraw-Hill Ryerson, 1978), 167.

105 Armstrong, *The Halifax Explosion and the Royal Canadian Navy*, 125.

106 *Halifax Herald*, July 18, 1918.

CHAPTER 9

107 *Halifax Herald*, December 4, 1917.

108 *Halifax Morning Chronicle*, May 2, 1918.

109 *Halifax Herald*, January, 17, 1918.

110 Ibid., December 4, 1917.

111 James A. Farquhar, *Farquhar's Luck* (Halifax: Petheric Press, 1980), 176.

112 Charles A. Armour and Thomas Lackey, *Sailing Ships of the Maritimes* (Toronto: McGraw-Hill Ryerson Limited, 1975), 207.

113 Johnston et al., *The Seabound Coast*, 662.

114 For more on this incident, see Keith Calow, "Rough Justice: The Court Martial of Lieutenant Robert Douglas Legate," *The Northern Mariner* 15, No. 4 (October 2005): 1–17.

115 David R. Gray, "Carrying Canadian Troops: The Story of RMS Olympic as a First World War Troopship," *Canadian Military History* 11, no. 1 (2002). Reprinted in *The Titanic Commutator* 30, no. 175 (2006).

116 Scanlon, *Catastrophe*, 37.

117 *Halifax Herald*, November, 1917.

118 Ibid., April 29, 1918.

119 Johnston et al., *The Seabound Coast*, 470.

CHAPTER 10

120 Chambers, "Halifax Explosion."

121 *Halifax Morning Chronicle*, December 19, 20, 1917.

122 Ruffman and Howell, *Ground Zero*, 442.

123 *Halifax Morning Chronicle*, December 14, 1917.

124 Ibid., December 7.

125 James F. E. White, "Appendix B: 'My Experience in the Halifax Disaster.'"

126 In his 1931 article in *Blackwood's Magazine*, Allan Baddeley included a photo of a wrecked ship that he claimed was the *Mont Blanc*. I have not been able to find any other references to it. I suspect it is the *Curaca*.

127 *Halifax Morning Chronicle*, December 14, 1917.

128 Log of HMS *Calgarian*.

129 The convoy register for December 11 lists thirty-five ships, including the *Beaverton*, *Cairncross*, *Marie Z. Michalinos*, *Pomeranian*, and *Saint Dunstan*, but elsewhere the register also shows these ships with later departure dates, indicating they must have been scheduled for the 11th but got delayed. *Highflyer*'s log reports thirty-one ships in the convoy. Admiral Chambers later wrote that there were thirty-three.

130 Pickford & Black registers.

131 Armstrong, *The Halifax Explosion and the Royal Canadian Navy*, 111.

132 Susan Speaker, "US Army Base Hospital # 4 Gets Royal Greeting in England," Historical Collections of the National Library of Medicine, May 24, 2017, circulatingnow.nlm.nih.gov/2017/05/24.

133 *Halifax Herald*, December 18, 1917.

134 *Halifax Morning Chronicle*, March 8, 1918.

135 *Halifax Evening Mail*, January 4, 1918.

136 Mary Frances Doner, *The Salvager: The Life of Captain Tom Reid on the Great Lakes* (Minneapolis: Ross and Haines, 1958), 169.

137 *Halifax Morning Chronicle*, April 20 and 25, 1918, and May 1, 1918.

138 *Halifax Herald*, July 17, 1918.

139 Ibid., August 1, 1918.

140 Tom Tulloch, "The Halifax Graving Dock and the 1917 Explosion," *Argonauta* 36, no. 1 (Winter 2019): 6–22.

CHAPTER 11

141 Alfred Kayford quoted in *Halifax Evening Mail*, December 21, 1917.

142 "Record of Proceedings," 403.

143 Ibid., 446

144 Ibid., 553.

145 Zemel, *Scapegoat*, 256.

146 Ibid., 277.

147 Ibid., 301.

148 Maybee, Aftershock, 75.

149 *Halifax Herald*, August 2, 1917.

150 "Record of Proceedings," 612.

151 "*Letitia* Inquiry Ruling," *Halifax Herald*, August 14, 1917.

152 *Halifax Herald*, January 10, 1918.

153 *Fifty-First Annual Report of the Department of Marine and Fisheries for the Fiscal Year 1917–18—Marine* (Ottawa: J. de Labroquerie Taché, 1918), 94.

154 *Halifax Morning Chronicle*, January 24, 1918.

155 *Pilot Service Establishment Book*, Department of Marine.

156 Maybee, *Aftershock*, 96.

157 *Halifax Herald*, August 4, 1917.

158 "Sessional Papers, Seventh Session of the Twelfth Parliament of the Dominion of Canada," Session 1817 vol. 2, 15.

159 "Record of Proceedings," 464.

160 Ibid., 696–700.

161 *Halifax Morning Chronicle*, January 29, 1917.

162 Joel Zemel, *Betrayal of Trust* (Halifax: New World Publishing Canada, 2017), 13–33.

163 Ibid., 682.

164 The other members of the pilotage commission were Captain Francis Rudolf (Halifax harbourmaster), Captain Neil Hall (port warden of Halifax), Halifax mayor Peter Martin, Dartmouth mayor Edward Williams, Walter Mitchell, J. E. DeWolf, see "Record of Proceedings," 553.

165 "Record of Proceedings," 571.

CHAPTER 13

166 Roger Sarty, "Incident on Lucknow Street: Defenders and the Defended in Halifax, 1915," *Canadian Military History* 10, no. 2 (2001).

167 Johnston et al., *The Seabound Coast*, 345.

168 *Acadian Recorder*, December 12, 1917.

169 *Halifax Morning Chronicle*, July 18, 1899.

170 Ibid., July 18, 1899.

171 Farquhar, *Farquhar's Luck*, 161.

172 Parsons, *In Peril on the Sea*, 62.

173 *Halifax Chronicle-Herald*, November 2, 2022.

CHAPTER 14

174 *Halifax Morning Chronicle*, April 16, 1918.

175 Johnston et al., *The Seabound Coast*, 529.

176 Zemel, *Scapegoat*, 296.

177 *Halifax Morning Chronicle*, May 6, 1918.

178 "Record of Proceedings," 513.

179 Ibid., 514.

180 Johnston et al., *The Seabound Coast*, 527.

181 Ibid., 520.

182 *Halifax Morning Chronicle*, January 25, 1918.

183 Scanlon, *Catastrophe*, 321.

184 Government of Canada, "Heroes of the Halifax Explosion," canada.ca/en/navy/services/history/heroes-halifax-explosion.html.

185 *Halifax Evening Mail*, December 5, 1931, 23.

186 Joe Scanlon, writing in *The Northern Mariner* 10, no. 4 (2000), states, "PRO, Admiralty (ADM) 53/44308, *HighFlyer*, Log, states explicitly that its crew did not know about *Mont Blanc*'s cargo."

APPENDIX A

187 *Halifax Morning Chronicle*, January 28, 1917.